PHYSICAL EDUCATION:
Concepts & Issues

PHYSICAL EDUCATION:
Concepts & Issues

Edited by
Dr. Sharad Chandra Mishra
Director, Physical Education,
Badri Vishal Post-graduate College
(U.P.)

Compiled by
Sandhu Varghese

SPORTS PUBLICATION
7/26, Ground Floor, Ansari Road, Darya Ganj,
New Delhi-110 002. Ph.: (O) 55749511, 55257538
(M) 9868028838 (R) 27562163

Published by:

SPORTS PUBLICATION
H.O.: 7/26, Ground Floor, Ansari Road,
Darya Ganj, New Delhi-110 002.
Ph. : (O) 55749511, 55257538 (R) 27562163, (M) 9868028838
E-mail: *ektathani@hotmail.com/ lakshaythani@hotmail.com*
Website : www.sportspublication.trade-india.com

First Edition 2006

I.S.B.N. – 81-7879-203-6

PRINTED IN INDIA 2006

Laser Typeset by:
JAIN MEDIA GRAPHICS, Delhi-110035. Ph.: 27190244

Printed by:
CHAWLA OFFSET PRINTERS, Delhi-110052

Price: Rs. 650/-

PREFACE

The fundamental purpose of the present book entitled ***Physical Education: Concepts & Issues*** is to serve as an introduction to the field of physical education and sports or sport and physical education. It is specially intended for the students of physical education and sports sciences and for the professionals in the field of sports and physical education.

The book proves as a handbook for the study of physical education for the students of physical education B.P.Ed., and M.Phil. researchers. It provides relevant informations about physical education and presents it as a field of study.

The book has been prepared in such a way that it can meet the needs of two different groups of people: (1) those who are using it from the standpoint of their general education, as part of a broad liberal arts and science background; and (2) those who are using it as an introduction to a field in which they will be prepared professionally, in addition to the general education function it can serve. Interestingly enough, it is very difficult to know just what name to give the field at present.

The terms physical education and sport and sport and physical education will be used interchangeably in this text. They are the terms that are recognized to the greatest extent on this continent and around the world.

Admittedly, they can probably be regarded right now as holding-pattern terms to borrow from airline nomenclature, although it is true that the entire list of names that one will find applied to the field of education.

A new introductory text for the field of sport and physical education offered to the profession. It is believed that this book has been conceived in such a way that it will meet the urgent needs of our field.

Such a text must concern itself forthrightly and strongly with both the professional and scholarly dimensions of our work with the so-called sub-disciplinary areas and with the concurrent professional components that we all face.

Diagnosis of the present situation indicates that the field needs redirection and rejuvenation. The health, physical education, recreation, and dance has now fully recognized that we are all separate but allied professions. As the reader examines the table of contents, he/she will notice immediately that there is a balanced approach between sub-disciplinary areas of our field and what might be identified as the sub-professional or concurrent professional components. By this it mean that what many have considered to be scholarly, scientific endeavour is regarded as professional writing too. Some may feel that this tends to redress the present imbalance too much, but it is believed that the present rift in the field between the so-called scholars and the so-called practising professionals must be significantly narrowed in the very least.

I owe my special heartiest thanks to all of people who assisted me in so many ways and the publisher who brought out this book in a decent manner. All suggestions from users on omission or shortcomings will be most welcomed.

— Dr. Sharad Chandra Mishra

CONTENTS

1. Physical Education—Meaning, Nature & Scope 1-33
2. Physical Education and Education 34-58
3. Principles of Physical Education 59-87
4. Class Management in Physical Education 88-124
5. Fundamental Statistics in Physical Education and Sports Sciences 125-160
6. Physical Education as a Profession 161-179
7. Managing Physical Education Programmes and Policies 180-263
8. Physical attributions and Characteristics in Physical Education and Sports 264-291
9. Physical Education and Sports Psychology 292-320
10. Tests & Measurements in Physical Education 321-340
11. Physical Education and Recreation 341-360

1

PHYSICAL EDUCATION—MEANING, NATURE & SCOPE

DEFINITION OF PHYSICAL EDUCATION

The word physical refers to body, and indicates bodily characteristics such as strength, speed, endurance, flexibility, health coordination and performance. It seemingly contrasts the body with the mind. The term education when used in conjunction with physical, refers to a process of education that develops the human body especially fitness and movement skills. Therefore, it transcends all misconceptions and misgivings about physical education as a field of teaching and being considered as an ingredient of general education.

A bird's eye-view of various definitions of physical education is essential. Physical Education as understood is such a cultivation of power and capabilities of student as will enable him to maintain his bodily condition in the best working order providing at the same time for the greater efficiency of his intellectual and spiritual life. It is proclaimed that physical education should aim to improve the mass of students and to give them as much health, strength and stamina as possible to enable them to perform the duties that await them after they leave their college."

These early definitions, laid emphasis on (i) the development of physical qualities which enable the individual to live his life successfully and efficiently and (ii) the process which is essentially educational in perspective.

Physical Education is rightly recognized as an integral part of education. The existence of man is primarily physical. The first lessons a human child learns are lessons of physical activity.

No education, howsoever ideal and exalted in its objectives, is complete without emphasis on motor activity. The human body is a sacred gift of Nature. Its growth, development and efficiency largely depends upon the quantity and quality of motor activities it performs. Compartmentalization of human personality into "body, mind, and spirit" is an over-simplification.

The mind and spirit do not reveal themselves without body. The body, being an observable material cause of mind, is an instrument through which man performs all mundane duties enjoined upon him by Nature and society. Sherrington aptly remarked that "muscle is the cradle of recognizable mind which seems to have arisen in connection with the motor act. Where integration progressed and where motor behaviour progressively evolved, mind progressively evolved"

Adequate muscular activity is not merely a biological necessity, it is the basis of "intelligent behaviour." The primacy of physical education over all other kinds of education, formal or informal, has to be recognized. At no point of time in the history of human civilization, did physical education receives so much attention as today. Several reasons may be cited for this dramatic change. First, since time immemorial physical activity has stayed with man as a survival reaction—the very core of "struggle for existence." Strength and fitness were crucial factors for protection against wild animals, and search for food.

With the onset of cultural revolution, man began to break away with his natural habitat, and rendered himself comparatively physically weaker to animals. Yet he could not completely cast away the mantle of" racially old" activities. The necessity to keep fit became a priority in the dramatically changing life style. Second, during the cultural epoch, human society organized its social institutions including education, Physical education, being a part of education, had to be organized and institutionalized.

The early Greeks are said to be pioneers in placing athletics at par with aesthetics, mathematics and ethics in the overall scheme of formal education. Third, the march of civilization characterized by rapid industrialization and urbanization has brought man to the brink of disaster. Endless pursuit of materialistic philosophy, hurrying-scurrying and robot-like routines leading to psycho-somatic disorders are inevitable consequences of scientific philosophy, hurrying-scurrying and robot-like routines leading to psycho-somatic disorders are inevitable consequences of scientific and cultural revolution. Intellectually man is a giant, physically a pygmy. In these "dark hours of degraded life", the only silver lining is vigorous physical activity which surely can bring back "the joy of living".

Hopefully, more and more people have begun to realize thee necessity to keep fit, to live vigorously and to keep cool and relaxed. Fourth, Physical Education turned a new leaf with the revival of the Olympic Games in 1896. Since the turn of the century, a tribe of specialized physical educators called coaches appeared on the scene whose inherent interest lay in producing record breakers in competitive sports. Although health, fitness recreation, well-being etc. continue to be general objective of physical education, specific focus shifted to highly competitive thrilled-packed sports. Finally, the insatiable thirst for Olympic gold amongst nations, has given a new turn to physical education.

Various aspects of human performance have begun to be studied in the bio-science laboratories. The physical educator has also crowned himself as a sport scientist. Spot and exercise physiology, sport psychology, sport medicine, sport sociology etc., have begun to play leading role in training of athletes for elite performance. No physical education curricula are complete without sport bio-sciences. Truly, physical education has grown into a huge banana tree whose tendrils cannot be easily distinguished from its main stem.

Misnomer Substitutes for Physical Education

Right from the beginning a variety of term has been used to denote physical education and in various cultural contexts; these terms might be a substitute for physical education but in the present day holistic view of physical education, they are archaic and misnomer. Physical education, in fact, is a very comprehensive endeavour and encompasses every thing which these singularly underscore. A segment cannot be used as an alternative for the whole. It is, therefore, necessary to explain these terms and their usage as well as the context in which they operate.

Physical Training

The oldest and the most widely used term for physical education is Physical Training. In common parlance, physical educators are still known as physical training instructors. In dictionary, physical training means "practical education in any profession" or "a course of diet and exercise for developing physical strength, endurance or dexterity". Physical training is a process by which an individual prepares himself to meet certain physical challenges. Comprising calisthenics, conditioning exercises, drills and gymnastic exercise etc., it is an essentialing radiant of the training of defence personnel and security forces. Specifically, physical training is meant to toughen the soldiers through vigorously mobile physical activities enabling them withstand the rigours and risks of war and fight calamities. These activities are graded and grouped according to severity. Repetition and generally rhythmic as they are, they aim to produce well coordinated, disciplined and tough body and mind. The idea is to produce men of steel for a specified job.

In physical training, the element of education is missing for it is a sort of regimented work out which permito no freedom of thought and action. Hence, using physical training in place of physical education is educationally unsound. Regimentation and education are diametrically opposed to each other. Hopefully, the term is becoming obsolete in the echelons of education.

Drills

Drill comprises precise and alacrity body movement performed to certain cadence. In the training of security forces, drill—with or without weapons—has an extremely important role to play. For each activity of the drill, the directions and sequence of movements are clearly demarcated and have to be followed without discretion. The main aim of drill is to develop co-ordination, rhythm, balance and perfection in the postures of sitting, standing, walking, running etc.

In other words, it is disciplining of the bodily movements. In physical education, emphasis on disciplining of the body-movements is laid and habits of correct posture are inculcated in children right from the very beginning. Still drill is not a perfect activity because its objectives are narrow. The word drill is also used to denote practice of fundamental skills of major games/sports. In this context, drilling means repetition—correct and precise. Skill-drilling leads to mastery over a game/sport.

In sum, drill is a means of training the body rather than educating it. Hence it cannot be accepted as a substitute for physical education.

Physical Culture

Physical Culture has its origin in the Greek phrase "body beautiful". It underscores development of a "shapely" body which could be appreciated on aesthetic standards. It is wedded to the philosophy of "outward" appearance of the body especially its shape, musculature, curvatures etc. Nations of the Eastern Bloc of Europe prefer to use Physical Culture in place of physical education. The best physique contests for men and "beauty contests" for women at national and international levels seem to have their genesis in "body beautiful" concept of physical culture. "Good looks, pronounced muscles," nowadays, are developed by using a variety of body-building equipment, weight training techniques etc. The stress is laid on the development of muscles only and not on speed or endurance or any other component of physical fitness. That is way physical culture is considered a lop-sided system vis-à-vis physical education.

The elements of movement education are altogether missing. A beautiful body has no meaning unless it can perform beautifully.

Play

Play primarily refers to such activities as provide to the participants, especially infants and children, fun, and freedom of action and thought. It is an instinctive activity which helps the child to develop physically and intellectually. "Play", is a joyful, spontaneous, creative activity in which man finds his fullest expression. Largely non-competitive in nature and developmental in function, play shapes human personality during formative years.

Infant's play is mostly individualistic, that of a child more gregarious. Play sans competitive spirit becomes a dull and drab affair. Play requires no formal teaching. Children play whatever and whenever like to play. Play neither needs nor knows any rules. For the child, play is an educative activity. As the child grows, the pattern of his play goes on changing dramatically. An adult and a child differ in their play activities. Elementary education ought to be all play. Outcomes of play are important for children in general rather than for serious athletes.

Gymnastics

At times used as a substitute for physical education in some countries, gymnastics has become a full-fledged sport usually involving agility exercises. Originally a gymnasium was "a public place or a building where the Greek youths exercised themselves, with running and wrestling grounds, baths and halls for conversation" and gymnastic composed "exercises devised to strengthen body" largely, feats or tricks of agility.

Today, gymnastic refers to those physical exercises which are performed with or without certain apparatus in the gymnasium specifically built for this purpose. The modern forms of gymnastics has had its origin in Sweden, Denmark and Germany who drew inspiration from the ancient Greek Civilization. The Russians, romans, Japanese and Chinese have shown performance par excellence in gymnastics. Besides floor exercises, gymnastic exercises are also performed on Roman rings, horizontal bar, parallel bars, vaulting box vaulting horse, trampoline etc. Educational gymnastics, aesthetic gymnastics, rhythmic gymnastics etc. are its variations very well-known the world over.

National and international gymnastic competitions are held separately for men and women. Although athletics, swimming and gymnastic are considered mother sports, at higher level of performance, they become specific disciplines enabling only a few to excel. That is why, from the viewpoint of complete education, gymnastics have its limitations. However, a few elements of physical fitness such as body poise, suppleness, balance, coordination etc. are developed only through gymnastic activities.

Sports and Games

Sport is, "carrying away from work", indicating an absolute freedom of activity. The major aim of sports is recreation. Having becomes highly competitive, sports today are seen in a much broader perspective than ever before. Sport, in fact, is an attitude of mind. For most people, sport is recreation, for others it is competition—the means to excel and achieve high standards in performance. Sports are largely individual events such as athletics, archery swimming, shooting etc., wherein the participant tries to compete against his own previous standards as well as those of others. Organized sports of today are refined and well-defined activities bound by rules and perfection in performance of skills. A number of sports has a carry-over value. They can be played even in old age.

Games refer to team events in which more than one person forming a group compete against the similar group for supremacy. A game is a co-operative affair in which team-mates play in accordance with certain well-defined set patterns. Football, hockey, basketball, handball, volleyball, etc., are commonly known as games rather than sports. Organization of team events is more elaborate and is based on rigid rules and regulations.

Although games and sports constitute a bulk of physical education programme, they are highly competitive in which only a selected few can take part. In fact, they are not mass activities but cater to only a class of people. They hardly aim at total well-being. Games of low organization such as minor games, lead-up games, relays etc., have a mass appeal but games of high organization become selective in which all may not participate. Only a few with a high ability, skill and persistence may rise to the top of the spiral. In the formative years of the child, games and sports not only develop physical qualities, they serve as an excellent medium of socialization and social adjustment. However, they lose educational value when to much of emphasis is placed on winning, supremacy, superiority, excellence etc. That is why games and sports cannot alone replace physical education which is "a wholesome endeavour" ensuring "balanced development of the individual in body, mind and spirit."

Unfortunately, their still prevails skepticism amongst the academic community about physical education as an inseparable aspect of education. For them physical education as an inseparable aspect of education. For them physical means morning jerks, dips and squats or free play only for the development of physique. In the modern scenario, this is simply a partisan view. Physical education offers much more than what meets the eye. Little is known about the fine elements of physical education. From simple play activities of infants and children to highly competitive sports, physical education covers a wide range of activities suiting all age groups and sexes. Its objectives are essentially educational and its medium physical activity.

A whole-some physical activity programme does not blunt the brain, it keeps in fine fettle the apparatus i.e., neurons, nerves and muscles, which is the very cause of intelligence. Physical education needs to be understood in its wider perspective. The 'whole' is always greater than the sum of its parts.

Physical education as "the accumulation of wholesome experiences through participation in large muscle activities that promote growth and development". The child's growth is the very core of all educational endeavour. Play has always been considered as a potential medium of child's growth. Rousseau laid greatest emphasis on play as a means of education. The impact of his ideas was clearly seen in physical education also. That is why, in the early phase of its development, physical education also. That is why, in the early phase of its development, physical education was brought closer to education with the introduction of "play-way" method of teaching. Physical education came to be understood as "the process by which changes in the individual are brought about through his movement experiences", and "........the sum of those experiences which came to the individual through movements". From these ideas sprang the concept of "movement education" which, in due course, strengthened thee foundations of physical education as an academic discipline.

Physical education is the sum of man's physical activities selected as to kind and conducted as to outcomes". While planning the physical activity programme, consideration ought to be given to two things. First, activities should be selected taking into account age, sex and situation. Second, the outcomes must be more than physical.

Besides, health, fitness and vigour, physical education must take care of mental and social aspects of man's personality. Considering physical education as an integral part of total education process, Butcher defined its aim as "thee development of physically, mentally, emotionally and socially fit citizens through the medium of physical activities that have been selected with a view to realising these outcomes". "Physical education," said Bucher & Wuest, " includes the acquisition and refinement of motor skills, the development and maintenance of fitness for optimal health and well-being, the attainment of knowledge and the growth of positive attitudes toward physical activity".

Over the decades, physical education has outgrown its limited objectives i.e., strength and vigour. It now encompasses diverse activities and programmes—formal, informal, recreative, competitive—for individuals as well as groups. Lumpkin believes that "physical education is a process through which an individual obtains optimal physical, mental, and social skills and fitness through physical activity". In the highly mobile and socially volatile life style, acquisition of variety of skills is necessary in order to economise on one's energy. Physical education surely makes people skilful directly as well indirectly. A physically trained person can take on any eventuality because he is fit, tough, courageous and energetic. This apart, skills learnt on the play ground, when transferred to life situation, help people to lead a happy, healthy and well-adjusted life, Adequate participation in large muscle activity, free play, sports, exercise, aerobics, dance etc., turns out physically educated people. This value should be one of many values of the liberally educated person. It becomes meaningful only when its is related to the totality of the individual's life. Barrow defined physical education as "an educational objectives are achieved by means of big muscle activities involving sport, games, gymnastics, dance and exercise". Barrow clarifies that "big muscles" are muscles of the movements of these muscles lead to gross motor skills which constitute the core of entire physical education programme and on which stands the bulky superstructure of games and sports.

A National Plan of Physical Education and Recreation the earliest document prepared by the Central Advisory Board of Physical Education and Recreation in India, says, "Physical education is education. It is education through physical activities for the total personality of the child to its fullness and perfection in body, mind and spirit". Immediately it is concerned with the development of physical fitness. In striving for such fitness, physical education has necessarily to train child's mental, moral and social qualities, arouse its awareness of environment and develop alertness, presence of mind, resourcefulness, discipline, cooperation and the spirit of respect, sympathy and generosity towards others—qualities that are essential for a happy and well- adjusted life in a free and democratic world.

From an overview of various definitions the following salient features of physical education emerge:

1. Physical education is essentially education for it is a means through which body, soul and intellect get moving—efficiently and vigorously.

2. In physical education, the main stress is "big muscle" or "large muscle" activity—an innate quality of the human organism. No wholesome experience is derived unless activity programmes are selective as well as elective and imbibe values other than physical alone.

3. The worthy outcomes shall accrue only when the individual participates in the activity programme. Nobody can learn to swim unless he gets into water.

4. The physical, mental, intellectual, spiritual, and social aspects of a "wholesome" personality are interrelated. Physical education strives to maintain and strengthen the body-mind spirit integration.

5. No where do the aim and objectives of physical education come in conflict with the objectives of education. In fact, they are like hand in glove.

6. Physical education is the only unique discipline which uses "physical activity" as the medium for human development. Its approach to its objectives is natural and unambiguous.

During the last three decades, tremendous developments have taken place in the field of physical education at the global level. Too much of emphasis on "excellence and performance" has catalysed research in various areas like sport sciences, management, teaching technology, training methodology etc. As a consequence, the very perception of physical education has begun to differ from person to person. Even the physical educationists themselves have criticized the adequacy of the title field. They suggest variety of titles, which they feel, can be used as alternatives for physical education. Some of these titles are Human Movement Arts and Sciences, Movement Education, Kinesiology, Sports Education, Development Motor Performance etc. Arguments for and against these titles are still going on.

The crux of the matter, however, is that physical education is a doing phenomenon whose roots lie in a variety of arts, sciences, humanities and activities. Like a bunyan tree it has grown in dimensions so much that the distinction between the trunk and the branches has almost vanished. Yet the bunyan tree retains its name and fame. Since physical education is basically and immediately concerned with "body and its movement", and identifies itself with education—"a life long process"—its present title is apt and appropriate. Any attempt to replace its name with any other title is likely to make it a lop-sided discipline both in terms of its efficacy and importance.

PHYSICAL EDUCATION AND ALLIED AREAS

Health education, recreation, dance and games and sports are distinctly complete disciplines and yet more often than not identified with physical education. From the view point of course-content physical education draws substantially from these areas. On account of their close proximity to physical education, a brief discussion on each of these allied fields is of great importance for physical educators.

HEALTH EDUCATION

Health education is a process by which the individual acquires adequate knowledge about (i) diseases, ailments and disorders and their preventive and curative aspects, and (2) fitness—both physical and mental. World health Organization defines health as "that state of the body and mind in which one lives most and serves best". Health is a very wide spectrum and is always discussed in its physical, mental and social aspects. To enjoy an optimal level of health one has to satisfy certain genetic criteria and environmental conditions.

Physical exercise is one of the most important

ingredients of healthy life. Health education, some believe, is a complete discipline within the framework of medical education. So far as general health of the people is concerned much of the responsibility lies with the individual, parents and, to some extent, teachers. People go to the doctors when they fall ill. Educational institutions are the best venues where health education needs to be imparted to the children right from the beginning. No other teacher is directly concerned with thee health problems of the children than the physical educator.

Health instruction, health supervision and health environment are the major sub-domains of health education.

Heath instruction addresses itself to creating awareness about health through verbal and non-verbal media. Health instruction should include the knowledge about common diseases, their causes their preventive and curative measures. Each individual needs to be guided in such matters as care of body, correct posture of sitting, standing walking running etc. Children also must have a fair knowledge about first aid, fitness, fatigue, personal hygiene etc. They must be made to understand the relationship among nutrition, physical activity and health. Practice and not precept should be the keynote of school health programme.

Health services or supervision refers to that aspect of health education in which the educational institutions requisition the services of medical and paramedical personnel to look after children suffering from ailments and diseases, and those who get injured on the play field. Educational institutions generally do not have enough resources to provide regular health services. Periodic medical check up of students is a must. Physical educators can maintain health records of students and supervise personal hygiene. Beyond this, they should not venture.

Heath environment take care of the surroundings, and ecology which ought to be clean and healthy. Rapid changes in the environment due to industrialization and urbanization have created health hazards. Over-population and fast depleting natural resources of life have added fuel to the fire. Unhealthy environment—biological and social—may not permit the individual to maintain high standards of health.

Healthy environment is created and maintained through healthy practices. Educational institutions, local self-governments, public health departments, social organizations and parents have to cooperate and make a concerted effort in providing disease-free environment. At the moment, there is a need to stem the high-rising tide of green-house effect. Schools and colleges have to play a significant role in bringing the humanity back from the brink of disaster.

Physical education and health education complement and supplement each other. One has no substance without the other. The role of physical educators in this behalf is well-defined.

RECREATION

Recreation is another significant area of physical education. In fact, thee basic purpose of physical education is recreation. All games and sports—minor or major—are utilized, by common man, as recreation. However greater emphasis on competition and excellence has changed their complexion. In Europe and the United States, recreation has developed as a separate subject. The recreation movement had its origin in the United States. Recreation is anything one wishes to do and as he pleases to do. Informality, freedom of choice, sense of accomplishment, variety, relaxation–both mental and physical—are the hall mark of recreation. Recreation is an escape from monotony and boredom resulting from set routines of life. From highly passive activities like listening to music, playing cards, reading etc., to the most active activities like athletics, game, hiking, trekking, dancing, camping etc., everything is recreation. Whether indoor or outdoor, recreation is fun, thrill, enjoyment and satisfaction. If is an attitude towards life expressed in variety of activities.

Agencies of recreation are numerous but the most effective agency is the school where children engage in active recreative activities as a part of physical education. Recreation has a much greater educational value than ever before because it satisfies children's need for physical activity and helps them utilize their "exuberant energy" in order to be physically strong, mentally alert and sharp, and socially well-adjusted. All educational institutions provide for recreation clubs.

DANCE

Since time immemorial dance has been an important aspect of human life. In its simplest from it appeared as folk dance and as a part of religious ceremonies it shaped into a variety of classical forms in the Eastern as well as Western civilizations. As a wholesome physical activity dance has no peer.

The ancient Greeks attached great important to dance. For them, every occasion of life was an occasion of dance. They danced at birth, they danced at death, and they danced at the funeral games. Therefore, dancing is a legacy of the past persisting in the present. It is a racially old activity stressing body-mind integration. Aesthetics, and social interaction. Physical education and dance are closely related because both deal with movement. No other physical activity involves as much of music and rhythm as dance does.

It is certainly a deft combination of athleticism and aestheticism. Folk dances of various states of India are a fine example of activity, beauty, joy, rhythm and vigour. They stimulate the developmental processes on the one hand, and stir the soul on the other. Physical education without dance is body without soul.

GAMES AND SPORTS

Games and sports form the bulk of physical education. Since the revival of Olympic Games, more and more emphasis is being placed on the competitive aspects-of games and sport. The craze and quest for winning in international sports competitions have started a rat race among the nations for the development of new techniques and methods of athletic training and performance. The use of modern technologies for identification of talent at a very tender age, stress on very hard physical training, introduction of exotic infrastructure and equipment have changed the very complexion of games and sports especially at the top level. Contrarily, this new focus has helped broad-basing physical education. Competitive sports have raised the standard of human efficiency and performance. They have revealed incredible human capacity. They have initiated and strengthened research programme in sport sciences. If sports are removed from physical education, much of its charm would be lost. In its top form, each game/sport is a discipline in itself. However, the teaching part of games and sports in educational institutions is a responsibility of the physical education teachers who are expected to be specialized at least in one major sport.

THE NATURE OF PHYSICAL EDUCATION

Whether physical education should be construed as an academic discipline like history, economics, philosophy or physics, or a profession like medicine, engineering or law, or simply a programme of activity continues to be a debatable point. Movement or activity, however, is the very crux of physical education.

Movement is learnt and performed; it is scientifically analysed and studied; it requires highly specialized people to teach. Physical education has its tendrils spread in all directions. An academic discipline has a "body of knowledge" that has evolved, over a period of time through observation, research, tradition and human experience. Henry considered an academic discipline to be "an organized body of knowledge collectively embraced in a formal course of learning." It may need not have a practical application. "The content is theoretical and scholarly as distinguished from technical and professional.........a focus of attention, a unique body of knowledge and a particular mode of inquiry" is all constitutes a discipline, believes Kenyon.

Human movement is the sole focus in Physical education. Movement for fitness, for performance, for excellence, for recreation and for health is all that is emphasized, advocated, preached and practised in physical education. The multi-dimensional movement requires multi-disciplinary approach to creating a theoretical foundation for physical education.

Physical education has its theoretical base in a variety of sciences and humanities. Biology, physics, chemistry, anthropology, psychology, sociology, education, management, ethics, philosophy, aesthetics etc., contribute a lot to the development of theory and practices of physical education. The entire structure of "body of knowledge" is well-knit, having movement as its axis. Whether in making the nation fit and healthy or in preparing thee athletes for super performance, physical educators have to have a sound knowledge of the principles which govern movement.

As theoreticians and sports scientists physical educators add to the body of knowledge. This is what makes physical education a discipline "with its focus on fitness-play concept". Incredible performances in various sports are chiefly due to the sound body of knowledge which the physical educators have evolved in the recent past. Vigorous research in bio-sciences and humanities in the context of exercise and sport is widening the frontiers of knowledge with tremendous speed. Physical education is, there for, an expanding discipline. The establishment of full-fledged faculty of physical education in more and more universities in the country and abroad truly justifies the status of physical education as an academic discipline. A couple of decades ago it was not so.

While an academic discipline is characterized by a well established theoretical background and body of knowledge, a profession is characterised by its "practical application and thee service it renders to thee society". Any area of knowledge may be both a discipline and a profession. Physical education has emerged as a profession because physical educators serve the humanity as teachers, health education leaders, sport scientists and specialized coaches. They are both mercenaries and missionaries. They constantly pursue the objectives of fitness and health for all and excellence in performance for those who are talented and capable.

The word profession is best understood when it is distinguished from trade. Precisely, trade is governed by certain set rules of economic and its chief motive is profit. Profession, on the other hand, is guided by ethics and its major objective is service to the society. This, however, dies not preclude the professionals to receive pecuniary benefits. Abraham Flexer has listed six strict criteria for a profession : theoretical basis i.e., intellectual activity, a practical use, research resulting in new knowledge and ideas, self-organization, the capacity for communication and altruism.

By all standards physical education deserves to be called a profession for it succinctly fulfils all these conditions. First, physical education has a very strong theoretical foundation. Its principles are derived from a variety of sciences and humanities. Activity is a very complex phenomenon.

It has physical, physiological, psychological and sociological implications. The physical educators engage in research and intellectual activity in order to strengthen the bases of their practices and policies and not merely borrow from other disciplines. It is interesting that 80% of the sport scientists today are basically physical educators. The recent thrust on exercise and sport-specific research has given birth to sub-disciplines like exercise physiology, sport psychology, sport sociology, sport management etc., within the domain of physical education.

Second, in order to be certified as teachers, sport scientists, managers, coaches etc., physical educators have to undergo long period of professional training in general as well as specialized areas of exercise and sport. The academic curricula—both theoretical and practical at the teacher's training institutes of physical education are of high standard and can be compared with the curricula in any other professional area. From undergraduate courses to highly intellectual and research-oriented doctoral courses, all levels of professional training contribute to the development of competent leadership. Physical educators are not drill or skill masters, as they used to be called. They are teachers, professors, sport scientists, coaches, administrators and organizes. Third, physical education is a highly organized profession.

The emergence of national and international associations of physical educators, sport scientists, coaches etc., has strengthened the foundations of physical education as a profession. Periodic meetings, conferences, seminars, symposia, workshops etc. at the global and national level afford opportunity to the physical educators to exchange ideas, debate controversial issues, prepare ethical guidelines and thrash out professional problems. Physical educators have received recognition and parity with teachers because the society has conceded to them a professional status.

Fourth, like any other professional people, physical educators are highly skilled in activities. All physical educators are required to achieve a reasonable performance standard because in order to teach, they have to perform. Besides, they have to acquire skills for teaching, communicating, managing, organizing and researching.

In no other profession are the professional skills so diverse as in physical education. Fifth, the knowledge and skills which physical educators acquire are not only useful to them alone, the society in general and sports-persons in particular benefit the most from them. High performers in sport are created through the application of scientific knowledge and methodology. Performing skills are unique to physical education.

Sixth, physical education is assimilating new ideas from other disciplines as well as professions such as business, management, engineering and medicine especially in construction of infrastructure, organization of competitions and training of athletes for high class performance. All this is being done with a professional approach and precision. As a profession physical education is turning a new leaf. Finally, physical education is rendering yeoman's service to the society in maintaining a high degree of health and fitness with a view to increase production and productivity. No other profession is so directly concerned with health and fitness as physical education.

EDUCATION AND PHYSICAL EDUCATION

Man is an indivisible integration comprising "body, mind and spirit". Attempt to drive a wedge between the bodily functions and mental processes would be an exercise in futility because the organism acts and reacts as a whole and not in parts. The age-old myth that body and mind are separate entities has since been exploded. While the body is considered as the gross, concrete and solid aspect of the universal matter, mind and spirit represent its fine, ethereal and celestial qualities. Soul without body, mind without matter and education without 'movement' are meaningless concepts. The basis of man's existence is primarily physical. The cognitive, intellectual and social aspects of personality stand on a secondary plane. They exist and develop in relation to the physique only. According to the law of Nature, the first lesson of education a child learns, is the lesson of "body movement". Movement is the basis of growth and development. The development of neuro-muscular system is a prerequisite to perceptual and cognitive development. Therefore, the primacy of 'movement education'—informal or formal—in the orbit of education is well-established. Children become conscious of their body and its movements much before they become conscious of mental processes and abilities.

Eduction may mean different things to different people but the essence of all definitions of education is that it should afford equal opportunities to all for optimal development of their potential. It should draw out the best in child. This broad-based and comprehensive view of education takes cognizance of all the factors that contribute to the harmonious development of human personality. The development of brain without corresponding development of the brawn is hazardous. Therefore, thee importance of physical education as a core curricular activity must be recognized.

Both education and physical education are doing

phenomena. Modern educationists do not subscribe to "knowledge-acquisition" as the sole purpose of education. Rather stress is laid on "learning by doing". Physical education is an activity-oriented endeavour the main thrust of which is on "doing and learning". Activity is a binding buckle between education and physical education. The classroom academic activity and physical activity on the playfield must compliment and supplement each other for the balanced growth of human personality. Playfields, gymnasia, stadia etc., are the temples and laboratories of physical education where children receive practical training of life. Not only do they improve heir fitness, health and vigour but also learn how to be confident, mentally resolute, tough, cooperative, tolerant and decisive. Physical education is not simply breathless repetition of physical skills and exercises, it is education of the whole man through wholesome activity programme.

Bucher set four major objectives of education. They are: Objectives of self-realization. Objectives of human relationship. Objectives of economic efficiency, and Objectives of civic responsibility. Specifying a variety of goals and subgoals under these objectives, he vouched that physical education must play a significant role in helping children achieve them.

The objectives of self-realization include an enquiring mind, knowledge of health and diseases, family and community health, skill as a participant and spectator, utilizing leisure in mental pursuits and appreciation of beauty. Organized physical education cuticula should afford opportunities to all sorts of people to (1) actively explore and interact with the social and physical environment. (2) know their physical and mental capabilities, strengths and weaknesses. (3) acquire knowledge about personal, family and community health. (4) learn how to be competitors and spectators. (5) utilize leisure wisely in sport and other mental activities, and (6) develop a keen aesthetic sense. Self-realization comes to the individual by doing things, interacting with the environmental forces and assimilating varied experiences. No other discipline offers more objective method and techniques of self-assessment than physical education. For ancient Greeks, education was in complete without "athletics".

The objectives of human relationship refer to human welfare in general and that of participants in particular, rich social experience, cooperation, courtesy, fairness and sportsmanship, family welfare and home-living. Physical education must ensure human welfare, and provide recreation which is an antidote to such vices as apartheid, aggression, political vendetta etc. Sports, games, and adventurous activities like mountaineering, rock-climbing, sky-diving, marathon racing etc., may be highly competitive, challenging and risky in nature but not devoid of humanistic approach to global problems. Playfields should be a leveller of inequalities—racial, social, lingual and economic. Play activities must result in a rich and abundant social experience which underscores such qualities as co-operation, co-existence, fair play, courtesy, obedience, sportsmanship, honesty, spirit of tolerance etc. Practice but not preaching, example but not precept should be thee guiding principles on thee playfield. The players must learn to play the game in the spirit of thee game, transcending all barriers of caste, creed, religion and status. The Olympic Games were revived with the sole objective of creating international understanding and human brotherhood.

The objectives of economic efficiency entail good workmanship, vocational placement, successful work, professional growth and wise consumption of goods and services. Doubts are sometimes expressed as to the direct link of these goals of education with physical education. The reality is that physical education ensures a very high degree of health and fitness in the participants. Production and productivity—the main props of economic efficiency—cannot be increased without health and fitness of the masses. Physical education, in fact, indirectly contributes to these educational objectives. By offering myriad avenue for vocational placement to participants and athletes, physical education helps people improve their economic status. Outstanding sports-persons can undergo suitable vocational courses to serve as physical educators, coaches, sports administrators, managers, sports scientists, sports journalists and the like. Physically-educated persons must also learn how to be economical in the expenditure of their energy and use of goods and services. Only fit and healthy people can ensure a nation's economic efficiency and professional growth.

The objectives of civic responsibility involve humanitarianism, tolerance, conformance to laws, civic responsibility and democratic living. Playing games necessarily requires participants to be obedient, to conform to rules and regulations of the game, to act as responsible members of the team and follow thee principles of democratic living. Sportsmanship and sportsman's spirit are always referred to as the most cherished qualities of an amiable personality. Physical education must purge the individual and the society of negative feelings, pent-up emotions and destructive tendencies which often cause social turmoils and political upheavals. Participation in and organization of sport and recreational activities at school, and college, club, community centre, state, national and international levels offer grand opportunities to the people to learn lessons in civic responsibility, humanitarianism conformance to laws, and receive practical training in democratic living.

SCOPE OF PHYSICAL EDUCATION

Physical education is not simply a programme of physical activities done in isolation, it is a multi-dimensional field of human endeavour. There are at least four clear concepts which shed light on the dimensions of physical education i.e., physical education as a discipline, a field of study, a field of activity and an area of professional practice or service.

As a primary scientific area of human knowledge, physical education today is recognized as an academic discipline. The theoretical base of physical education lies in various applied science and art disciplines. Like any other subject—history, physics or mathematics—physical education is taught and practised in educational institutions. Recreation, fitness, health and play—both in theory and practice—make physical education a unique discipline in the technical sense of the term. There is no dearth of skeptics, within and without physical education, who do not subscribe to this view.

They believe that theoretical principles of physical education originally come from other well-established disciplines. There might be some truth in what they believe but there is no denying the fact that physical education is an emerging discipline in the changing spectrum of academics.

A field of study, physical education indeed is. A field of study, it is believed, result from the integration of knowledge derived from several disciplines and applied to one or more professional practices. Emphasis on research, more specific to practices, adds a new dimension to physical education as a field of study. Physical activity, ranging from simple play pranks in infancy to highly competitive Olympic sports, is the central focus of physical education and a reality of modern life. Excellence in sports is impossible to achieve without scientific back-up. Bio-sport sciences such as sports medicine, sport & exercise physiology, sport psychology, anthropomorphic, bio-mechanics, sport sociology etc., have crystalized as exciting and vitally important fields of research exclusively wedded to exercise and sport. The physical activity sciences are defined as field as field of study devoted to (1) "the understanding of all aspects of human physical activity and (2) the application of this understanding to meet the needs of the entire population. Physical activity sciences, therefore, supply the principles which help to weave the texture of activity programme. They also bring together individuals from different background, training, and interests. Doctors, engineers, architects, academicians etc., make significant contribution to physical education as an ever-widening field of study and practice. Human physical activity is a indisputable reality that is and will continue to remain an extremely important field of study by researchers of varied interests and backgrounds. It is estimated that 80% of the sport scientists today are physical educators themselves; 20%

come from other allied fields but their discussed and researched in the classrooms and laboratories of other art and science subjects, even though, as a field of study, they are largely nurtured in faculties, schools or department of physical education throughout the country.

As a field of activity, physical education is marked by variety. Games, recreation, fitness programmes, yoga, adventure sports etc., all comprise physical education. Irrespective of age, sex, geographical and cultural boundaries, one can choose any activity one likes to participate in. In general physical education includes thee following:—

(1) Games & Sports :- Archery, athletics, badminton, basketball, baseball, gymnastics, hockey, swimming, football, kho-kho, kabaddi, wrestling, tennis, table tennis, volleyball, adventure sports, water sports and the like. They are specific skill-based activities.

Some are individual sports, others team games. Excellence in these activities can be achieved through hard, vigorous and sustained participation and practice. Some games and sports do have carry over value.

(2) Self-defence activities:- Combatives—dual and mass—such as wrestling, boxing, judo, karate, stunts, stick fight, dagger of sword fight, martial arts etc., are included in this group of activities, thee major aim of which is to defend oneself against human or animal attack and develop such personal qualities as confidence, courage, determination, daring and decision-making.

(3) Gymnastics:- As a distinct discipline, this group of activities comprises educational gymnastics, etc.

Gymnastics is considered as a mother sport which aims to develop a sense of rhythm, balance, suppleness, agility, flexibility etc. Highly specialized gymnastic activities are a purview of the fees who are blessed with rare qualities of head and heart.

(4) Rhythmics :- Rhythmics serve as an interface between dance and gymnastics to some extent. Set-drills, mass rhythmic activities folk dance, lezium, tapir, drill and marching etc., are an excellent form of physical activity for school children. Mostly developmental in nature, their major objective is to help enfoldment of motor qualities, improve body posture, develop unity and uniformity in movement, and create a sense of rhythm.

(5) Correctives :- Corrective exercises purport to rectify posture defects—both genetic and acquired. Generally physio—therapists make use of limb and muscle modalities to activate the attached body parts. If not removed in childhood, clumsiness of structure and movements causes psycho-social problems for people in later years.

(6) Recreation :- Marked by hurrying and scurrying, the modern life-style necessitates recreation for physical and mental relaxation and diversion from monotonous routines. Any physical or mental activity done for its own sake—indoors or outdoors—may be termed recreation. However, outdoor active activities such as walking, hiking, camping, trekking, fishing, nature study etc., are considered as the best forms of recreation. Vigorous physical activity becomes much more enjoyable when performed as recreation for it invigorates the body and lets the soul soar high.

(7) Yoga :- As a traditional system of philosophy and exercise, yoga has been a way of life for all sorts of people

since time immemorial. Beginning with as both static and dynamic—which purify and discipline the body, the logic exercises help to control the disarrayed tendencies of the mind and finally lead to spiritual awakening. In physical education, yogic exercises are of utmost importance because they help the participants and elite athletes to streamline somatic functions, conserve psychic energy, develop a high degree of concentration and keep the individual mentally relaxed under highly charged competitive environment.

Physical education is essentially a performing art and activity is its very soul. Without "wholesome activity experiences, physical education has no existence. Activity for growth, for fitness, for health and for excellence is all that physical education stands for.

Physical education has emerged as a profession. Physical educators, coaches, sport scientists and sport administrators are its missionaries. They are suitably paid, awarded and rewarded for the services they render to the society. Amateurism in teaching or coaching is simply unthinkable in this age of economic astringencies on the one hand and pursuit of materialistic philosophy on the other.

2

PHYSICAL EDUCATION AND EDUCATION

In establishing the position of physical education in the pattern of general education it is important to present in brief the role of physical education in the past, and to indicate in what way the purposes of physical education are in accord with, or contribute to, the goals of education. This will be done in the light of the present day philosophy of physical education as it is reflected in modern courses of study, in the significant writings in the field, and in the need of physical education in our society.

From a brief review of the evidence of the past well shall see that the amount and type of physical education practised by a people reflects its philosophy and frequently reveals the dominant purpose of the state. Some people of the past who believed in subjugating the body as a means of elevating the soul discouraged enjoyable physical activity and, as a result, did very little toward developing a physical education program.

However, the Egyptians, Babylonians, and Hebrews, with a higher regard for the physical, encouraged and engaged in numerous sports and, consequently, developed more extensive physical education program. Persia, under Cyrus, a dominant leader, revolted from

Media about 558 b.c Cyrus had a philosophy of conquest and a major purpose that physical education could serve. He needed soldiers who could fight well and who could take care of themselves on the march. Consequently, he took young boys at about the age of six and trained them in discipline, running, jumping, javelin throwing, mounting, raiding, and other skills that would build more efficient fighting men. To test and develop his troops, Cyrus held long hunts which were severe ordeals. Extended marches, little food, and meagre protection from the elements characterized this phase of training.

The education of boys stressed primarily the physical and moral aspects-those moral aspects that would make for better fighters. Since the girls were not needed as soldiers, their education was neglected. About two centuries later, a philosophy of ease coupled with corrupt practices led to a neglect of rigorous training and to disregard for physical efficiency. This undermined the strength of Persia and, as a result, Alexander conquered her with ease. The Spartans, somewhat after the time of Cyrus, had a philosophy and purpose similar to that of the Persians and developed the same type of physical education.

The boys were take by the state at about the age of seven housed in barracks, and trained in those attitudes and forms of physical activity that made for stoic, rugged soldiers. Jumping, running, wrestling, throwing weights, and mimic dances of warfare were among the important physical activities. To provide more surely for strong fighting men, the weak and poorly formed babies were exposed to die. Spartan girls were trained physically so that they would become better mothers. Athens had military needs comparable to those of Sparta and Persia, but had a somewhat different philosophy. Learning, beauty, and grace loomed larger in the picture of Athenian life; less rigor and more freedom was the standard for men.

The physical education of women was given very little consideration. The physical activities were practically the same as those of Sparta, but additional aspects of performance were stressed. Beauty, grace, and sportsmanship were added to speed, courage, strength, and skill. This philosophy spread and made, itself felt during Greek control of the Panhellenic games, the most noted of which were the Olympic games. During the growth and rise of Rome as a would power hard work and physical exercise that prepared the young for war were dictated by a philosophy of conquest. At the crest of its power, and especially during its decline, Rome was aflame with a desire to see blood.

The physical activities of its great arenas reflected this desire. Dangerous chariot races, gladiatorial contests, beast baiting, miniature battles, extremely rough fighting, and brutal ball games marked this epoch of Roman Life. The Dark Ages, with the revival of asceticism, produced a general lack of interest in physical activity. Centuries later Jahan, of Germany, used physical activity and its accompanying attitudes to build to ward the great German goal of defeating France. Ling, of Sweden, saw in formal physical drill a means of improving the efficiency of the Swedish army.

This fear of neighbours and the desire for conquest have been responsible for certain types of physical education down through the ages. Even England, with her island seclusion and the resulting protection which permitted more athletic games and less mass drill, outlawed golf at one time because it interfered with archery practice. The Puritans and other early settlers in America, who had a great deal of work to do, frowned upon those types of play that did not consist of some work form. Wood-chopping contests, corn-husking contests, and rifle matches were popular. More recently, however, increased leisure, greater freedom of thought, and a philosophy of success have led to a variety of vigorous, competitive games in the United States not modelled after work forms.

The depression, with its enforced leisure for millions, stimulated recreational centre activities. The military draft figures for World War I disclosed numerous physical defects, and as a result many states enacted compulsory physical education laws.

Although the intention was good, there is not much that additional physical education laws and activity courses can do to reduce defects of the type that cause draft rejection. Draft figures from World War II supports this point. We see, then, that the philosophy of a people, which is always formulated in part by its needs, determines both the form and the amount of its physical activity. Hence, it is important that we consider the organization and administration of those forms of physical activity that are in harmony with our present philosophy, for those are the forms with which we shall have to deal. Certain activities, formerly discouraged, are now important units in our physical education programs; others, once of major significance, are now of only minor concern. We must follow our educational philosophy, which is influenced considerably in its application by public opinion.

With What Are Organization and Administration

Concerned?

Sound organization and administration are concerned with setting up or planning the total purposes and activities of the department or unit and carrying these out to the end that all important aspects involved are accomplished. Organization includes setting up the over-all pattern or plan, whereas administration deals with putting it into operation and keeping it functioning. In the physical education department the major phases with which organization and administration deal are over-all policies, facilities and equipment, human relations, budgeting and finance, staff selection, programs of physical and academic activities, details of class and team management, publicity, student problems, and aims and objective.

It is desirable that the student at this stage realize that a course in organization and administration is a summary type of course in organization and administration is a summary type of course which touches upon and re-emphasizes many phases of the program which have gone before and which ties together the entire offering in the field of physical education to give an overview of the whole departmental offering. In the whole process should be developed the viewpoint that the administrator who would accomplish his purposes best must act wisely, be friendly, strive to keep associates happy, make decisions, be reliable and honest, have a good general understanding of the entire unit involved, and be willing to accept responsibility.

The Present Outlook

These are some of the outstanding elements in our philosophy that point to the wisdom of dealing with the organization and administration of certain phases of physical education, along with some of the topics they indicate as worthy of consideration:

1. Realization of the fact that physical education should be educational.—Relation of Physical education to general education.

2. More concern about thorough establishment of bases upon which to operate a program.—(a) Aims and objectives of physical education and (b) administrative policies and activities.

3. Concentration upon developing better content and methods in physical activity classes.—(a) The physical education service program and (b) physical education class details.

4. Emphasis on more adequate preparation and higher certification standards for faculty members.—Physical education staff.

5. Increased interest in the teaching of health.—Health education.

6. Greater national and local emphasis on providing more and better school facilities.—Physical education plant.

7. A marked interest in interschool athletics.—Interschool athletics.

8. More enthusiasm for athletics for all.—Intramural athletics.

9. A conviction that we must learn to do by doing, to lead by leading.—Student leadership.

10. Tendency to check more carefully on school expenditures.—Budget making and finance.

11. Greater concern about securing and maintaining safe, well constructed, nice-appearing equipment.—Purchase and care of equipment.

12. Recognition of the value of maintaining friendly relations with the public.—Public relations in physical education.

13. Greater concern about the legal responsibilities involved in conducting a physical education program.—Legal liability for injuries.

14. More emphasis on efficient office procedure.—Office management.

15. Increased interest in national and local organization and societies.—Physical education organization.

16. Strong emphasis on research and evaluation of public performance.—Tests and measurements in physical education.

Major Topics to Be Considered

A survey of the courses dealing with organization and administration of physical, and related subjects, in a number of the leading schools of physical education shows that the above topics are given marked consideration in many of them. Current writings in the field also emphasize the importance of the above topics in the area of organization and administration of physical education. Consequently, in the remainder of this book the following major topics will be considered in turn:

• Relationship of physical education to general education

- Aims and objectives of physical education
- Administrative policies and activities
- The physical education service program
- The physical education staff.
- School health education
- The physical education plant
- Interschool athletics
- Intramural athletics
- Student leaders in physical education
- Budget making and finance
- Purchase and care of equipment
- Public relations in physical education
- Legal liability for injury
- Office management
- Physical education organizations
- Tests and measurements in physical education

Physical Education an Integral Part of Education

Physical education is that part of education which proceeds by means of, or predominantly through, physical activity; it is not some separate, partially related field. This significant means of education furnishes one angle of approach in educating the entire individual, who is composed of many component, interrelated functional units, rather than of several distinctly compartmentalized faculties. The physical, mental, and social aspects must all be considered together. Physical education, when well taught, can contribute more to the goals of general education than can any other school subject; not more to each goal than any other subject but more to all goals than any other school subject.

This is made possible, in part, by the fact that participation in physical education is very largely on the level at which the youngsters live. They grant their coaches and teachers great authority; the instructors in physical education have less need to demand it than do most other teachers. Opportunity for excellent achievement knocks continually at the door of the physical educator, making physical education one of the most keen-edged tools in the educational kit. With it he may sculpture beautiful figures or hack to pieces and mutilate the already partially shaped raw material that comes to him. In discussing contributions, we assume that a reasonably skilled teacher is in charge, for even the most perfect system or machine will not function well without competent direction.

The Goals of Education

The seven objectives presented in Cardinal Principles of Secondary Education are generally accepted as adequate goals of education. They are health, command of the fundamental processes, worthy home membership, vocation, citizenship, worthy use of leisure, and ethical character. A committee of leading educators appointed by the national Education Association in 1913 spent three years preparing this bulletin. Many years have passed since the bulletin appeared, and still the basic ideas of these objectives have not been replaced by others for the great mass of educators.

However, some have altered them a little here or there

to balance their own personal equation. Certain writers have overemphasized particular cases; sporadic attacks have been launched from time to time by others; and many have expressed the same ideas in different terms; but these seven objectives still stand as adequate and acceptable goals of American education. It is worth noting in this connection that the Educational Policies Commission, an outstanding committee of the National Education Association, has this to say of the bulletin; "It is probably the most influential educational document issued in this country." The commission, in its The Purposes of Education in American Democracy, then goes on to restate or reclassify the objectives of education.

This commission lists four major objectives: (1) The objective of self-realization, which covers in general the same area as covered by health, command of fundamental processes, worthy use of leisure, and ethical character of the seven cardinal principles group; (2) The objective of human relationship, which deals with members of the family and community group and is akin to worthy home membership, citizenship, and worthy use of leisure of the seven cardinal principles objectives; (3) The objective of economic efficiency, which covers in general the same area as vocational preparation and worthy home membership; and (4) The objective of civic responsibility, which is essentially the same as the objective of citizenship in the seven cardinal principles group. Since physical education is a part of education, it has the same general goals. The closeness of this relationship can be shown by pointing out the numerous ways in which physical education contributes to these goals.

Major Contributions to Health

These contributions can be made to both physical and mental health. The proper functioning of the social life of the individual is considered under ethical character and citizenship. Health is considered as that condition, mental and physical, in which the individual is functional, well adjusted internally as concerns all body parts and externally as concerns his environment.

Physical exercise and development of the muscular system have furnished an incentive to develop the other body systems in the advance from the lower to the higher forms of life.

In the amoeba, the simplest form of animal life, the one cell carries on all of the functions of the organism. Living in water, it gets nourishment by absorption from particles around which it wraps itself; in this process there is a secretion which helps digestion. Excretion is simply unfolding and moving away from the waste products remaining. As a means of locomotion it throws out a pseudopodium and rolls and drags itself over toward it; one piece is extended and the remainder of the cell then works over to it. Respiration is performed by absorbing oxygen from the water through the surface of the cell. There is no true circulation-the process is about like the diffusion of bluing in water.

There is no known nervous system, but if the amoeba is properly stimulated it responds. Reproduction takes place by division of the cell into two; these two in turn divide to produce others.

The sponge, a slightly higher from of life, has specialized reproduction cells and a skeleton, but otherwise shows no great functional advance over the one-celled amoeba except in the combination of cells.

The hydra, a coelenterate, shows functional advancement in that it has crude muscles and nerves and gets nourishment from "outer surface" cells.

In the earthworm we note a marked advancement over the hydrainage regard to functional systems. It has a co-ordinated muscular system which provides for locomotion. The energy necessary for even the relatively slow movement of the worm is immense as compared to the amount required in the life process of the practically immobile hydra. The extra muscle needed to move the worm about must be maintained during periods of inactivity as well as during times of action.

The hydra not only does not need to provide the energy for appreciable motion but is entirely free from the task of supporting a muscle mass of any consequence. With this gradually increasing muscle mass, requiring proportionately more nourishment, the developing worm is faced by a great problem; some better method of securing food than taking it through the outer skin must be provided. The answer to this problem is the development of a digestive tract or long hollow tube with some secretory tubes along the sides of it—a marked advance toward a digestive system. The worm is divided into numerous small segments, united end to end. Each segment has two primitive kidneys for excretion, and the whole organism has an outlet for waste other than the body surface.

A circulatory system is developed to carry food to the cells and waste products away from them. By no means the least important addition is the directing or nervous system, which controls and regulates all other systems. In the worm there are separate nodes for each section and a larger or more important ganglion in the head section. These various centres exhibit a rough kind of teamwork in action. A special reproductive unit is in evidence here too. Of those body systems that are primarily concerned with the individual's own life, the muscular system is the oldest and furnishes the main reason for the others' existence. However, the muscles existing in the earthworm compare only to our trunk and neck muscles; our other muscle groups came later. This phylogenetic development might be traced on up the scale of life, showing how the various parts originated. The muscles comparable to our shoulder and hip muscles appeared at the time of the fish; those of the arms and legs at the amphibian stage; and so on until the development of the hand muscles, which first appeared in the primates.

It must be remembered that although it came into being in a rudimentary form in the reptile, one of the very last regions to develop in its great complexity was the cerebral cortex, which develop in its great complexity was the cerebral cortex, which developed almost concurrently with the nerves and centres controlling the limbs and the delicate hand co-ordinations. The muscles and nerves that are phylogenetically old are larger, stronger, and less complex than those that are not so old.

These large-muscle groups with their controlling nerves are called the fundamental groups in that they came first or are phylogenetically older and are basic units. Those structures and functions which developed later—the cortex, the smaller muscles of the arms and legs, and vocalization—are called the accessory groups, because they are developed later as structural and functional additions to the earlier fundamental units. It seems to be a rule in nature that an adequate functioning of the fundamental groups is essential to a proper functioning of the more recently added accessory structures. That is, long continued proper functioning of the cortex depends upon exercise of the large muscles, particularly during the growing period. Before birth, ontogeny roughly repeats phylogeny as far as the physical organism is concerned. There is some small evidence of this trend after birth. The nervous system and the brain, however, develop relatively early, and growth of the various body parts is anything but uniform in progress; but when a system is started, it follows crudely the life history of the race. There is far less evidence of recapitulation after birth than before, for it is in attitudes, urges, and mental condition that the implied recapitulation takes place, and accurate evidence concerning attitude and urges is difficult to obtain.

The hypothesis advanced here is not that the specific physical changes are marked or noticeable, but that the general plan is followed; that, since big muscle action has ushered in progress of the various organic systems in the racial past, the plan is still used for proper development of those systems during the individual's growth. Nature discards very slowly the principles, constructions and devices that have, at some time, proven useful. Physical exercise and a great deal of it, is advocated as one of the necessary means of attaining a healthy development.

The child who exercises plentifully becomes tired and will rest better; gets hungry and will eat more; has more need of oxygen, and breathes more deeply and more rapidly; has more waste content to be carried from the cells and needs more nourishment for the cells, causing increased circulation; all of these contribute their bit toward better elimination of waste. This concentration on the other functions of the body strengthens the higher and lower directing centres, which are responsible for all action, but it does not require great action of the cortex. This is as it should be, for in youth the cortex is not ready to respond to extreme demands.

There are three fairly well differentiated stages of growth gradually leading from the first to the last; pure growth, developmental growth, and approaching maturity. During the period of pure growth, which is almost entirely an increase in mass, practically no exercise is needed. About all of the body parts except the cortex and some of the accessory muscles have passed through that stage at birth, and are ready for developmental growth, which should include increase in both mass and function but should not undergo intense exercise. The cortex is still so close to the pure growth stage for some time that only a small amount of exercise is needed. Any effort to improve upon the original plan an rush the developmental process is apt to produce harmful results, in terms of chorea, nervousness, and similar disturbances. Experimenters have used tadpoles in testing out the proposal that nature can be hurried along. Since the tail is absorbed to be replaced by hind legs, anyway, the tails of some were cut off in an effort to hurry the appearance of the hind legs. The hind legs did develop sooner than in the non-mutilated tadpoles, but they were deformed.

The penalty for violation of the general developmental principle was deformity. This experiment offers guiding advice to those who would neglect the physical and rush mental development. The third stage of growth is that of approaching maturity when marked activity is necessary to finish off properly the functional growth of the various parts. In general, the large-muscle groups are one stage ahead of the cortex and of the accessory groups in terms of development. In case of any doubt, it is safe to allow and advise additional physical, and less cortical, activity during childhood. Our present generation is nervous and unsettled. What can be expected of the next if concentration on cortical activity crowds out still more of the physical? This line of reasoning can be advanced one step further.

The other body systems still depend upon the action of those same muscle groups for stimulation to proper functioning during adult life. However, the amount of exercise required is much less than was needed in the first few years of life. This reduction in amount of required exercise has been taking place gradually. As the cortex reaches the more advanced stages of growth, it can stand more exercise and consequently should have more. In adult life, or even earlier, it has completed the period of developmental growth and more of the time of education can be devoted to "mental pursuits." This does not mean that physical activity is no longer necessary but, rather, that the body needs proportionately less exercise as age advances. Those who have neglected the physical and concentrated on the mental have suffered. It is the office workers and other men who use their cortex and inner hand muscles to the neglect of the large-muscle groups who have nervous breakdowns, rather than the day labourer, who exercises chiefly his large-muscle groups. These phylogenetically young members of the total body equipment, the interpretative and emotional controls of the cortex, and the fine hand co-ordinations, are the weaker ones in terms of stability and endurance.

They are the ones that give way first in the presence of sudden, immediate strain and also under long continued strain. Exercise of the older groups seems to build up strength in the new or to recharge them. The human system may be likened to a motor vehicle in regard to certain functional purposes, provided the analogy is not pressed too far: let the engine, or motive power, represent the large-muscle groups, and the battery, with its control over the lights and starter, represent the cortex. Assuming normal functioning conditions, then long driving or use of the engine charges the battery, strengthens the starter, and furnishes plenty of electricity of the lights. Suppose, however, that the lights are left on and the engine is started often but very little driving is done. After a time the battery will not be strong enough to start the engine and the lights will be dim. It is much the same with college students who neglect the physical in an effort to concentrate upon the mental. The average undergraduate does not suffer much, but the graduate student who is convinced that since he is a man in the realm of academic advancement he must put away may of the childish things of the undergraduate, including exercise, is very apt to suffer., Hence we conclude that physical education contributes to physical and mental health through the use of the fundamental muscles, which stimulate action of the other body systems and tend to "charge the cortical battery." Physical education contributes in other ways also. School children need some joyous excitement and will have it. Activity can substitute for dissipation, delinquency, and carousing by giving youngsters something interesting to do. Free time, once spent on playgrounds, on hikes, in gymnasiums, or in other areas of physical activity, is used up and hence cannot be spent in some unfavourable environment.

The evidence indicates that juvenile delinquency decreases as supervised play areas increase in number. Team games provide an excellent means of keeping certain youngsters' mind off sex matters. Especially at the adolescent age there is much dreaming and planning about things that appeal. In many unfortunate cases this centres around sex. With adequate direction, the team and its success can become the centre of plans, dreams, and activity; and, thanks to the much maligned coach, they often do! Then, too, vigorous play tires the growing boy, and his bed becomes a place for sleep rather than one for sleep and day dreaming. Students acquire sound habits only by practice, not by reading or hearing about them. Athletics, a large part of physical education, contributes well to health in this respect.

In order that the individual may be a better player now, or at some time in the future, he will gladly practice health habits. He will avoid some stimulants and poisons, establish regular and sufficient hours of sleep and rest, select more carefully the foods he eats, and, in general, practice better habits of living. We must never forget the value of play as mental relaxation.

It takes the youngster's mind off his worries and troubles; it provides a change in the emphasis of his concentration. Something new and vital to think about provides mental rest just as change of occupation provides physical rest. When we realize that one half of the hospital beds in the United States are occupied by mental cases, the importance of the mental aspect of health becomes readily apparent. During adolescence especially, but during young generally, there are emotional stresses and strains brought on by the conflicts between one's own plans and actions and the plans and actions of others. This emotional tension, flavoured with anger, fear, and the other strong emotions, provides increased internal secretions of adrenaline and the like.

It is better to work off the products normally through vigorous activity than it is to force the vital organs to make the adjustment of returning to the normal condition without the aid of such big-muscle activity. There is relatively clear evidence to the effect that exercise carried to the extent of marked fatigue leaves an individual more susceptible to certain diseases than he would have been without the exercise. However, competent physical educators discourage the practice of exercising to the point of extreme fatigue just as they do other excesses. The loss of resistance to infection is partially compensated for by the fact that regular, adequate exercise builds one up to the place where he is less readily fatigued. Then, when emergencies arise which demand an extra output of physical activity, he will be less fatigued than he would have been had he not build up his endurance. By practice the threshold of fatigue can be raised through developing greater endurance.

Contribution to the Attainment of Fundamental

Processes.

The point here is to support the contention that there are "fundamental processes" in physical education; once this is established it is readily apparent that physical education contributes to their attainment. Those fundamental processes are the physical skills common to America in general and to one's own locality in particular.

They are fundamental chiefly because the child needs them now for happy living, but also because future physical education endeavours and many life occupations are based upon them. As was pointed out before, children live on a different level from that of adults. In play situations the good performer is the hero and the poor performer is pushed into the background. Much of child life is play life, and a large share of it deals with physical sills; whereas only a small part of adult life is play, and good performance is not stressed so much. If an adult loses at golf or does poorly in a ball game at a picnic, it matters little, for success in those areas is not particularly vital; there are many other things that influence happiness so much more.

The child does not have those numerous other phases of endeavour to which he can turn for success if he fails miserably in his physical skills. He must master the fundamental processes or suffer the consequences of loss of standing and recognition among his fellows in one of the major fields of youthful endeavour. That is one of life's most severe punishments, and it can be avoided by improving physical abilities. Many unhappy, insignificant boys have become leaders in their school because of improvement in their fundamental skills. Whether boys and girls go on to college or into other walks of life, training in the fundamental skills is necessary.

It is unpleasant and unprofitable to remain below the elementary school athletics and leisure-time sports activities demand a thorough grounding in the fundamental physical activities and skills. Certainly physical education contributes largely to the attainment of an adequate command of may of the important fundamental educational processes.

Contribution to Ethical Character, Worthy Home Membership, and Good Citizenship.

Since many of the qualities that make for achievement in any one of the above provide for achievement in the other two, the three are grouped together. Health, which helps to a larger degree in attaining worthy home membership and citizenship and less in attaining ethical character, is any exception worth noting. Physical education is one phase of school work that lends itself particularly to the development of character. Student interest prevails, activity is predominant, and relatively great authority and respect are accorded those in charge.

The physical education class provides more than just a place to discuss character education theory; it furnishes a laboratory for actual practice. We develop character much more surely by living it out than we do by hearing about what should be done or should not be done. It is one matter to decide upon the correct response to a tense situation when merely looking on, and an entirely different proposition to decide and act correctly when in the midst of heated combat. One contestant may foul another, unnoticed by the official, near the end of a close game and thous prevent an opportunity to score. The player fouled cannot take his ensuing action under advisement and decide some time later what to do about it. He must decide at once and give his answer immediately by what he does.

This splendid educational laboratory demands actual responses to tense situations just as much as life in general does. The whole setup provides real rewards and punishments which with proper guidance will serve to encourage sportsmanship, co-operation, sociability, self--control, leadership, and those other qualities of character and citizenship which we stress. The competitor is an active citizen, not a passive one. It is the acting citizen who receives training. There are lows or rules that must be obeyed as he drives on toward his major ambition of winning the contest or performing well. There are penalties imposed immediately upon any infraction of the law. Opportunities to give, to take, to obey, and to co-operate are numerous. Here is the ideal setting for developing the good citizen, the worthy home member and the individual of ethical character, provided, of course, that the situation is well handled and well regulated. In no school situation arc the goals adequately attained if those in charge are incapable or indifferent. As in the case of health, the dominant drive for a winning team or good performance leads to the development of good habits. Sane character habits, such as controlled sex life and abstinence from the use of alcohol, are steps in the direction of good citizenship that can be prompted by athletic competition. In order that he may be a better player, the youngster will practice these and other habits of good citizenship. In the long run as well as in the immediate situation, clean living builds for success. Habits of clean living and good citizenship tend to carry on just the same as do undesirable habits. Enough good ones crowd out some bad ones. Out personality with its basis of character is, after all, the sum total of our responses to the social situations in which we find ourselves. We establish characteristic reactions to familiar situations. Pursuit of interesting, desirable goals during the period of habit formation will help to develop desirable reaction patterns.

It may be unreasonable to contend that the boy who displays co-operation and consideration in game situations will ask a tired mother to permit him to do the dishes in the evening: it is probable that he sees no common elements in these situations. All good traits certainly will not carry over completely from one situation to another; but, if there are many, at least a few may be expected to carry over to similar situations. When all other phases of school life contribute their bit toward good citizenship, worthy home membership, and ethical character, generalizations of fairness, sportsmanship and the like can be build up that will have some carry-over value. The identical elements involved should also carry over to similar home and community situations. Some of the skills learned contribute to worthy home membership and citizenship as well as they do to command of the fundamental processes. Other things being equal, the more skilful home member is more worthy than the less skilful one.

Contribution to the Worthy Use of Leisure.

Within the last 30 years, the hours of labour for children and adults have been drastically reduced. Many informed people predict further reduction.

Whether or not this anticipated reduction comes to pass, there is a vast amount or leisure time to be spent now; much more than ever before in the history of this country. It is not during the hours of labour that unsocial conduct develops but in the hours of relaxation and freedom. Since it is during free or play time that those who enter crime prepare for that regrettable adventure, steps must be taken to employ that time more profitably. It is to this phase of guidance and development that physical education is eminently qualified to contribute. It is provides a means of interesting, active, and constructive adventure instead of an approach to unsocial conduct. Inherently youth desires physical activity, competition, co-operation, fellowship, and many of the other elements in our program. It is well to note that adequate provision for the leisure time of adolescents is more important than is the preparation for their leisure time when they will be adults.

If the problem is adequately administered in youth, there will be little cause for anxiety about it during the time of adult life. It is a mistake, then, to criticize many of our more vigorous team games on the count that they do not provide carry-over activities for later life; they do not need to do that in order to justify themselves for they serve the cause of leisure time right now. In meeting the leisure needs of youth, they may render a greater service than those less vigorous games which carry over into adult life. One reason for this lies in the fact that children have much more free time than adults: the greater need offers the greater opportunity for service. Another reason which has been touched upon above, is that proper training and correct habit formation in youth may carry over into adult life. Adult habits cannot revert to a youth that is past.

It is most valuable to occupy the leisure hours and days of youth harmlessly and constructively. Since team games attract strongly, they have the power to pull youngsters to them who might not be attracted otherwise. To be sure, our games that have carry-over value as entire games into adult life need to be included among the physical activities of adolescents, but they must not be used to the exclusion of the more vigorous team games.

3

PRINCIPLES OF PHYSICAL EDUCATION

There are very rare physical educators who does not long for a better sense of direction, who does not ask: What is my purpose here? What should I be doing with and for these students? To answer these and other related questions, he must first critically examine his basic beliefs. Not until after asking what is life all about, what is the real nature of the world, and what is of greatest significance in life, can he make discriminating decisions about what and how to teach. All of us hold certain beliefs about life, of course, but many of use may not be able to state them explicitly and may never have submitted them to sharp scrutiny. A physical educator who wishes to burst out of this cocoon of complacency can profit from examining philosophical explanations that endeavour to make our existence intelligent and meaningful and to give direction and purpose to our activities. Philosophers are concerned with three basic problems: What is reality? What is truth? What is of volume?

The problem of reality forces them to decide what is fundamental, real—what is the ultimate nature of being or existence. The problem of truth or knowledge makes them probe into how man arrives at knowledge and how he can be certain that it is true. The problem of value causes them to consider the worth of things. They may, for example, give attention to ethical, aesthetic, religious, social, educational, recreational or health values.

Their basic concern is to ascertain what is good in human conduct, in social organization, and in art. Adherents of various philosophical schools have come to somewhat different conclusions about the nature of reality, truth, and value. The idealist believes that ultimate reality lies in a thinking being—a self, mind, spirit—rather than in physical things—matter. Men live in a world of ideas; what they know of the physical world is what their minds have created. In contrast, the realist believes that reality is independent of human experience; it exists in the laws and order of nature which are neither subject to the human will nor dependent upon a human mind for their existence. The pragmatist contends that the only reality we know is that which we actually experience each day. He does not believe in an all-inclusive reality, an unchanging order.

Reality is not something that is static or everlasting—it is an ever-changing flow of experience. The existentialist contends that ultimate reality resides within the individual human person. Reality is a man's own experience of being: the awareness of his moral self and his irrevocable responsibility for making choices that will fashion his essence. How do the various philosophies differ in regard to the nature of truth or knowledge? The idealist believes that true knowledge consists of universal or ideals that are eternal and purposeful. Man discovers them through mental activity, insight, and intuition.

The realist believes that true knowledge consists of the real things in the physical world—the laws and order of nature. These laws exist by themselves; they are independent of the mind and self. Man discovers them through sense perception, through scientific reasoning, through objective means that are free of any personal, emotional, or subjective approach. The pragmatist believes that knowledge is discovered through experience, and he questions the possible absoluteness of truth. To him, truth is a matter of consequences. If a suggested solution to a problem works in a given set of circumstances, it can be considered as truth for the time being.

But, to the pragmatist, truth may change as circumstances change; what is true today may not necessarily by true tomorrow. As men gain greater insight into the world through experience, they will continue to revise and correct their knowledge. The existentialist does not believe that truth is forced upon him by an external or objective reality, but rather that the individual is the final court of truth. He contends that all knowledge, all intuiting, all experiencing, arise within the heart and mind of the individual and receive certification by him. Knowledge—truth—is what exists in man's consciousness and feelings as a result of his experiences and the meaning he has given to them. How do the various philosophies differ in regard to the nature of value? To the idealist, the essential values of life are eternal, fixed, and man discovers what is good or bad, beautiful or ugly, right or wrong, but the values themselves do not change.

The realist believes that a thing is good, right, or

beautiful if it conforms to the laws and orders of nature, that it is evil, wrong or ugly if it does not, and that these values are not variable. The pragmatist is skeptical of fixed and immutable values. He contends that value is based on human judgment. Man creates his own values through purposeful action and the interpretation of his experience. Good is that which the group discovers, works out satisfactorily in practice—not in a selfish sense, but in a social sense. To the existentialist, the final arbiter of what is good or beautiful is the individual. He rejects the uncritical acceptance of value systems that have been established by social, political, scientific, or theological groups, because he does not want to forfeit his essential existence—his freedom to choose.

The existentialist looks within himself for an understanding of what is good and beautiful, and establishes his own value system. He assumes full responsibility for contributing to the moral and aesthetic essence of man, through personally deliberating about and practising what he decides is best for himself and mankind. The idealist, realist, pragmatist, and existentialist look upon education in light of their particular beliefs, concerning reality, knowledge, and value.

Consequently, they develop different, but not mutually exclusive philosophies of education. It is rather difficult to generalize concerning their beliefs because adherents of each philosophy express various shades of opinion, and members of different schools embrace similar as well as different views. In bold outline, however, eliciting answers to the following questions will tend to set these philosophies apart.

(i) What is the objective of education?

The idealist encourages a vigorous, full development of the individual's creative powers in a manner that will bring him into harmony with the highest ideals. Seeking ever greater individual perfectibility includes the development of the body and good health. This objective is placed at the bottom of the hierarchy of values, but it is considered basic for the realization of the social, moral and spiritual aims. The realist does not emphasize the "self"—the individual—for he believes that reality exists in the laws and order of nature.

Hence, the objective of education is to acquire verified knowledge of these laws and to mould youths so that they will live in conformity with them. The educator is to build competencies in youths that will enable them to understand and make an adequate adjustment to the real, external world. The pragmatist is not interested in absolute ideals and inexorable laws, but in the obvious realities of life—the here and now. His objective is to have students solve successfully the problems of life as they arise. He strives to stimulate a desire for continuous growth and helps students become functional members of society by providing opportunities for everchanging experiences.

In brief, he seeks many sided social efficiency. The existentialist elevates the individual to a position of central prominence, for he contends that self-determination is the ultimate objective of pedagogical attention. Education is to awaken the student to a knowledge of his moral self. It is to make him understand that the responsibility for choosing what he will become and for living with what happens as a result of his decisions rests with him alone.

ii. What is the nature of the student?

To the idealist, the student is not merely a biological organism that is shaped by the physical environment; he is a "mind , personality, soul"—a "self" whose body is responsive to his will. As Horne explains, "It is not so much the stimulus shaping the individual, as the individual responding to the stimulus". To the realist, the student is biological organism with a highly developed nervous system that interacts with the physical environment. The physical stimuli within and without the student determine his behaviour—not his personal whim, his will, or blind chance. To the pragmatist, the student is an active, doing organism who grows through effective interaction with the ever-changing, social-physical environment.

Upon meeting problems in life situations, he proposes hypotheses and tests them to find workable solutions. To the existentialist, the learner is a unique, autonomous individual who independently makes the commitments and takes the action that determines what he will.

iii. What is the nature of the curriculum?

The idealist is primarily concerned with content that consist of ideas—the humanities, but he includes physical education in the curriculum as a means of providing for the full development of the individual and the realization of an ideal society. To him, any content or activity is acceptable that acquaints students with the accumulated wisdom of the race and permits them to recreate truth, goodness, and beauty in their own thoughts, feelings, and actions. The realist believes in a rigorous, systematically organized curriculum that places emphasis on the transmission and mastery of content—particularly scientific facts and principles.

The contents and sequence of the curriculum are scientifically determined. The realist is primarily interested in quantitative subject matter, and the idealist is interested in qualitative subject matter. The pragmatist utilizes any activity that gives students experience in applying the scientific method of solving problems. The curriculum is not a systematic structure consisting of rigid work units that are presented in a particular sequence. It may consist of related or disparate units of work and may utilize any content that will help the problem at hand.

The curriculum is closely related to pupils' interests and to community and current problems; new activities are added whenever there is a need for them. Emphasis is placed on "group activities", "cooperation", "doing", "problem solving"; hence, sports and games provide an excellent medium for instruction. The existentialist believes that the curriculum cannot be prefabricated for the child. Rather the child is made aware of his moral self and of a wide variety of alternatives, activities, and tools. He is absolutely free to appropriate those that will help him fulfil his unique purposes.

In the existentialist curriculum, individualized activities would probably predominate. Group activities would be self-chosen. A deep conviction of the need to act with others to become the person that the individual wants to be would cause him to join or organize group activities. The objective of the group would not be to impose the will of the majority on members, but rather to help on another bring about a realization of their individual essence and develop a genuine relationship with society. The curriculum would not shield the child from the wholeness of life—it would make him aware of evil and he could prepare himself to meet them squarely as a part of life.

iv. What is the nature of the teacher and his methods?

To the idealist, the teacher is more important than facilities, equipment or any physical thing. He is a firm, friendly individual who thoroughly understands his subject and pupils. His personal example of wholesome, vigorous living and the attention he focuses on personalities and works of inspiring greatness stimulate students to develop their full creative powers. His pupils are surrounded with positive influences and are shielded from deleterious ones. They are provided with inviting opportunities for creative effort; challenged to put all of their powers into their performance; and given ample opportunity for discussion, self-initiative, and self-direction.

Students learn—fashion their character—through making decisions, judgments, and analyses. Whenever possible interest is utilized to evoke effort, but external discipline may be employed to stimulate enough effort to cultivate interest and establish the habit of self-discipline. When evaluating pupils, the idealist is not especially concerned with quantitative assessments of mechanics of an activity and the reproduction of specific knowledge, but rather in the changes in self.

The views of idealist's are being rejected by realist. In his classes, pupils are brought into contact with the real work through demonstration, experiments, field trips, and audio-visual aids. They are exposed to clear, distinct facts in an objective and logically ordered manner and are drilled in the mastery and application of scientific principles. External discipline is utilized, if necessary. Learning proceeds inductively; it starts with elements and details and builds toward a systematic whole.

When selecting techniques, the realist makes decisions upon the basis of scientifically demonstrated facts. When evaluating students, he employs objective rather than subjective tests and seeks quantitative measures of achievement. The pragmatist guides students so that they can find successful solutions to problems as they arise. The emphasis is placed on how to think rather than on what to think. The teacher serves as a co-worker and co-learner who helps students identify problems and apply the scientific method of solving them.

In this socialized approach to learning, group decision making is stressed. Ample opportunity is given for the free interchange of ideas and continuous evaluation of progress. Little emphasis is placed on systematic lectures, terminal tests, and traditional coverage and organization of subject matter. The learning environment is often extended beyond the walls of the classroom. The pragmatist believes that if students tackle problems that intensely interest them, they will spontaneously put forth the effort required to seek solution. Consequently, the teacher will neither have to lure them with external rewards or have to serve as a drill master or moralizer.

The existential teacher is not a transmitter of information, nor a director of projects, nor a model to imitate. He is a provocateur of thought who awakens the child to the moral dimensions of life. Through posing moral and intellectual questions, he causes a student to think seriously about who he is, what he is in the world for, and what he should make of his life. The existential teacher establishes an intimate, exploratory communion with the student in which an atmosphere of free association prevails. After getting the student authentically concerned about moral issues and encouraging him to search for facts, to examine alternatives, and to consider probable consequences, he strictly refrains from prescribing a course of action.

The student is required to make his own choices in light of what he thinks man ought to be and is held strictly accountable for what happens as a result of his decisions. The existentialist sees little value in traditional testing procedures that are based on group norms and that measure prescribed subject matter. Inquiring into the nature of his beliefs, appraising his teaching practices in light of what they imply about his beliefs, weighing whether his beliefs and practices are worth retaining or need to be revised will be a disturbing but an exhilarating experience. The physical educator may decide that one school of philosophical thought is most compatible with his beliefs and provides the most meaningful insights for clarifying his educational problems and directing his professional life.

On the other hand, he may find that his beliefs do not fit into the straight jacket fashioned by any of the existing philosophical approaches. Becoming familiar with views of the world and concepts of the purpose of education that others have developed in detail and have submitted to rigorous examination should sharpen his critical consciousness, but blindly accepting beliefs, standards, and practices that others impose upon him cannot be condoned. A physical educator must engage in a never ending personal quest to clarify and to coordinate the concepts that constitute his personal act of commitments.

Building, broadening, and depending his own philosophy of physical education, eliminating inconsistencies, and developing the capacity to articulate his ideas to others is a professional responsibility of the highest order.

The Contributions of Physical Activity to Social Development

Thoughtful people agree that emotional and social learnings are important, for real education is an emotional and social as well as an intellectual experience, and that there must be an effective curriculum for personal-social education that parallels and often intertwines the academic curriculum. The direction for improving social education demands the utilization of insights and studies from many disciplines from which health education, physical education, and recreation draw their basic principles. We must, therefore, look not only to the research and thoughtful study of specialists in the areas of biology, psychology, and medicine, but also the social sciences of sociology, cultural anthropology, and social psychology. There must be some cause and effect laws in the way human beings behave just as there are cause and effect laws in the way steel, rubber, or the atom behaves.

Where do we look for these principles? The behavioural sciences provide possibilities of honest, exhaustive, intelligent, interdisciplinary searching for facts and their meaning or implications with reference to any given problem in our field. In the area of psycho-social development it is exceedingly difficult to establish functional relationships between numerous variables involved. This makes the task of validating causative explanations of individual behaviour a terrifically challenging and difficult one.

Social Development in a Culture

Culture consists of the things that we have learned to do, to make, to believe, to value, and to enjoy in our lifetime. Our culture expresses the basic values of our society. The forces which interact on the playing fields, in the gymnasium, and elsewhere provide for children a steady flow of motivations and feelings which gradually shape the personality. In the sense that we as teachers have a part in controlling or influencing to some extent these factors in our culture, we become guardians and developers of personality by influencing the dominant attitudes and goals of that part of our culture related to games, sports, and recreation in general.

Social Psychology

It is well known that participants of a culture or in a group take on the existing values or norms of the group. A democratic climate produces democratic values, and a sportsman-like climate produces attitudes of sportsmanship. We perceive these situations in terms of the norms we bring from the group situation. We deal here with the role of suggestion in the formation of attitudes. Using parent rating and child behaviour rating scales, Baldwin found that democratically raised children were more active, were more extroverted, and were favoured in their group. They rated high in intellectual curiosity, originality, and constructiveness. The variable indulgence seemed to produce the opposite effects of democracy. Sherif found that individual subjects tended to be strongly influenced by others in the group, the degree of influence being effected by the prestige and leadership qualities of certain group members. His findings have implications for values stressed in games and sports, for major attitudes, are derived from groups to which we related ourselves or of which we regard ourselves as members.

Dunker found it feasible to influence nursery school children's food preferences through social suggestion. After determining the children's preferences and their tendency to imitate others, stories were told to present certain foods in an attractive light and other foods in an unattractive light. Sixty-seven per cent of the children in the experimental group chose the food presented as attractive against only 13 per cent of the children in the control group.

Implications may be drawn for seeking character education outcomes through play situations. Symonds, studying normal adolescent boys and girls, concluded that the greatest need of these adolescents was opportunity for social participation and that the greatest personality handicap was social and isolation. Physical education and recreation activities are indicated.

School and Teacher as Social Forces

The school represents a social structure and system of its own—of students, teachers, administrators, and service personnel. In the various social sub-groups which are constantly forming and reforming, pupils get to fill social roles in many different groups, such as classes, clubs, athletic teams, orchestras, student councils, and a host of others. The experiences in these various groups provide the social and psychological settings and conditions for the development of many aspects of social learning—knowledges, attitudes, skills, and values. The teacher and administrator must find ways in which all participants relate themselves to one another so that new social learnings result not only in greater social integration and efficiency but also in individual satisfaction of needs.

Todd in a sociometric study on the senior high school level, demonstrated the value of the democratic method of physical education class management by objective data showing greatly increased acquaintanceship and significant decrease in the number of unpopular and unwanted girls during a one-semester experimental period. Anonymous questionnaires revealed that the pupils found the sociometrically selected squads more enjoyable and efficient than any other grouping method they had ever experienced.

Nedelsky indicated that the child's first social world is his family; he then shifts to a world in which his orientation grows out of being a part of a group of other children whom he accepts as equals. The school then becomes the social system which is an important setting in which children relate to one another.

McGuire and Clark reported upon two alternative indexes of peer status that have been recently developed. The two forms seem to approximate essential aspects of the level of acceptance of subjects in classroom groupings and in age-mate societies. It appears that level of acceptance could be a variable for distinguishing and identifying individuals and subgroups in a population for further study.

Swensen and Rhulman in analysing questionnaire

responses from 1217 university sophomore men and women concerning many aspects of their extracurricular activities, found that the four chief reasons for the participating were relaxation, working with people, professional reasons, and opportunities for service. The highest percentage of participation in campus activities was in social living groups. Athletic events were the most popular spectator-type activities.

Social Development

Much social interaction centres around physical skill. The child lacking motor skills is often barred or not accepted in social participation. Human personality cannot be developed apart from the social group and since our children are destined to live in a highly organized social order, the physical activities of children and youth should be used progressively from kindergarten through high school to develop social learnings and a gradual intensification of social consciousness. The social implications of play and sports are revealed in several studies.

Bunker studied 50 male college students active in physical education and sports and 50 who tended to be inactive in these activities. Histories indicated that participation in team games by the actives was consistently greater through the upper grades than for the inactives. While 64 per cent of the active reported that the greater part of their daily play as children was in neighbourhood groups, only 36 per cent of the inactives so reported. Bunker concluded that the bases for active participation must be laid in the elementary grades.

Foehrenbach, when inquiring into the social motives

operating to make high school girls participate in after-school sports, found that going with the crowd and imitation of older girls were prominent in the thinking of junior high school girls, while making new friends was a stronger motive for senior high school girls. Fear of failure to do well kept about one-sixth of the junior high girls from participating, and the fact that they had no friends who were participating restrained one in ten.

Shugart, while a psychiatric case worker in the receiving ward of a large neuropsychiatric service in a naval hospital, invariably found histories of meager play experiences in men being referred to the hospital. Patients experienced lack of interest in play as children, and deficiencies therein were evident in both quantity and quality. Further study, elsewhere, of the play histories of 60 psychotic children showed that these children had suffered serious deficiencies which assumed characteristic forms of expression.

Studies of holding power of secondary schools have revealed that extracurricular activities are important means of keeping students in school.

Gough used four high school senior classes in his study. Students who had a high number of extracurricular activities seemed to be characterized as: (i) frank, unpretentious; (ii) self-disciplined, but tolerant of others; (iii) broader cultural and intellectual interest; (iv) identification with and acceptance by the group; (v) possessed effective social skills; and (vi) optimistic, with higher levels of drive and energy.

Thomas studied high school drop-outs and discovered that not one person who dropped out before completing the third year had engaged in even one activity, and that 89 per cent of those who finished, had. Since intramural and interscholastic athletics are administered as student activities in practically all high schools, it can be seen that few drop-outs participated in sports activities.

Comparing academically successful and unsuccessful children, Volberding found that the child considered most likely to succeed is more intelligent, better adjusted socially and personally, more interested in active play, prefers play in competitive groups, attends movies less often, and listens to radio more frequently.

Duffy studied 16 nursery school children, age 2 years, 11 months to 3 years, 10 months. His observations suggested a possible correlation between muscle tension and various aspects of behaviour, such as number of physical contacts in free play, number of words used, degree of restlessness, and degree of inattention.

Resnick studied the relation of high school grades to satisfactory adjustment as judged by scores on several standardized inventories and found that pupils earning the higher grades also secured the highest mean satisfactory adjustment scores. In general, categories related to adjustment in relation to other pupils, to social competency, social participation, satisfying work, recreation and interpersonal skills were significantly in favour of the student with higher honour point ratios.

Betz found low but significant relationships between several physical fitness test variables of adult men participating in an afternoon adult physical fitness class and certain personality traits as determined by Catell's 16 Personality Factor Inventory items.

Partridge studied factors of leadership in six different Boy Scout troops totalling 226 boys by using a five-man-to-man plan of rating. He found that outstanding leaders excelled others in age, intelligence, athletic ability, scout rank, scout tenure, and physique.

From a larger group of normal children, Rarick and McKee selected for investigation 20 third graders. Ten had a high level of motor achievement and the other 10 a low of motor achievement. Though a small number of cases were observed, those children who attained a high level of motor proficiency tended to be more frequently well adjusted in school and personal relationships. Also they appeared to have fewer irregularities and difficulties in infancy and early childhood.

Antisocial Behaviour

Children's insecurities and frustrations show up directly or symbolically in their free play. The aggressive, destructive, unsocial, or antisocial attitudes are acted out in play. As professionally mature physical educators, health educators, and recreation specialists we must try to decipher the real meaning of these activities as sensitive indicators of personality development. We must try to structure play situations that will facilitate release and expression of impulses, feelings, and fantasies. Games and sports often become substitute responses which redirect behaviour and satisfactorily reduce the original instigation by satisfying emotional and social needs.

In tracing the evolution of play therapy, Lebo concludes that if play therapy had developed solely from the theoretical explanations of play it would be used to educate children to play properly.

Cox, in studying sociometric status and individual adjustment before and after play therapy, found that sociometric status was shown to be an effective index of adjustment for a group of 52 orphans, aged 5 to 13 years. The findings supported the theory that the sociometric status is a sensitive and valid index of behavioural change.

Bernstein asserts that play is a natural means of expression for the child and can be clinically useful in diagnosis, therapy, and research. Play may diminish anxiety in children and be helpful in evaluating the need for psychiatric help.

Shaw found that an inconsistent or conflicting environment retards the development of socially sanctioned behaviour. He showed quite dramatically the influence of the group, or small segment of society and its mores, upon attitude and behaviour of individuals.

Cox, in studying sociometric status and individual adjustment before and after play therapy, found that sociometric status was shown to be an effective index of adjustment for a group of 52 orphans, aged 5 to 13 years. The findings supported the theory that the sociometric status is a sensitive and valid index of behavioural change.

Wattenberg noted that in any group of full-fledged delinquents, the first signs of behaviour difficulties appear in later childhood, often before the age of ten. For eleven year old, poor school performance and gang activities are strongly related. Frustration met in school may have led to hostile feelings which were vented in destruction of property or fighting. The author suggests that for those who failed in efforts to earn social recognition in sports or scholarship, daring deeds of theft and bravado may have been a compensation.

Chittenden used play situations as a means of helping children get a better understanding of their own problems and as a means of finding whether they gained in understanding. Play was used also as a means of direct teaching of manners and techniques that would help children to avoid quarrels.

Personal Social Adjustment

Adjustment is the dynamic process by which organism meet their needs. Physical education and related activities satisfy many of these needs by siphoning off dammed-up tensions in wholesome and socially acceptable ways. It satisfied in opposite ways, neurotic or delinquent behaviour may be the result. Studies reveal that socially well-adjusted persons tend to be more successful in athletics, physical fitness, and physical education activities than are persons who are less well adjusted socially. Jones, Hardy and Wenger found some relationship between muscular function and social adjustment. In Jones' study subjects with high strength scores were rated high in popularity and social prestige and were well adjusted, whereas subjects with low strength scores had social difficulties, inferiority feelings, and personality maladjustment.

Hardy found substantial positive correlations between being esteemed by one's classmates and leadership, health, cooperation, I.Q., and E.Q., and between general behaviour traits and school attitudes, muscular strength, and physical achievement. Wenger found positive correlations which confirmed the hypothesis that individual differences in characteristic level of muscular tension in skeletal musculature are positively related to differences in (a) frequency of overt muscular activity, (b) speed of movement, (c) emotional behaviour and instability of response, (d) aggressiveness, and (e) irritability.

Using a rating scale for measuring character and personality of persons in physical education classes, Blanchard found that desirable character and personality traits are stimulated by participation in physical education activities. Walsh reported that girls whom others seek as team-mates and playing companions seem to be the ones who can perform well in physical activities. Edwards found that performance in the Cowell Athletic Aptitude Test correlated .389 with the Partridge Leadership Ballot, and .371 with the Cowell Personal Distance Ballot. These correlations obtained with pre-adolescent faculty sons, were significant at the 1 per cent level of confidence. Also using the Cowell Personal Distance Ballot, Stover found a correlation of .661 between this measure of social acceptance and a 12-item battery of physical achievement.

Reynolds found an r of .414 between scores on the Cowell Personal Distance Ballot and performance on the Pursue Motor Fitness Test, using pre-adolescent boys as subjects.

Several investigators related social adjustment to physical education performance. Cowell found that social adjustment ratings by teachers and by classmates were positively and significantly related to physical education grades. Breck found correlations ranging from .27 to .90 between choice of friends and skill ratings in activity classes at the University of California, Los Angeles, with those selected as desirable friends having the higher skill ratings.

Another group of studies revealed a relationship between athletic achievement and social adjustment. McKinney found that well-adjusted college students tended to be more athletic, to be more interested in the opposite sex, to participate more in extracurricular activities, and to be of a social nature. Brace found a marked relationship between athletic ability and social status among pupils in grades 6 through 9.

Sperling and Signorella found differences in adjustment between athletes and non-athletes. Sperling found athletes to be more extroverted and ascendant. Signorella found that differences in amount of athletic participation were moderately related to scores on the Cowell Social Adjustment Index.

Henry obtained a positive correlation between general athletic ability and favourable attitudes about physical education. The correlation was highest in performances demanding extreme sustained physical exertion and lowest with agility and coordination. Similarly, Biddulph found that students ranking high in athletic achievement showed a significantly greater degree of personal and social adjustment than students ranking low in athletic achievements.

Zeleny indicated that researchers on leadership are in practically unanimous agreement that leaders are superior to non-leaders in intelligence, scholarship or knowledge, vitality, social adaptability and athletic ability. Stogdill's summary of leadership research to 1947 found height, weight, energy and health, and especially athletic prowess all associated with leadership.

Tuddenham pointed out that the Reputation Test can

be used to reveal problems for social maladjustments much earlier than they are ordinarily detected by adult observers. Thus test diagnoses a child's social adjustment to his peers.

Studying students' objectives in physical education, Schurr found that 450 freshman high school girls most want to learn to get along with and understand others, to learn to control emotions and be a good sport, and to learn to lose graciously.

Comparing them with active junior high school boys, Cowell found that fringers were less acceptable, socially to other boys and girls as compared with actives and were deemed less able to fill school positions.

Sociometrics

Sociometrics is the study of the patterned relationships between members of groups. Data from which such studies enable us to try to understand and adjust those currents of influence that unite or separate the individual members of any group. Health, strength, and physique determine to a great extent what, and especially how well, a child plays. Play skills, in turn, are of major importance in companionship and friendship in the social relationship of children. The physically excellent child has opportunity to lead in games and to learn thereby the very important techniques of leadership and co-operation. Many studies demonstrate that athletic prowess contributes to social status.

Tuddenham applied the Reputation Test to boys and girls in grades 1, 3 and 5. He found that athletic competence, daring, and leadership were source of prestige for boys, while attractiveness and demure friendliness were important for girls. Tryon found that in middle adolescence social excitement is directed toward the athletic leader or one whose physical, dramatic, social or intellectual skills give status. McGraw and Tolbert reported a moderately high relationship between sociometric status and athletic ability in almost all groups of junior high school boys in a school in Texas.

Kuhlen and Lee studied 700 children in grades 6, 9 and 12. They found that those most acceptable were judged more frequently to be popular, cheerful, happy, enthusiastic, friendly, and those who would enjoy jokes and initiate games and activities. Todd states that squads chosen on the basis of sociometric information are likely to produce happy, cooperative work and play.

Furfey showed that when boys selected chums, physical development had a larger correlation with companionship than did intelligence. Flowtow and Ondrus both found that members of athletic teams had higher social status than others not able to make the team. Along somewhat the same lines, Marks pointed out that boys with higher sports scores were more sociable than those with lower sports scores. This indicates the social stimulus value of strength and physical ability among adolescent boys.

However, at the sixth grade level, Austin and Thompson found that being skilful in games were sixteenth on the list of reasons for choosing someone as a friend. In another study of reasons for choosing friends, Williams found that among adolescents such items as full of fun, fair and square, good sport, athlete, and the like were prominent. Bretsch further verified that sports participation is related to social skills and activities of adolescents which distinguish socially accepted from unaccepted adolescents.

Lieb in pre-Nazi Germany found that both boys and girls mentioned physical superiority most frequently as a basis for leadership. Wellman found that differences in size, strength, and health seemed to be more important factors in social adjustment than are moderate differences in intelligence. With quite similar findings, Bower pointed out that popularity was unrelated to intelligence, height, home ratings, or school achievement but was significantly related to strength and to physical ability.

Two investigators studied drop-outs and social status. Kuhlen and Collester found that drop-out was related to such factors as health, unhappiness, and a sense of lack of status. Kuhlen and Bretsch found that those who dropped out of school were less acceptable socially to their classmates and were judged by their classmates to possess traits of personal and social maladjustment.

Success in the classroom and social status were investigated in three studies. Grounlund and Whitney showed that sociometric status in the classroom is a fairly reliable index of pupil's general, social acceptability among his peers. Buswell concluded from her study of a classroom of boys and girls in the early and upper grades that in general those who are succeeding in their school work will also be succeeding in their social relationships with their peers. Bonney and Powell, studying first graders, found that the highly acceptable differed from those sociometrically low by smiling more frequently; engaging in some form of cooperative, voluntary group participation; and making more voluntary contributions to their groups. They were also less likely to be alone during free play or activity periods.

Activity Preference, Physique and Personality Characteristics

Studies of personality and somatotyping suggest that there are fundamental types which influence choice of physical activities. These findings have implications for planning physical education on an individual basis. Thune conducted a study to discover some of the differences in attitudes and personality traits which may exist between weight lifters and other active team sport athletes. He found that training which weights appeals to a certain personality group. Weight lifters tended to be strong and dominant individuals who received more satisfaction in winning an individual championship than being a member of a winning team. They definitely disliked traditional sports.

Nelson studied the personality and attitude differences of those who chose ROTC in preference to the physical education program. The military students were less in favour of physical activity and competition, and displayed a withdrawing disposition in social situations. They preferred organized uniformed groups and had a more favourable attitude toward authority and position.

Hanley reported on the relationship between body type and reputation as measured by a reputation test of the who's who type along two groups of boys, ages 16-20. Boys of mesomorphic build were described as good at games, real boy, takes chances, and leadership. Ectomorphic boys were bashful, untidy, not quarrelsome admissive.

Personality was found to be a factor in selecting physical activities by Flanagan. Results indicated that fencers seemed to be more dominant, more feminine, and more extroverted than those engaged in badminton, basketball, volleyball, boxing, and swimming. Volleyball players seemed to be more submissive, more introverted, and less emotionally stable.

An analysis of data covering ten years at the United States Military Academy by Appleton, revealed significant positive relationships between physical ability of cadets at the time of entrance and the criterion of success or failure to graduate from the Military Academy.

Cabot, in studying the relationships between characteristics of personality and physique in adolescents, found that a good physique disposes boys to develop traits of self-expression, social acceptability, and physical vitality.

Ragsdale compared 45 women physical education majors and 45 non-majors in the ratings given by high school principals. The two groups were equal in appearance, manners, and purposeful use of time. The physical education group was superior in leadership and initiative, and more of this group displayed a high degree of emotional control. Bayer and Reichard reported that somatic androgyne indicates a relationship between physique and certain psychological reaction patterns.

Social Mobility

The social mechanism called social mobility involves many factors which become social sifting device for selecting, promoting, or demoting individuals and distributing them in terms of social class. Athletic sports and games, as common denominators, bring youth from various socioeconomic levels together on a common basis. The athlete in school tends to become more socially mobile than the non-athlete and, other things begin equal, has greater opportunity to achieve upward social mobility. La Place studied personality traits in relation to success in professional baseball. Results indicated that major league players were better able than minor league players to apply their strong drive toward a definite objective, to adjust to occupations requiring social contact or the ability to get along with others, and to exercise initiative.

Annarino found a critical ratio of 9.0 favouring greater campus social mobility for Purdue athletes as reflected by their dating girls in socioeconomic levels superior to their own. Popp had five administrators and teachers select ten boys most nearly like sons they would like to have and ten boys least like sons they would like to have. Of the boys who fell into the desirable category, 69 per cent had high PFI's; of the boys in the undesirable category, 75 per cent had low PFI's.

Social Integration

An integrated social group is one in which there is a great deal of social interaction within the group and people are bound together by such organizational bonds as common goals and purposes. A good team and a good school as miniature societies illustrate integrated social groups. The quantity and quality of friendships developed by students in a physical education class or on an athletic squad should be a concern of a good teacher. They are also personal concerns of students. In a well-integrated social group each individual would tend to accept every other individual in the group at a close personal distance.

Erwe found a positive statistical relationship between employee participation in the sports activities of a large industrial plant and the merit ratings of supervisors. The merit ratings were based on aspect of dependability, accuracy, efficiency, safety, and social adjustment.

Gustad, in summarizing the research literature dealing with factors associated with social adjustment and maladjustment, noted that those participating in social activities tended to have fewer significant scores on adjustment inventories and to exhibit less maladjustment. They were generally more extroverted, stable, and dominant than non-participants. Participation in extracurricular activities was associated, with above average academic achievement. This was complicated by the fact that social leaders tended also to be brighter than the average student. There was no evidence that a reasonable amount of extracurricular activity affected grades.

Walters presented an analysis of the change in social adjustment of motivated and non-motivated groups in a seven-week bowling class. The results seem to indicate that though both groups became more socially adjusted as a result of group participation and acquaintance, the motivated group became better adjusted than the non-motivated.

4

CLASS MANAGEMENT IN PHYSICAL EDUCATION

All students have basic motives and needs for learning. Motivation impels students to learn—to work toward achieving success in learning. Whether or not one takes a position that student's motivation is self-generated, residing totally within each student, teachers do make a difference. They do this by managing and directing instruction to improve student's motivation for learning and to prevent or minimize disruptive student behaviours in their classes. A safe, orderly, and positive learning climate helps students attend to the work assigned. Need for recognition, approval, acceptance by teacher and peers and the class as a whole are all important needs to consider in planning motivational strategies.

Teachers who believe that student's learning is enhanced through their instruction, match their modes of instruction with the abilities of their students. Teacher's expectations, their belief that what they teach is important, and their belief in their ability to teach and the ability of all their students to learn, influence student's behaviours in learning. Teacher's expectations of success have positive effects on student's motivation to learn and structures the class climate for all students. Each student is expected to achieve. Parents, too, influence their children through their expectations for them. Parents involvement in the instructional process, their value and attitudes toward program goals and objectives, their supportive efforts for the program and their home instruction all facilitate their children's involvement, their desire to learn and, consequently, their achievements.

A FRAMEWORK FOR PLANNING

There are many motivational schemes that teachers can consider in planning class management strategies.

Other Considerations: Students with Special Needs

Teachers are often concerned with establishing and maintaining favourable student attitudes, acceptable patterns of behaviours with students who have special needs. Here are some suggestions that have been useful in different classes based on two strategies found in the literature: role playing and source credibility. Role Playing. Role playing can be an effective technique to introduce students to individual differences in learning. Role-playing techniques are consistent with several instructional activities for learning discussed under motivation. Here are ideas for:

Role Objective: A student with special needs.

Objective: Experience a physical condition.

Materials: Special equipment to produce a particular condition.

Procedure: Create a physical condition in yourself by:

—full and partially covering eyes;

—using earplugs to fully or partially block hearing;

—using a wheelchair;

—wearing a brace;

—any combinations;

Give attention to problems with

—physical layout of classroom, barriers and obstacles;

—methods used for giving directions to students;

—student distractions or outside influence.

Other Activities

Role Play: Puppets

Carnival: Booths.

Credibility: At times students need a highly credible source to influence their attitudes. For example, often messages on television are considered a reliable source by students.

Research Project

Objective: Help students become aware of contributions made by individuals.

Materials: Readings, chalkboard, and chalk.

Procedure: Present a list of persons with handicaps who are living or have died. Ask students to select one person and research his or her life for a report. Each report must include:

—nature of handicap and how it occurred;

—how handicap affected the person—education, home life, friends, job and recreation/leisure;

—what problems were encountered as a result of handicap;

—what are or were the accomplishments, contributions, goals and future hopes of that person; artists; inventors/scientists; athletes; politicians, others.

Other Activities

Films: Help students become aware of handicaps and their influence on people's lives, reduce stereotypes and myths about individuals with handicaps. Present one or more films pertinent to age group of class. Follow up with discussion.

Other Suggestions: Although these ideas may increase student's awareness and acceptance of students with special needs, involving students in planning activities is the best procedure. Here are a few more suggestions that have been found effective.

Define: Who has a handicap, a special need?

Objective: Help students examine their perceptions.

Materials: Chalkboard and large charts.

Procedure: Write the word handicapped on the chalkboard. Have students give a definition. List words in that students suggest. Ask them why they associate each word with the term handicapped. List reasons on board.

Other Activities

Objective: Gain awareness of the concerns of students with special needs: at home, at school, at play.

—a buddy or peer in a class or gym class; assist in teaching motor skills in elementary classes.

Visitors: Speakers or sports personalities with special needs.

These strategies focus primarily on preparing classes for students with special needs who are or will be assigned to the teacher's classes. One important strategy is for teachers to get to know the student before entering the class. The student, parents and related school personnel may be the best sources for helping teachers focus activities for the individual student's needs and motives. Using instructional strategies discussed under motivation for learning applies equally to all student's basic needs and motives for learning.

Planning Class Management Strategies

Class management strategies include all the skills, and techniques that are primarily intended to control student's behaviours. These strategies are most relevant when they are used to increase student's involvement in learning and, consequently, student achievement. Strategies that promote student involvement, engaged time in learning within allotted instructional time, tend to improve student's behaviours in learning, preventing a minimizing disruptive or interfering behaviours. Student behaviours that are disruptive are not always the result of managing and directing instruction.

Students can provide their own source of interference through forms of withdrawal, disinterested, defensive, or hostile behaviours. These behaviours may represent adjustment mechanisms developed by students in trying to deal with what they feel to be intolerable situations. Reasons are numerous. The ultimate cause lies somewhere between the motivational problem and the learning problem. Numerous, but high on the list are:

—repeated failures and frustration in past efforts;

—lack of motivation, purpose, relevance, interest;

—rejection at home or by significant others;

—lack of ability and peer relations.

Class management strategies focused on controlling student's behaviours to increase student's involvement are presented under two areas: selecting principles for designing strategies, and using a variety of strategies.

Selected Principles for Designing Strategies

Effective class management strategies to prevent or minimize student's disruptive behaviours are based on seven general principles. These principles provide teachers with guidelines for planning and managing instruction to help students develop and maintain appropriate behaviours in learning.

(i) Know the Learner: Regardless of how many strategies teachers know, they will be of limited assistance without the knowledge of individual students. Managing and directing instruction appropriate for individual students require teachers to know the learner.

Learning. Teachers need knowledge of student's skill levels, learning styles, and interests in the instructional program.

Personal-Social. Teachers need to be aware of their student's frustration levels, self-esteem, expectancy of success, responsibleness, and attitude toward the teacher, peers and school.

Health-Physical. Teachers need to know what the student can do—strengths and health and safety factors in the environment.

What teachers do makes a difference. Students who are defensive or fearful, for example, require strategies that are quite different from those needed for students with low self-esteem. Defensive or fearful students may benefit from short, simple tasks, guaranteeing success; students with low self-esteem typically respond to positive reinforcement. Students also respond differently to rewards for success in learning. Some respond to tangible rewards, such as award cards, free choice, praise by the teacher, or being selected to demonstrate for the class.

In short, individualizing instruction is the selection of appropriate class management techniques to meet class and individual student's needs.

(ii) Select Target Behaviours: Teachers need to focus on specific target behaviours. The target behaviour must be manageable. Global statements such as, "The student is disruptive" or "The student does not pay attention" or "The student is lazy", have little meaning. Similarly, teachers who intervene with too many behaviours, important or trivial, are spreading the effects so thin that it is doubtful that any strategy will be successful. Teachers must select target behaviours that have greatest disruptive or interfering effect for student or for the class during instruction. Teachers should not attempt to manage each and every inappropriate behaviour that occurs within a few seconds.

For example, if a student comes late to class, moves noisily about the gym talking loudly to another student, gets equipment clumsily and takes it to assigned space and the teacher uses a series of verbal statements as interventions, such as "You are late, No Talking, Watch where you are walking, Pick up the equipment quietly, please," there is little effectiveness. The teacher's effectiveness is improved if a single target behaviour has been selected, such as "being on time". The other behaviours would be unimportant if the class had not started. Behaviours that are symptomatic of a condition are of critical concern when working with students with special learning needs.

Loud vocal noises emitted by hearing-impaired students, the inability of a student with cerebral palsy to remain still in time, the confusion about time and class organization by a learning-disabled student, are examples of symptomatic behaviours. If students have no conscious control of these behaviours, they should be tolerated. Tolerance does not imply a lack of structure for these students. It does imply a learner's leeway before the teacher intervenes with direct intervention. The teacher may need to work with related support personnel in identifying manageable target behaviours as well as the most effective intervention strategy. Focusing on student's target behaviours, teachers are instructional managers.

They are not forced into the role of a disciplinarian. By identifying target behaviours, intervention strategies can be planned. The limits of appropriate behaviours can be defined. These limits can be clearly communicated to students. Appropriate behaviours can be explained and demonstrated. Students can provide examples of what is desired or not desired. Once behavioural limits are established, these limits need to remain consistent.

(iii) Set Routine Structures: A routine structure should be set and followed. Specific student behaviours are defined as appropriate in particular activities. For example, specific assignments to begin and end a class session, moving from one area to another, sharing equipment if necessary, or taking turns in different class formations. Unplanned situations do occur during instruction; for example, interruptions by school announcements, class pictures, school assemblies, or even substitute teachers.

Regardless of these interruptions in class routines, structure is important. Students need security of predictability. They need teacher consistency in managing and directing instruction.

(iv) Use Sensible Rules: Teachers can make too many rules of conduct. Neither the teacher nor the students can remember all of them. Too many rules provide no consistency in their enforcement and/or reinforcement of appropriate behaviours. Rules established to regulate behaviours that personally annoy the teacher but have no visible impact on learning should be avoided. For example, these might include pulling the hair, picking the nose, or dirty hands and face, which have little impact on learning. These kinds of behaviours need to be handled outside of class time at appropriate times when positive reinforcement of appropriate behaviour can be given.

(v) Provide Positive Reinforcement and Feedback: One of the most powerful tools available to teachers is the selective and systematic use of positive reinforcement: the continuing use of a stimulus resulting in an increase or maintenance of the target behaviour. Positive reinforcement is another name for what turns the student on. The reward can take many forms. It is a motivational technique to increase or maintain appropriate student behaviour or performance in a skill.

A list of example motivational techniques as rewards for performance is provided below. These techniques are easily adapted for use with student behaviours in the learning environment:

i. Decrease the amount of practice time by one minute for each additional correct response/or decrease of one or more error responses.

ii. Give points or verbal praise of beating yesterday's score.

iii. Give free time for daily, improved performance.

iv. Have the student beat the teacher's best rate.

v. Give days off if the skill is mastered early .

vi. Hand out merit or award cards for aims that were met.

vii. Keep a student chart of the skills mastered; follow the mastery of every fifth skill by something specific the student chooses to do.

viii. Omit practice time altogether if a student demonstrates a better rate of performance today that yesterday.

ix. Have the students select where they would like to practice and continue to let them select the location as long as performance improves.

x. Let students select the persons who will monitor the daily check and help chart progress.

Frequently provide reinforcement feedback during the initial learning of appropriate behaviour. Reinforcement schedules and timelines for rewarding students vary with each student as well as for the class as whole. The goal is for students to become self-directing, the reward intrinsic to the act itself: skilled performance and acting appropriately in varied situations. Teachers can develop, with students or teams, a record keeping system of appropriate student behaviours.

Charting correct responses, appropriate behaviour in a given situation can serve as a type of reinforcer for student, team or class. For example, a sample record sheet with a column for desired behaviour followed by a column to record reinforcer and dates when given can be drawn on construction paper and covered with a clear, plastic sheet.

(vi) Reward Appropriate Behaviour: Teachers need a systematic plan of rewarding students who are performing appropriately in the learning environment: students, who are completing their work, working on target objectives, or working quietly with others. Students who are disruptive can learn from their peers that appropriate behaviour is rewarded. Even the most disruptive student performs appropriately sometimes within the class.

For every assignment the disruptive student performs correctly, minimal as it may be, should not go unnoticed. Reward the appropriate behaviour, catch the student doing something correctly. Teachers need to address the current student behaviour, i.e., here and now. Reminding the student of past problems in behaviours serves no useful instructional purpose. It may, however, promote feelings of failure or resentment on the part of the student. Teachers must not signal to students that their past behaviours, or behaviours of other students, will continually be used to evaluate current performance. For example, using such statements as, "You did this for the last two weeks", or "How many times must you be told" or "Look how correctly you are performing compared to the number of times 1 had to tell you". The current problem should be dealt with and past problems or other students should not be discussed. Teachers must target current behaviours that afford the student the opportunity to change and to achieve success.

(vii) Define Limits, Set Consequences, and be Consistent: One of the most important class management strategies to define, limits, set consequences and consistently enforce them. This strategy helps prevent inappropriate behaviours, thereby reducing the number of discipline problems. Some students seem to find pleasure, their own reward, or reinforcement, in continuing inappropriate behaviours disruptive to instruction.

This is particularly true when there are no defined limits or consequences. Consequences selected need to be practical to carry out, related to the behaviour violation, fair and reasonable, and help students learn appropriate behaviours. For example, the students are playing a game of tag and two of them begin pushing and hitting. The teacher approaches the students and asks them to stop. They do not stop. What is the consequence? Send students to the principal's office? Report them for detention? There are too extreme for the violation. Should they be removed from the game until class is over? This consequence may not help them learn to play with appropriate behaviours. The teacher finally decides to have them sit out for two minutes and then rejoin the game. Students finish the game with appropriate behaviours. The teacher praises their performance and the performance of all student in the game. Whenever possible, teachers should avoid threatening, negative reinforcement of inappropriate behaviours.

Negative reinforcement is referred to as aversive control, which motivates students to avoid negative consequences or to escape from undesirable consequences. Examples of this type of motivation include sending students to the principal, threatening detention or loss of privileges, verbal harassment, giving students signals that they will get it later, or other specified consequences of non-performance. In some instances, these procedures may be necessary. Teachers need to communicate clearly the limits and consequences of inappropriate behaviours to all students and explain the appropriate behaviours in instruction for all students.

Demonstrating these behaviours and knowing that the students understand them is important. Consistent and predictable enforcement of class rules procedures, routines and consequences is required, and periodically reviewing these limits and consequence is important for the whole class. Feedback and positive reinforcement of appropriate behaviours for the whole class, as well as for individual students, are effective class management strategies.

Using a Variety of Techniques

Teachers must use a variety of techniques to minimize discipline problems. No technique, however, can replace the teacher's knowledge of the students and knowing which situations are likely to create problem behaviours. With this knowledge, teachers can plan and devise instruction to prevent or to minimize the occurrence of the problem behaviour. Motivation for learning and instructional and management strategies previously described provide teachers with a variety of techniques.

Positive approaches foster motivation and

management of student behaviours to build teacher and class cohensiveness and consensus. They establish task-related emphasis in learning and develop positive teacher-student and student-student relationships. Techniques that control student behaviours, using pressure and force, appear to be significantly less effective in promoting student achievement, appropriateness of student's behaviour in learning. The motivation and class management strategies discussed focus on developing and maintaining appropriate student behaviours. They are strategies, teacher behaviours, useful in controlling student behaviours directly relevant to increasing student's involvement in learning—time-on-task. These strategies are designed to prevent or minimize the discipline problems and the need for more extreme intervention strategies and consequences for non-performance. These student behaviours destroy the class climate conducive to learning for all students. Extreme discipline problems—destruction of property, fighting, shouting, profane language and hostile, argumentative activities—require immediate teacher intervention strategies. These strategies require supportive assistance and a specified set of consequences established by school personnel.

No matter how well an initial ABC program plan is designed, it is never perfect. The initial program plan provides a foundation upon which a dynamic, constantly improving physical education curriculum can be developed. Accepting that all programs can be improved, the question becomes one of how program weaknesses can be identified and remediated. The process of evaluation specifically addresses these issues. Evaluation in the ABC model is a process by which program merit can be systematically determined.

Program merit is the identification of strengths in the program, whereas lack of merit is the identification of weaknesses.

The process of evaluation seeks to determine these strengths and weaknesses by comparing program expectations with actual program products. Data related to the identified weaknesses often provide information as to why the deficiencies exist and the insight necessary to design alternatives that will remediate identified weaknesses. Program, can refer to instruction related to a specific objective, a unit, a year, an instructional level, or an entire K through 12 program. It can also refer to a program for an individual or a group.

The evaluation process always begins at the instructional objective level and works up. Teachers must evaluate instructional objectives first since they make up the units, and by looking at the effects of several units, they can evaluate the results of a year, multiyear, or the entire program. Therefore, whenever the term program is used, simply substitute objective, unit, year or program. As indicated, the goal of evaluation is to determine merit. The role of evaluation is multifaceted. Teachers can evaluate a total program, a program component, an individual's program, or the program of a particular population group. Similarly, teachers can evaluate the ends of a program, the means to the ends, or the degree to which the program meets some external standards. The more common purposes of evaluation are to:

i. Document the validity or importance of the expectations of the program.

ii. Document the way in which the program is being implemented.

iii. Determine the effect of the program on its participants.

iv. Provide information-based recommendations for revisions necessary to reduce identified weaknesses.

v. Document compliance or noncompliance with legislative mandates.

vi. Document the relationship between program costs and effects.

Of particular importance is the information necessary to enhance orderly growth of the program to a stable condition that has benefited from current staff members but is not dependent on them. Such a program is dynamic in that it would improve each year as staff identified and remediated weaknesses of the program. The result of the application of evaluation procedures can be as many and varied as the roles that evaluation can serve. The more important for physical education are:

i. To describe the expectations of the program and to communicate the rationale and/or importance of these expectations to everyone involved with the program.

ii. To describe how the plans and procedures designed to result in identified expectations are being implemented.

iii. To describe the results of implementing the program in terms of student performance gains.

iv. To identify strengths and weaknesses of program implementation and effect.

v. To make recommendations for improving the program.

vi. To design in-service sessions based on observed weaknesses in the program planning, implementation and evaluation.

Currently, many models are available to guide educational evaluations; unfortunately, most of them cannot be used readily by physical education teachers. They are too complex, written generically, and designed to be used in a wide variety of educational settings. Consequently, it is often difficult to apply these models to specific physical education evaluation needs. More important, their complexity is overwhelming, not only from the standpoint of evaluation design but also from the standpoint of implementation time.

Physical education teachers simply cannot allocate the time necessary to conduct a formal evaluation as described in most models. A primary value of the evaluation models, however, is that they provide a framework from which a solid evaluation plan can be built. The objective-based structure underlying the ABC model ensures that it has already met certain criteria in its organization and implementation. Teachers, therefore, can get right through much of the content of other formal evaluation models and get right at the evaluating questions that must be answered to continuously refine the program. The simplified evaluation procedures proposed for use with the ABC model are not meant to reduce the quality of the evaluation process.

Rather, they are suggested on the premise that a workable evaluation that is completed and results in positive program change is much better than a sophisticated evaluation plan that is not workable and therefore is never implemented. Physical educators must have an evaluation model that:

i. is consistent with the concept of quality;

ii. is simple enough to be workable;

iii. can be applied to a total program or program elements;

iv. can be applied to an individual, group or groups;

v. can be conducted in a short period of time with little or no data collected beyond that which is already available as a result of implementing the program; and

vi. can be conducted as part of the program's regular implementation.

Student Evaluation and Reporting

Student evaluation is the process of determining and reporting the degree to which targeted goals and corresponding instructional objectives have been achieved by the students in the program. The student evaluation process is based on reassessment and yields information for represcribing and student reporting. The procedure for conducting student evaluations include:

i. assessing student entry status on the instructional objectives selected for inclusion in the program;

ii. reassessing student change continuously during the course of instruction to provide:

—feedback to the student,

—feedback to the teacher regarding the appropriateness and effectiveness of instruction,

—information necessary for reporting student status and change at the end of instruction;

iii. determining what aspects of instruction were

effective and what aspects of instruction were not effective; and

iv. determining and reporting to appropriate audiences the amount of change observed subsequent to instruction.

Assessing Student Entry Status

Student entry assessment data allow the teacher to set student performance expectations, prescribe instruction, and make appropriate placement decisions.

Reassessment and Prescription

Reassessment is designed to measure the performance level of a student subsequent to instruction. Reassessment provides the information necessary to keep the student working on the next higher performance level of each instructional objective and thus in the success-breeds-success cycle. For this reason, reassessment should occur continuously during instruction. Reassessment in this context, refers to the constant evaluation of student performance included as a part of the instruction that results in feedback to the student as well as information for the teacher.

Each time students attempt a skill and receive feedback regarding some aspect of their performance, reassessment and representation have occurred. The students have received positive feedback regarding their performance and direction regarding what needs to be worked on next. The teacher has received feedback regarding the quality and effectiveness of the prescribed instruction. Although this form of ongoing evaluation is at the informal end of the assessment-reassessment scale, it nonetheless is associated with good teaching and is a major determinant for improving student on-task-time and thus increases the probability of students making significant gains in performance.

All re-assessments are not formally recorded. This does not imply, however, that many of these observed changes in performance should not be recorded. It would be desirable if all re-assessments were recorded. Such a practice, however, could often demand more instructional time than would be justifiable.

Reports: Content and Grading

Meaningful reports to students, parents and others are extremely important if the program is to maintain credibility. Complete student progress reports should include the following information:

i. The content that was taught.

ii. The student's entry status on the instructional objectives.

iii. The student's exist status on the instructional objectives.

iv. The amount of change that occurred on each objective.

v. The student's relative to his or her own continuous progress.

vi. The student's status relative to his or her peers.

Not all of the above information needs to be provided on every report. These data should, however, be available on request to the interested student, parent, administrator, teacher, or IEP committee.

Content Information. The reporting of student achievement must be based on the content that composes the instructional program. Accordingly, a student progress report should be based on the degree to which the content has been mastered. As simple and logical as this may seem, student performance in physical education has not been evaluated and reported in this manner. Student evaluations are typically based on some standardized test of motor performance, motor development, fitness, and/or select sport skills. To the extent that these tests measure the objectives included in the program, they may yield some usable information; however, these tests are generally not selected for their match to the instructional content taught in the program, thus making this type of evaluation unacceptable for identifying and reporting student gains. With an ABC program, student evaluation with respect to test content is clear. Students are tested on the degree to which they have mastered the objectives they were instructed on.

The performance standards of the instructional objectives comprise and criterion-referenced test items and the assessment and reassessment process provides the evaluating data. Reporting student progress, therefore, automatically includes the content that was taught by the fact that there are scores reported for each instructional objective. Student performance data in relation to the instructional content should be reported at two levels. The first is the unit level and the second is the program level.

The unit level of reporting is confined to the student's performance on the instructional objectives taught during the specified reporting period. No information is included about objectives covered previously or about those that will be taught in the future. The program reporting level is a cumulative report that indicates the student's performance throughout the program. This report shows the instructional content covered in the entire program and the student's achievement on those objectives to date.

Entry and Exit Status. Entry status on instructional objectives is often omitted from most reporting formats used in physical education. Entry status, however, is necessary for calculating the amount of gain that has occurred on the objectives as a result of instruction. Omitting entry status prohibits the recipient of the repot from knowing whether or not any improvement was made. Entry status can be reported in raw score form or, more commonly, in the form of a standardized score. Exit status in more commonly reported in many reporting systems. It may be reported individually for each instructional objective or summarized as a per cent or grade representing progress on a cluster of instructional objectives.

Exit status is traditional information that most students, parents, and other recipients of the report expect and want to know. Exit status represents the degree to mastery the student has attained on the content covered within a reporting period. More specifically, it indicates the degree to which a student has mastered the components, of a skill or skills along an absolute continuum. Exit status alone does not indicate the amount of learning that occurred but instead only the student's present degree of mastery. Although exit status scores allow for comparison between student's degree of mastery, the usefulness of these data is limited in the absence of how much was learned.

Status Relative to Self and Peers. All of the reports presented thus far have been individual reports. These repots show only the individual student's performance in relation to objective mastery and/or targeted expectations. This form of reporting clearly communicates the student's performance on the program objectives. If the student is not achieving as expected, appropriate changes and modifications can be made in the program and/or in instruction. A second dimension that can be added to these individual reports is peer comparative data. This dimension allows the recipient of the report to also interpret the student's progress and performance on the program objectives in relation to other student populations. This form of evaluate information also aids the teacher in identifying individual student strengths and weaknesses which is helpful in making appropriate programmatic adjustments such as adjusting the amount of content covered, the student's placement, or the level of performance expectations set. Profiles represent a comprehensive reporting system that incorporates the content covered, student entry, exit and change status on the instructional objectives included in the reporting period, information relative to the individual student's own continuous progress, and the student's status in relation to significant others.

The pictorial nature of profiles allows them to communicate much information that can be easily interpreted by the report recipients. If per cent/letter grades must be assigned, they can by readily derived and justified from the student's profile. Graphic profiles can be produced by hand or by computers. The greatest obstacle to widespread use of profiles as a reporting format in physical education is the time required to make them. The ever-increasing number of microcomputer in the public schools and the multipurpose data base management programs available to use on them makes the feasibility of using computers to generate profiles a reality in almost all schools.

Physical educators must be willing, however, to explore and harness the use of computer technology to best serve their needs. The notion that a teacher must be a computer programmer or a math genius to use a computer is a myth. Many computer programs that could be beneficially used by physical educators only require a few hours of training and practice to use efficiently and effectively.

Student Report Formats. Letter grades or their percentage equivalent have been used traditionally by many schools to report student progress in physical education. Letter grades by themselves fail to communicate much of the information needed to report student progress effectively. No information is communicated in a letter grade regarding the content taught, the student's entry or exit status on the instructional objectives, and whether the grade is based on student gain or only student exit status. If letter grades must be used, they should be accompanied by either a narrative report or a graphic profile to substantiate how they were derived. Although narrative reports can be developed to meet all the report criteria outlined. In practice they rarely do in physical education. Most narrative reports used in physical education employ open-ended general descriptions of student performance. Narrative reports of this nature are used quite commonly at the elementary school level; unfortunately, they communicate no more information than the letter grades they were designed to replace. The graphic profiles are the recommended reporting formate to be used in conjunction with an ABC in physical education.

Student Evaluation Summary

Student evaluation is important for feedback to the student, teacher and for modification of instructional prescriptions. It is also a prerequisite to accurate reporting of student progress. A complete report of student progress must either incorporate, or have a sound rationale for not incorporating, each of the following elements: the content covered, student entry, exit and change status on the objectives, included in the reporting period, information relative to the individual student's own continuous progress, and the student's status relative to significant others. Though many formats for reporting student progress are available, the student profile is the recommended reporting format to be used with an ABC in physical education. It can be readily seen that the ability to document student progress is a prerequisite to completing any kind of program evaluation and refinement.

Physical educators must be able to document the success and failure of students both individually and collectively to systematically alter the instructional program to improve its benefits to all students. The information that students, their parents, and selected other school officials want and need is also essential information needed by physical educators to make appropriate program changes. Data collection and reporting are thereby critical components of instituting a quality ABC physical education program.

Program Evaluation and Modification

Program evaluation and modifications are an extension of the student evaluation procedures. Program evaluation is necessary to identify program merit and to systematically improve the procedures of planning, implementing and evaluating instruction to maximize the results or outcomes of the evaluation process. Program evaluation is designed to evaluate three basic questions:

i. Is the program plan appropriate?

ii. Was the program implemented as intended?

iii. Did the program produce the desired results?

The evaluation and modification procedures associated with each of these questions are discussed in the remaining section of this chapter.

i. Is the Program Plan Appropriate?

Although the first question reads, "Is the program plan appropriation?" remember, the words "program plan" could apply to a K through 12 program, a program level, a unit, an objective, and the question would still be relevant. Similarly, the question could be stated as "Is the program plan appropriate for a particular child or for all children?" The key to the question is the term appropriate.

The program plan must be appropriate for the individual and/or population group for which it was designed. If the program plan is found to be inappropriate, the physical educator should then skip the next evaluation questions, and deal directly with the question "What needs to be changed to improve the program plan?" Many evaluation questions related to program appropriateness can and should be addressed prior to the program implementation. Although the use of internal experts is the most efficient form of evaluation during program development, the use of outside experts to review the final program plan is probably one of the more commonly used evaluation techniques.

When this option is considered, it is critical that the experts be selected based on their established experience in program evaluation and demonstrated link with ongoing quality programs and not because they have a fancy title. The more comprehensive a review undertaken prior to implementation, the greater the likelihood that a number of potential implementation problems will be avoided. When discrepancies or problems are identified, appropriate changes can be made using the different procedures. When the program is finally judged appropriate, it is ready for the ultimate test—implementation.

ii. Was the Program Implemented as Intended?

Before the degree of student gains can be evaluated, it is necessary to identify how the program was implemented. Teachers must know whether they are evaluating the planned program or modified form. The program can be modified as long as the modifications are known and recorded sufficiently so that the program can be evaluated and replicated. Self-monitor forms designed to identify program discrepancies can be used by the staff. Although the goal of any teacher of staff member would be to achieve 100% mastery on all evaluation items within and across units, each discrepancy must be interpreted independently. On one item, 80% mastery might be considered acceptable while on another, nothing less than 100% might be acceptable. Acceptance levels therefore should be established in accordance with local values. When individual or group discrepancies or problems are identified, appropriate modifications can be designed to remediate them. This evaluative data can also be used to determine such things as:

i. inservice priorities for staff training;

ii. the need for additional administrative support;

iii. rationale for changes in scheduling or class sizes;

iv. reallocation of resources; or

v. a variety of other programmatic changes.

In addition, this evaluation process also identifies strengths of both the program and individual staff members. Systematic evaluation of a variety of different approaches to addressing various problems will allow the poor practices to be discarded and the successful practices to be identified and replicated. If, during the program's implementation, it becomes apparent that changes are needed, they can and should be made. This, however, becomes an evaluation resulting from an attempt to implement the program forcing an immediate refinement to allow implementation to occur.

Such a change is the result of a discrepancy between a planned occurrence or expectation and actual implementation and therefore must be resolved. The resolution then becomes the new planned expectation for the next implementation trial. Accumulations of such refinements are what allow the program to grow in its effectiveness and are therefore the desirable products of an evaluation. When changes are made in the program either as a result of an implementation attempt as suggested, or through the implementation of another evaluation technique like the teacher checklist, they must be recorded in two places. First, the change must be added to the description of the program so that it does not have to be rediscovered during another implementation attempt. Second, the change should be reflected in a modification of the monitoring form, if appropriate, to assure that the form is sensitive to the implementation of the new procedure. It is critical to the stability of a program that such refinements be written into its description or they may be lost and emerge as problems at another time. When no adequate description of the program exists, this constant refinement and growth is lost.

It is not uncommon for refinements that were created over years by an excellent instructor to be lost when he or she leaves the system. This occurs when these changes are not incorporated into the description of the program. A new employee hired to replace the experienced staff person must start all over to build the program without the benefit of information learned and previously integrated into the program. This is a tremendous waste of public resources and a serious disservice to the students.

Did the Program Produce the Desired Results?

Evaluation of the program is merely an extension of the evaluation of individual students. Evaluation of individual students within an ABC model is straightforward in that the program's organization, implementation and evaluation are based on program objectives. In the "Student Evaluation and Reporting" section we discussed that teachers evaluate student progress to the degree to which stated instructional objectives are achieved. Student gain is simply the student's status upon entry subtracted from their exit performance. Program evaluation concern itself with the number of students enrolled in the program who are making the desired gains on the objectives taught. If the proportion of gains is large enough, then the program can be said to be effective; if sufficient gains occur, the program is in need of revision. Program evaluation can be completed by the implementation staff with information primarily available as a result of regular implementation of the program.

Professional and legislative mandates require that instruction be delivered by using the ABC model where instruction is prescribed based on an assessment of student entry status and represcribed as a result of changes monitored during the course of instruction. The student change data necessary to determine program effectiveness therefore are already available in records associated with assessment and reassessment data. Accordingly, program evaluation can be completed by good record keeping and simply aggregating the individual student change data already available. Although the teacher effectiveness value is a good indicator of whether the program is having the desired effect, it must be recognized that this value is dependent on the teacher's ability to set appropriate target expectancy levels for each student.

If the teacher consistently underestimates each student and sets a lower expectancy, the effectiveness value achieved would be proportionally too high. Conversely, the opposite would occur if the teacher consistently sets exceptations that are too high. A second indicator, program effectiveness, is the relationship between student actual gain and the standard set for meaningful gain during program planning. Although meaningful gain is also somewhat of a subjective standard, represents the combined estimate of the staff involved in planning the program. Since the targeted meaningful gain is also directly related to the amount of instructional time scheduled for an objective, failure to consistently achieve meaningful gain on an objective might indicate a need to increase the amount of instructional time allocated. The key to successful program evaluation is the maximum use of available information. The teacher implementation mastery values were taken from the various Teacher Unit Implementation Evaluation Checklist. Teacher effectiveness and program effectiveness values were calculated from the class performance score sheets. This composite provides a clear picture of the program's implementation and effect from which strengths and weaknesses can be identified. Where anticipated implementation or effects have been achieved, the teacher can then attempt to refine the program so that the same results can be achieved with less time, effort, and cost.

Where expectations were not met, the teacher must determine why and initiate appropriate changes. When the program begins to produce consistent positive results, the physical educator can start a good public relations program advertising the quality of the program. Program evaluation summary data should be reported annually to all relevant audiences. Although summary implementation and effectiveness evaluation data provide clear indications of where weaknesses exist, they frequently do not explain why. Only by identifying why can revisions be made to remediate the weakness. It is usually easy to determine why a weakness has surfaced in program implementation. Often it is the result of a lack of knowledge related to planning, implementing, and/or evaluating, or simply a situation of not following through and doing what was planned. Determining why a sufficient number of students did not make meaningful gains on one or more of the program's objectives is a more difficult task.

There is, however, a simple approach to this problem that is systematic and consistent with procedures recommended in large evaluation projects. The procedure involves systematically identifying the differences between those who made the expected gain and those who did not. Large evaluation studies investigate this evaluative why question by conducting many correlational analyses student gain data and many other variables. Categories of variables that are typically used include:

i. characteristics of the students;

ii. characteristics of the teachers;

iii. characteristics of the instructional setting or school-related factors; and

iv. implementation characteristics.

In each category there are many variables measured on many students that are all interrelated in such a way that the strength of the relationships are documented. The stronger the relationship between student gain and some variable or group of variables, the more likely the reasons for insufficient achievement may be attributed to the identified variable or variables. For example, if the instructional objective run were taught to a group of students and only 20% of them achieved the targeted gain, an obvious weakness in the instructional program could be identified. Suppose that an analysis of the relationship between gains in running and other measured variables showed a strong relationship to the variable age.

Review of the gain data of the students on running shows that the younger students comprise the majority who made no changes, whereas nearly all the gains were made by the older students. Such an analysis would suggest one or more of the sample reasons listed below regarding why only 20% of the students achieved the expectancy level.

i. The expected amount of gain was too high for younger students.

ii. The instructional materials used to direct the lessons were inappropriate for younger students. Games, drills, and/or organization were such that the student did not get a sufficient number of trials and/or appropriate feedback.

iii. The teaching method and/or approach was more appropriate for older students or less appropriate for younger students.

iv. The instructional context was appropriate for older but not younger students.

v. The younger students did not have the necessary prerequisite skills to benefit from the lessons.

This type of analysis can isolate potential causes for an achievement weakness. Such an analysis, however, is fine for large groups of students in large evaluation studies where the resources to do sophisticated computer analyses are available, but what about the single teacher working with one class and only limited data collection on potential relationship variables? Obviously, he or she cannot conduct a large self-investigation into the evaluative why question of the same magnitude as a large-scale evaluation project. There is, however, a similar and realistic approach that can yield equally beneficial results. In essence, teachers can get the same information by informally comparing the characteristics surrounding the instruction of the students who were the best achievers with those who achieved the least.

Informal implementation of this technique requires no data collection beyond that which is already available. Assuming there were appropriate record keeping, systematic implementation of an ABC model yields the information necessary to identify potential answers to why achievement expectations were not met. For example, a teacher implementing an ABC in physical education would have the following information available:

i. Class performance score sheets that include student entry and exit levels on each of the instructional objectives included in the various units.

ii. One page overview of the units showing the amount of time allocated to teaching each instructional objective.

iii. Lesson plans.

iv. Teacher implementation data for the unit.

v. Information regarding the student's learning, personal-social, and physical and motor characteristics obtained from the student needs profile.

To make a high-low comparison, select 10 to 15% of the highest and lowest achievers on an objective or set of objectives and determine how they differ from one another. Such a comparison can be conducted mentally within a short period of time or by actually comparing the screening profiles of the high and low achievers item by item. Consider every difference for its potential in influencing the lack of learning that occurred for the low group. Where potential influencing factors are detected, they become criteria for making appropriate planning, implementing or evaluating changes.

Often, surprisingly powerful notions emerge regarding achievement. From these notions, changes emerge that must be developed, implemented and re-evaluated to determine their effect in subsequent implementations of instructional objectives. This process should be continuous. Initially, changes should be identified and remediated to eliminate weaknesses related to student achievement on all possible instructional objectives. When this occur, the evaluative effort can be shifted away from mere remediation of weak spots toward improvement.

Improvement in this context refers to either meeting increased expectation levels or meeting the same levels of expectation while reducing the amount of instructional time. If instructional time can be reduced, additional instructional objectives can be added to the program. To create a dynamic program, the recommended changes must be included in an updated program description.

Fostering Student Motivation for Learning

A major key to planning appropriate class management strategies is concerted focusing on student's motives and needs for learning. To accomplish this task, a list of pertinent student needs or motives for learning helps to structure the process, to identify class management needs of the students, and to design appropriate strategies. This process helps teachers manage and direct instruction for all students and target their efforts on one or several needs of individual students. Examples of ten pertinent student's motives or needs for learning, identified by the different teachers, include the need to:

i) trust others;

ii) feel self-worth;

iii) act responsibility;

iv) accept one's own strengths and weaknesses;

v) communicate appropriate with others;

vi) use appropriate behaviours in varied environments;

vii) interact appropriately with peers and adults;

viii) cope with stress;

ix) control anxiety;

x) control impulses.

Examples of class management needs, identified by teachers, have included the need for:

i) participation in planning, monitoring and evaluating one's progress in learning;

ii) clear and detailed statements of rules, procedures, and consequences;

iii) consistency and predictability in the class routines;

iv) consistency in reinforcing rules and procedures;

v) encouragement and support from peers and adults;

vi) appropriate learning tasks and expectations;

vii) positive reinforcement, immediate positive feedback in learning new skills or in new situations;

viii) rewards for success in learning desired by students, positive consequences following learning that motivates the student.

The inclusion of these examples does not preclude the importance of other need areas. These examples focus on student's needs, basic motivations for learning, and consequently, the managing and directing of instruction.

5

FUNDAMENTAL STATISTICS IN PHYSICAL EDUCATION AND SPORTS SCIENCES

Statistics is only a body of substantive knowledge, but also a body of method for obtaining knowledge.

In other words, statistics in the measure of properly of the sample through various statistical method. For example mean, median, mode, standard deviation etc.

— Statistics or sample statistics are the measure of the property of a sample e.g., mean, median, mode of height of the International basket ball player.

— It also refer to the body of analytical procedure or techniques employed in the manipulation of numerical data.

— Statistics is information communication in a numerical form e.g., number of football players in a institution.

— Statistics means by which a set of data may be described and interpreted in a meaningful manner and also a method by which data may be analysed and inferences and conclusions may be drawn.

According to Yule and Kendle "Statistics we means quantitative data affected by a marked extent by multiplicity of cause".

Croxton and Cowden has defined statistics as:

"Statistics may be defined as the collection, presentations, analysis and interpretation of universal/ data".

There are the following four stages in a statistical investigation:

1. Collection of data
2. Presentation of data
3. Analysis of data
4. Interpretation of data.

There can be one more stage that is 'organisation of data'.

Dhananjoy Shaw has defined statistics as: "science of collection, organisation, presentation, analysis and interpretation of numerical data".

According to Walls and Roberts: "Statistics not only a body of substantive knowledge but also a body of method for obtaining knowledge"

In other words, "statistics is the measure of property of the sample through various statistical methods for example, mean, median, mode, standard deviation for inferring population characteristics. Thus, the world 'statistics' refer to quantitative data information or to a method of dealing with quantitative information.

Statistics or sample statistics is the measures of the property of the sample e.g. mean, median and mode which serves as an estimator of the relevant parameter. Some property varies from sample to sample in composition which can be averaged for good estimation of the parameter.

A population or universe in statistics is a vast group comprising of all animator, non-animator, individuals, objects or cases that possess the specific property, characteristics or quality under investigation, e.g. Athlete, Non-Athlete, Male, Female, Plants, Diabetic Individuals etc.

Parameters is the measures of the properties of population e.g. mean, median and mode of Indian height.

Direct population/parameter measurement is not economic for experimental method. These parameter can be estimated upto a specific degree of probability with the help of sample statistics. Sample is a relatively small group of individuals. Objects of cases, drawn from a population for an experimental test or survey.

Statistics can also be defined on the basis of its nature:

1. Information communicated in a numerical from e.g., number of player in a institute, average height of student. Thus, statistics certainly useful to the decision maker. Statistical data are the raw material on which the structure of analysis is built.

2. The word statistics is also employed to refer to the body of analytical procedure or techniques employed in the manipulation of numerical data. To generate useful information, it is often necessary to subject the data to statistical analysis prior to their in corporation in the decision making process and also for more effective initialization of information.

History of Statistics

The word statists, statistics and statistical have been derived from Latin word 'states', Italian word states and German word 'statistisk' meaning a political state. Statistics is the science of collecting and analysing data. It is being used more and more in various applications.

In government many people are involved in collecting data from censuses and surveys and monitoring trends in economic and financial indices. Such data are often referred to as "official statistics". They are used to evaluate and improve, current policies. On a smaller statistics used in medicines, for example, to assess which of used treatments is better. By company data statistics can make some judgement as to which disease is affecting the patient. The term statistics is used either as a substitute for the word 'data' be scientific method of studying data.

Originally it meant the official words data. This use of statistics, as data, has been in vogue for a fairly long time for example, more than 2000 year ago. Indians had a idea of the utility of data, official and administrative records were kept. This tradition was carried forward in medieval ages and we find extensive collection of agriculture, land revenue, administrative and other data. The famous hand and revenue, administrative and other data. The famous hand and revenue minister of Akbar, Raja Todormal, maintained good records of land and agriculture statistics. Similarly in many other ancient countries like Egypt, Rome and Greece, statistics on military strength of the national vis-a vis the enemies were frequently collected and records of deaths and births maintained. Statistics was projected as 'the science of statecraft'.

However, the use of statistics as a scientific method is not very old and its origin is easily traceable. During the mid-seventieth century, gamblers of France and England discover the challenging problems of games of chance to mathematicians and scientists, who attacked and solved those problem and, in the process, laid the foundation of the theory of probability. Pascal, Farnet, Bernoulli, Laplace Gauss, Demoivle are some of the prominent names associated with the early development of this theory. Thus, in the early stages of the development of statistics, it was the theory of probability that received the greatest attention and by the time other techniques were evolved, this theory had already gained from foundation. This can be seen from the fact that around 1800 A.D., the theory of probability had already gained a mature stature while the other techniques of analysis were developed mostly after 1800 A.D.

Francis Galton in his study relating to the inheritance of stature found that offsprings of abnormally tall or shorts parents 'regress' to the average height of the society. Thus, he introduced the concept of 'regression' in statistics.

Karl Pearson was a pioneer in the field of correlation studies and the coefficient of correlation known as product-moment correlation coefficient was devised by him. W.C. Gosset introduced the famous t-distribution in 1908 and considerably enlarged the scope of statistics.

Perhaps the most important of all the name is that of Prof. R.A. Fisher who introduced and developed considerably the concepts of point estimation. Analysis of variation, various tests of significance, design of experiments and many other statistical tools and such diversified field as biochemistry, education etc. Making statistical methods very popular in the process. In olden days facts and figures were required by kings for their administration. Therefore, in post statistics was known "science of kings". Buts its scope now days has been widened.

In Indian contexts, in the year 1932 the Indian Statistical Institute (I.S.I.) was registered, Calcutta as a learned society for advancement of statistics in India.

Now this Institute is the pioneer centre for training and research in statistics and related fields. The Indian journal of statistics, entitled 'sankhya' published by the Indian Statistical Institute.

In 1959, in recognition of the role of statistics in as a key technology of the modern times and the importance of the institute in the development and application of statistics. The International Statistics Education Centre, established in the institute in 1950, in collaboration with the International Statistics Institute under the auspicious of the UNESCO & Govt. of India (I.S.I.).

In his article Psychologist Robert Bollers makes a attack against the use of statistics and he says that "One should avoid statistics whenever possible and get on with the Business of Science" specially, he suggests the scientists should measure thing rather than test hypotheses, they should look for the obvious. And they should look at the data rather than the statistics. Statistics techniques are tools that are only as good as the individual who uses. Statistical procedures are very helpful tools in arriving at answers to those questions.

Indian Statistical Institute

Professor Prasanta Chandra Mahalanobis founded the Indian Statistical Institute in the Presidency College in Calcutta. Within a few years the Institute's achievement in teaching, research and project work undertaken for the Government of India brought recognition not only in India but also in the world of statistics, by excellent library, facilities in modern computers and specifically for its long tradition in providing professional and technical help in promoting national development.

The Institute initiated and promoted the interaction

of statistics with natural and social sciences through collaborative research work; this is still the unique feature of the Institute.

Following are the main objectives of Institute:

1. To promote the study and dissemination of knowledge of statistic, to develop statistical theory and methods, and their use in research and practical applications generally, with special reference to problems of planning of national development and social welfare.

2. To undertake research in various fields of natural and social sciences, with a view to the mutual development of statistics and these sciences.

3. To provide for, and undertake, the collection of information, investigation, projects and operational research for purposes and operational research for purposes of planning and the improvement of efficiency of management and production.

The Institute has acquired a special distinction in India for its activities since 1930's relating to collection and analysis of information on social, economic and demographic characteristics in India in particular through the national sample surveys, agriculture surveys, socio-economic enquiries, research in national income, cooperation in the preparation of national economic plans and specific project work pertaining to national development and social welfare. The early research work in the Institute, especially by Professor P.C. Mahalanobis, Prof. R.C. Bose, Prof. S.N. Roy, and Prof. C.R. Rao, had won the Institute a unique place in the world of statistics.

The Indian Journal of Statistics, entitled Sankhya, published by the Institute, has not only established the contributions and fame of the Indian statisticians in the world, but also has acquired a distinctive position in the annals of statistics. A large number of Indian statistics and probabilities who have won international fame have been scholars or members of the Institutes faculty. The Institute has on its faculty several well-known statisticians, mathematicians and other scientists in different fields, among whom are fellows of the Indian National Science Academy, recipients of the S.S. Bhatnagar Memorial Award, Mahalanobis Memorial Medal and fellows of many other scientific societies in India and abroad. A special feature as well as the long tradition of the scientific activities of the Institute is the collaboration it receives from all the world over through the visits of eminent statisticians, mathematicians and other scientists, and their active participation in teaching and research in the Institute.

Sir R.A. Fisher was a frequent visitor and collaborator. Prof. J.B.S. Haldane joined the Institute in the late fifties and worked in the Institute for several years. The Institute has been offering formal courses in statistics leading to certificates and diplomas since the late thirties. Post M.Sc. advanced course in statistics was started in the late forties.

In 1959, in recognition of the role of statistics as a key technology of the modern times and the importance of the Institute in the development and application of statistics, the Parliament of India enacted the Indian Statistical Institute Act, declaring the Institute to be an Institution of National Importance and empowering it to grant degrees and diplomas in statistics. The B. Stat. (Hons.) and the M. Stat. degree programmes in statistics were introduced in the Institute following the enactment of the I.S.I. Act with the objective that the academic training of a statisticians should encompass the basic principles of statistics along with its theoretical and methodological development, not merely in abstract formulation, but also in relation to concrete problems arising from natural and social sciences. The curricula for these degree programmes were developed accordingly.

In 1950, The Electronic Computer Laboratory of the Institute was established. The first electronic computer in India, a HEC-2M, was installed in the Institute in 1956, and one of the foremost formal courses for computer science in this country started in the Institute in 1962. The Institute has a number of computer systems in Calcutta, Delhi, Bangalore, Madras and Hyderabad, and the computer centre at Calcutta has initiated a new generation computer system VAX-8650 and SUN PARCSTATION.

The diploma in computer science was started in the Institute in 1966 and upgraded to the M. Tec. degree course in 1978. The International Statistical Education Centre, established in the Institute under the auspices of the UNESCO and Govt. of India. This centre has been providing training in statistics to sponsored students mainly from Asia, Africa and the far East. In the early fifties the Institute initiated the use of Statistical Quality Control and Operations Research in India, and started to develop these fields through and applied research, practical training in industry and consultation work.

The Institute in Calcutta, its two centres in Delhi and Bangalore, and a network of service-cum-research units in other cities in India have many experienced and highly qualified personnel in S.Q.C. and O.R. The Institute had offered postgraduate diploma in S.Q.C. and O.R. till 1988.

Since 1989-90 academic session in M. Tech. degree

course in Quality, Reliability and Operations Research is being offered. The Institute's library in Calcutta has over 2,00,000 books and journal volumes besides many official reports, reprints, microfilms, microfiche and receives about 1339 scientific and technical journals regularly.

Calcutta, Delhi and Bangalore are the places where most of the research and teaching of the Institute takes place. Each campus has hostels for students, residential quarters for the faculty and a guest house, besides recreational and medical facilities. At each of these three campuses the Institute has a distinguished and experienced faculty in theoretical and applied statistics, mathematics and economics. In Calcutta, where the headquarter of the Institute is located, there are strong groups of scientists not only in statistics, mathematics and economics, but also in many disciplines such as computer science, physics, chemistry, biology, botany, embryology, geology, anthropology and human genetics, psychometry and sociology. These scientists are engaged in research work in their respective disciplines along with collaborative work with the statisticians of the Institute.

The Need of the Study of Statistics in Physical Education and Sports Sciences

Statistics is being used in physical education and sports sciences because of the following reasons:

i. To understand interpret and evaluate scientific literature—To study/understand interpret and evaluate different research articles in the scientific formals, thesis project etc., the knowledge of statistics is necessary.

ii. To determine the scientific worth of tests—Tests are either available in the literature of need to be developed, keeping in view the purpose and feasibility in terms of scientific authenticity.

iii. To prepare report based on the test results—For the preparation of annual report, progress report and preparation of a research articles, thesis, projects, for different tables, graphics, results and conclusions.

iv. Statistics is an important tool—To discriminate between satisfactory and unsatisfactory evidence in reports containing statistical analysis.

Importance of Statistics in Physical Education and Sport Science

Statistics is very important in physical education and sports science because of the following reasons:

i. It should be noted at the very outset that statistics usually not studied for its own sake, rather, widely employed as a tool-and a highly variable one-in the analysis of problems in physical education and sports sciences.

ii. To understand and interpret and evaluate scientific literature of physical education and sports sciences.

iii. To determine the scientific worth of a test.

iv. To prepare research sport based upon test result.

v. To discriminate between satisfactory and unsatisfactory results/performance.

(a) The teachers able to understand and profit from professional literature especially research publications.

(b) The knowledge of statistics essential to conduct research and report the result.

(c) It is important in order to effectively evaluate the

available teacher made test and standard test on scientific basis.

(d) Statistical analysis gives more meaning to test data and thus aids in the understanding interpretation of scores for both teacher and students.

(e) A knowledge of statistical technique can be of considerable help in grading and grouping process.

(f) Statistical methods and analysis are necessary part of the test construction, also useful to prepare, formulate and test the hypothesis and to develop theories.

(g) It helps in prediction while framing plans and policies.

Statistical Techniques

Basically there are two kinds of statistical tests:

(i) Parametric statistical tests: This type of test assumes that the data are essentially normally distributed, following probability principals, for different statistical inferences.

Non-parametric statistical tests: This type of tests are applicable to non-normally distributed data. These are also called distribution free test. These do not require normally distributed data.

Types of Statistical Process

There are three main types of statistical methods:

1. Descriptive Statistics: These methods are used for assessing or describing the properties of particular samples using the methods namely measure of central tendency, variability or statistics of dispersion, relationship.

2. Sampling Statistics: These are Used for statistical

inferences or sampling statistics use is the descriptive statistics of sample beyond the limits of the later and for a wide group, fixing simultaneously the amount of error due to the use of random sample, e.g. comparison, 't' test, analysis of variance test of significance etc.

3. Regression or Prediction Statistics: These are used to estimate and predict, the value of a dependent variable is an individual/sample from the known value of an independent from the known value of an independent variable is the same individual/sample on the basis of the relationship between the two variables. e.g. Regression coefficient.

In the broader concept statistical processes are of following five types:

1. Descriptive Statistics: The characteristics of a single group are described using various methods namely Mean, SD.

2. Comparative Statistics: The characteristics of two or more groups are contrasted, e.g. 't' test, 'F' ratio etc.

3. Relationship Statistics: The correlations between numerous human trails as possessed by the same, e.g., product moment correlation, partial correlation, multiple correlation, rank order correlation etc.

4. Inferential Statistics: Population are determined by observed data from a sample are used as a basis for generalizing about the total population from which the sample was drawn.

5. Prediction Statistics: Unknown facts about the individual are predicted on inferred from known measurable qualities. e.g., regression coefficient.

Variables and Attributes in Fundamental Statistics

A variable is any property or characteristics, which

varies from individual to individual in population and can have any particular value or type.

The specific set of values or types of a variable known as domain of the variable and set of observations forms the records or data of experiment test or survey.

Variables may be classified into following categories:

1. Quantitative Data: It is collected as numerical values which are usually expressed as scores on test. e.g., scoring in archery in FTTA Round, timings in 100 m., sprinting etc.

2. Qualitative Data: It is collected as non-numerical basis or grouping or subjectively nominated or ranked e.g. sex, ranks assigned by teachers, grades etc.

Attributes, Qualitative Variables

An attribute has a non gradient classification. e.g. Boys and Girls, Men and Women, Athlete and Non Athlete, Skin Colour, Black, Yellow and White. It is also called nominal scale. Colours of eyes or har, Race, known as qualitative variables.

They are two main types:

1. Nominal Variables: e.g. Sex, colour of eyes here the condition of the variable can be assessed and expressed in all or none manner only. Scores can be divided in groups or classes which differs from each other.

A nominal variable divided in two classes with real gap between the character is called a dichotomous variable. e.g. Sex = Boys and Girls.

2. Ordinal or Ranked Variables: This type of attributes which is distinctly in magnitude or intensity but this magnitude is not quantitatively measured, here the

given ranks may be in ascending or descending order.

These ranks refers the gross qualitative differences in magnitude and which helps for comparison among the individuals. e.g. ranking the player, teacher ranks or grades, the students according to their achievements. Here, poor, good, better and best individual do not contain measured numerical values of the variable.

Measurement Variables

This type of variables are like age, height, blood pressure, reaction time, body weight, can be measured or counted and their values can be expressed in numerical units as quantitative or numerical variables. They are as followings:

(a) Continuous Variables: This can be measured and expressed not only in whole units but also in any fraction of the unit, here the limiting factor may be the quality of the instrument or accuracy of the measurement or the method of testing. e.g. height can be measured in cm. and even to any small fraction of units. Another example, age can be measured by years-months-days-hours-minutes-seconds etc. Thus, it is observed that there is no real gap in between the scores, thus, produces continuous series or metric date.

2. Discrete, Discontinuous Variables: This can be measured and expressed in whole units number only and not in fractions of units. Real gaps exist between two possible consecutive values because of the impossibility or impracticability of further sub-division of the measure with a specific value that a never with fraction of unit, e.g. cells counts of blood, number of stepping, number of hockey, goals in football, basketball etc. which are obtained by simply counting and counting is limited to whole number.

Quantitative Data are equally scaled when the units increase or decrease in equal steps. They are as follows:

(i) Interval Variables: Here the scale does not include an absolute zero. The scale starts from an arbitratory zero level; Thus, such scale and the variable are known as an interval scale and an interval variable respectively. Such values can be added or substracted but cannot be multiplied or divided with one another, nor can be calculated for ratios. However, ratios of differences can be calculated. e.g. Scores for intelligence, attention and ability, very good, average, very poor etc.

(ii) Ratio Variables: This type of scale starts from an absolute zero level and which may indicate the total absence of a variable in some of the individual of a sample. It is known as ratio scale. e.g. Physical Properties.

(i) scales like gram, centimetre, foot etc.

(ii) variables like length, height, weight and numerical counts known as ratio variables which are conveniently comparable in magnitude with one another; may be added and subtract, divided and multiplied with one another, as well as ratio can be calculated.

Derived Variables

These are the varying relations between/among two or more measurement variables which have been measured directly and independently. e.g. rats, ratio, proportions and percentages are not counted in measured directly but calculated.

Other Ways of Classification of Variables

Whether variable is qualitative or quantitative, nominal, ordinal, interval, a ratio, they can be classified into another two classes:

Where some association or relation between/among two or more variable exists, the value of one of them changes when the value of the other is valid. The former is a dependent variable and later is an independent variable. e.g. weight and height, general structure and body weight.

In a study about the changes of a dependent variable corresponding to the variations of an independents.

There can be different kinds of independent variables:

(i) Classification Variables: Such independent variable is an experiment/test may change their values more or less freely due to their inherent nature but not due to the manipulation of the investigator. e.g. IQ, age, fitness, performance level etc.

(ii) Treatment Variables: Such independent variables are under extensive control of the investigator and values may be changed due to deliberate, predetermined and specific (per fixed) manner during a test/an experiment and which may lead to changes in the dependent variables, e.g. magnitude of load of exercise, magnitude of volume of exercise, intensity of exercise, methods of teaching/coaching.

There are two more types of special variables which may be useful for researcher in physical education and sports sciences:

vi. Intervening Variables: It is a sort of hypothetical variable, which is not directly observable but logically assumed variable, which is associated with intelligence, performance, habit etc. They are known as logical constructs because they serve as logical explanations in many experiments. e.g. Development of conditioned reflex, here connection or association is assumed between conditioned stimulus and unconditioned stimulus by repeating the former immediately before the later. Hence, such unobservable hypothetical and logically invented associating to connection are known as intervening variable.

vii. Suppression Variable: This type of variables are very much evident in multiple correlation.

For instance the correlation between performance and speed may be substantively reduced by the influence of another predictor variable strength and which has a high correlation with speed but not with performance directly in particular sports hence, this strength variable is known as suppression variable.

Variability and Statistics of Dispersion

It is the tendency of dispersion or spread of individual scores or values around the $\overline{X}$, Mdn, M_0 of a distribution.

— Variability is low in homogeneous group and high in heterogeneous group.

— Variability represents the spread and relative closeness of the individual scores within the distribution.

Range

It is the interval between the maximum and minimum scores of a set of observations and is expressed in the same units:

a. Applicable to all samples.

b. Range indicates only two extreme values but not magnitudes and frequency of intermediate values.

c. It is unstable, because greater the sample greater the range. Hence, range of unequal size is not comparable.

d. Extreme scores effects the range, thus introducing elements of error.

e.g. Body weight of MPE-I, a total of 25 students ranging from 50 (Minimum)-85 (Maximum) kg = 35 (Range)

whereas Mode 20 students having

R = Max. 60-Min. in 55 = 05

Mean Deviation or Average Deviation (MD or AD)

MD or AD is the arithmetic mean of the absolute deviations of the individual scores from the Mean ($\overline{X}$), Median (Mdn) or Mode (M_0) of a distribution.

(i) MD is not much used as a measure of variability particularly when N is large and grouped into regular class interval.

(ii) It is useful for skewed distribution.

(iii) MD of a sample is minimum when it is calculated about the Mdn.

Mean Deviation (MD) from $\overline{X}$ in the case, of symmetric distribution:

$$MD = \frac{\sum |x - \overline{X}|}{N} = \frac{\sum |x|}{N}$$

Where,

x = individual scores

$\overline{X}$ = Mean

$x = x - \overline{X}$ = deviation of an individual score from the mean.

MD, is the therefore, a measure of variability only of

the six, and not of the opposing directions.

MD from Mdn in the case of skewed distribution:

$$MD = \frac{\sum |X - Mdn|}{N}$$

Standard Deviation (SD or σ or S)

SD is the positive square root of the mean square deviation or as the positive square root of variance.

1. It is expressed in the same unit as scores.

2. SD of a population = σ

SD of a sample = S

Computation

SD from original and ungrouped observations when N ≥ 30 (large sample)

(i) $$S = \sqrt{\frac{\sum (x - \bar{X})^2}{N}} = \sqrt{\frac{\sum x^2}{N}}$$

(ii) $$S = \sqrt{\frac{\sum x^2}{N} - \bar{X}^2}$$

(iii) $$S = \sqrt{\frac{N \sum x^2 - (\sum x)^2}{N^2}}$$

Where,

x = Individual score,

$\bar{X}$ = Mean,

N = Number (size of sample)

$x = x - \overline{X}$

SD from Ungrouped Data:

When, N < 30 (small sample)

$$S = \sqrt{\frac{\sum(x-\overline{X})^2}{N-1}} = \sqrt{\frac{\sum x^2}{N-1}} = \sqrt{\frac{N\sum x^2 - \left(\sum x^2\right)}{N(N-1)}}$$

$$= \sqrt{\frac{\sum x^2 - (NX^2)}{N-1}}$$

SD from Grouped Data:

SD by short or code method from observations grouped in class intervals of equal size:

$$S = i \times \sqrt{\frac{\sum fx'^2}{N} - C^2}$$

$$\text{or} \quad S = i \times \sqrt{\frac{\sum fx'^2}{N} - \left(\frac{\sum fx'}{N}\right)}$$

Where,

i = length of the class intervals,

N = Number of observation,

f = Frequency in an interval,

x' = Code number of the interval,

c = Correlation term in code units.

Steps:

(i) The mid point of any class interval, near the centre of the distribution is arbitrarily chosen as assumed mean (AM or A) and given with a coded value of zero.

(ii) Code numbers x' of +1, +2, +3 ... etc., are assigned in an ascending order to the mid points of the intervals rising progressively higher than that containing A or AM, code numbers of -1, -2, -3 etc., are similarly given in a descending order to the mid points of the class intervals going progressively downwards from the interval of A or AM.

Codes gives positive and negative deviation from mid point.

(iii) The code number x' and the frequency (f) of each class interval are then multiplied with each other to get fx' and the algebraic sum of all these products (Σfx') is worked out.

(iv) The code number x' of each interval is again multiplied by the respectively fx' to give fx'^2 of that interval and (Σfx') is also calculated.

(v) The correlation term (c) in code units is obtained by dividing Σ fx' by N:

$$C = \frac{\sum fx'}{N}$$

or

$$C^2 = \left(\frac{\sum fx'}{N}\right)^2$$

(vi) By using the formula 'S' is computed.

Properties of SD

Standard Deviation has the following properties:

1. M ± 3SC contains 99% scores (frequency) of a distribution, likely M ± 1SD=68%, & M ± 2SD=95%.

2. Addition or subtraction of a constant amount of each individual value or score leaves the standard deviation unaltered, but multiplication or division of each score lay a constant number causes the same changes in the standard deviation.

Quartile Deviation (Q)

Q is another measure of the scatter of individual scores around the mean.

Co-Efficient of Variation (CV)

CV is defined as the standard deviation(s) expressed as the percentage of the mean $(\overline{X})$.

$$CV = \frac{100s}{\overline{X}}$$

It is ration and is expressed as a percentage.

it is a measure of relative variability.

CV is independent of any particular unit of measurement (unit free). CV is more suitable than that of variance or SD in comparing the variabilities of two groups of data expressed in two different units. e.g. weight and height in kg and cm respectively.

CV is suitable for comparing two groups of data widely divergent means belonging to same unit. e.g. Height of children & Height of adult. However, CV is not suitable as a measure of variability of the mean is close to zero, because such CV becomes to close to α.

$$CV = \frac{100 \times S}{0} = \alpha$$

Basics Concept of Probability

The word 'Probability or chance' is very commonly used in day-to-day conversation, e.g. 'Probably it may rain tomorrow'. or 'It is likely that Mr. A may come for taking his class'.

So, these words like probably, likely convey the same sense, i.e. the event is not certain to take place or there is uncertainty about happening of the event. Suppose you play some match then you are not sure that whether you will win or loss. In such cases we talk of chance or probability, which is taken to be a quantitative measure of certainty.

Probability means the degree of belief in the proposition of the person making the statement.

Trial and Event

Suppose any experiment gives you several possible outcomes. This experiment is called a trial and outcomes of the experiment are known as events.

Exhaustive Events

The total number of possible outcomes in any trial is known as Exhaustive events.

Favourable Events

The number of cases favourable to be happening of an event is a trial are called favourable events.

Mutually Exclusive Events

Events are said to be mutually exclusive, if the happening of any one of them precludes the happening of all others.

Equally Likely Events

Outcomes of a trial are said to be equally likely if taking consideration of all the relevant evidences; there is no reason to accept one in preference to the other.

If a trial results in 'n' exhaustive, mutually and equally likely cases and m of them are favourable to the happening of an event (E) then the prob. 'p' of the happening of an event E is given by:

$$P(E) = P = \frac{\text{Favourable No. of Cases}}{\text{Total No. of Cases}} = \frac{m}{n}$$

Now the number of cases favourable to the non-happening of the event (E) are n-m so the prob q that (E) will not happen is:

$$q = \frac{n-m}{n} = 1 - \frac{m}{n} 1 - p$$

Obviously p and q are non negative and cannot exceed unity.

so; $o \leq p \leq 1$, $o \leq p \leq 1$

If, P(E) = 1; then (E) is called a certain event.

If, P(E) = 0; then E is called impossible event.

Independent Events

Two or more events are said to be independent if the occurrence of any of them is not influenced by the occurrence of any other. e.g. if we throw two dice, the result obtained on the first dice has no effect upon the second, therefore, these events are independent.

Basic Rules of Probability

Addition Rule

1. If two or more events are mutually exclusive, the prob. 'p' that any one of these events will occur in a single trail is equal to the sum of the individual probabilities.

i.e. $P(E_1 + E_2 + \ldots\ldots + E'n') = P(E_1) + P(E_2) + \ldots. + P(E_n)$ or simply $P(E_1 + E_2)\ P(E_1).\ P(E_2)$

2. If two events are not mutually exclusive then the prob. of occurrence in a single trial at least one of them is equal to the sum of the individual prob. minus the prob. that the events will occur together.

i.e. $P(E_1 + E_2) = P(E_1) + P(E_2) - P(E_1).\ P(E_2)$

Multiplication Rule

If two or more events are not mutually exclusive then the prob. of occurrence in a single trial at least one of them is equal to the sum of the individual prob. minus the prob. that the events will occur together

i.e. $P(E_1 + E_2) = P(E_1) + P(E_2) - P(E_1).\ P.\ (E_2)$

If two events X and Y are dependent then we take the help of conditional prob.

$$P\left(\frac{Y}{X}\right) = \frac{P(XY)}{P(X)}$$

or $P(XY) = P(X)\ .\ P(Y/X)$

Binomial Distribution (Distn.)

The binomial distribution refers to a sequence of events which possess the following properties:

1. A sample experiment is repeated a number of times where the outcomes are independent.

2. Outcomes of each trial can be classified into two mutually exclusive i.e. success and failure.

3. The prob. of the success in a single trial denoted by a remains constant for all the trials.

4. The experiment is performed under the same conditions for a fixed number of trials.

Theorem

If s represents the probability of success in a single trial and t the probability of failure, as n becomes larger in a binomial distn. for N samples of n trials, the resultant histogram approaches to normal probability curve.

Conditions for Normality

If the distn. of the observation is to be normal the following conditions must be satisfied among the factors affecting the individual events that make up a given popn:

i. The casual forces must be numerous and approximately equal weight.

ii. These forces must be the same over the universe from which the observations are drawn.

iii. The forces affecting events must be independent of one another.

iv. Such forces affect the individual events in such a way that the maximum frequencies are clustered around the mean value and give rise to a symmetrical curve and further that the positive and negative deviations from this mean value are equally likely.

Mathematical Equation of Normal Prob. Curve

A random variable A is said to have a normal distn.

with parameters B (called Mean) and c (variance), if its probability density function or simply its basic form is given by:

$$P\,(a) = \frac{1}{\sqrt{2\pi}\,c} e - \frac{1}{2}\left(\frac{a - \mu}{c}\right)^2 \quad -\infty < a < \infty$$

where, P = 3.14159

e = 2.7183

and generally we denote it as

$$x \sim N\left[\mu, c^2\right]$$

Characteristics or Properties of the Normal Distribution

The following are the important properties of the normal curve and the normal distribution:

i. The normal curve is symmetrical about the mean. If the curve were folded along its vertical axis, the two values would coincide. The number of cases below the mean is equal to the number of cases above the mean, which makes the mean and median coincide.

ii. The height of normal curve is at its maximum at the mean. Hence, mean and mode of the normal distn. coincide. Thus, for normal dist. mean, median and mode are all equal.

iii. The curve is asymptotic to the base on either side. From the maximum point which occurs at mean, the height of the curve declines as we go in either direction. The curve approaches nearer and nearer to the base but it never touches it.

iv. Since there is only one maximum point, the normal

curve is unimodel.

v. As distinguished from Binomial distn. where the variable is discrete, the variable distributed according to the normal curve is a continuous one.

vi. The first and the third quartiles are equidistant from the median.

vii. The mean deviation is 4/5th of the standard deviation in the normal distn.

viii. Of all the important properties of the normal curve the most important property is the area relationship. The area under the normal curve between mean ordinate and ordinates at various sigma distances from mean is distributed.

Importance of the Normal Distribution

The normal distn. has occupied a central place in the theory of statistics. Its importance is clear from the following points:

i. Most of the distribution occurring in practice e.g., binomial, poison, hyper geometric distn. etc. can be approximated by normal distribution. Moreover, many of the sampling distn. e.g. students 't', F test, Chi square distn. etc. tend to normally for large samples.

ii. Even if the variable is not normally distributed, it can sometimes be brought to normal distn. by simple transformation of variable. e.g. if the distn. of x is skewed, the distn. of $\sqrt{x}$ might come out to be normal.

iii. Many of the distn. of simple statistic (e.g. the distn. of sample mean, sample variance etc.) tend to normally for large samples and as such they can best be studied with the help of normal curves.

iv. The proofs of all the tests of significance in sampling are based upon the fundamental assumption that the population from which the samples have been drawn is normal.

v. Normal distn. finds large applications in statistical quality control.

Finding Areas Under the Normal Curve

In normal curve, the probability that a given observation will fall between two scores is the area of the distribution contained within the given interval in relation to the total area of the curve which is taken to be one.

Normal Curve

Normal curve is bilaterally symmetrical curve, with high concentration of scores at the centre and sloping off towards the ends also known as normal probability curve.

Principles of Normal Curve

There are following principles of a normal curve:

i. Normal curve is based upon the probable occurrence of an event.

ii. When the probability depends upon chance.

iii. When each event has an equal chance of occurrence.

iv. Thus, occurrence of the event must be equally likely and must be mutually independent. e.g. non-occurrence having no influence on occurrence of an event.

v. Any divergent in the Normal Curve is due to the probable error (PE).

Properties of Normal Curve

Normal curve have the following properties:

1. Normal curve is bilaterally symmetrical.

2. Not all the symmetrical curves are normal.

3. The explanations of Binomial expansion gives the definite description of the normal curve. Thus, normal curve has a general equation that constricts it mathematically.

4. It is asymptotic to the base line (do not touch the base line to infinity).

5. Each points of inflection (point of changing direction) are each point of standard deviation from the ordinate of mean.

6. The height of an ordinate of given SD distance from the mean ordinate is an exact proportion of the height of a mean ordinate. Thus, the area under the curve included between the mean ordinate and an ordinate at any given SD from the mean will be an exact proportion of the total area under the curve.

7. In case of normal curves Mean, Mdn. and Mode are all exactly in the centre of distribution hence they are numerically equal. Hence, calculation of Mean, Mdn. and Mode are test of normal distribution.

Divergence from Normality

If sample size is large enough, we get NC from the frequency distribution of any physical, mental traits. But there are certain traits which are not normally distributed hence, deviate from normality due to some factors. i.e. learning, forgetting etc.

It has the reasons:

i. Scores obtained by using a very hard test or too easy test.

ii. Test is obtained anyway or non-representative.

iii. Test may clarify the small homogenous group within the sample likely to produce narrow high peak curve and vice versa.

There are two types of divergent from Normal Distribution:

a. Skewness

b. Kurtosis

a. Skewness

In this type of distribution the concentration of scores are significantly above or below at the centre in comparison to the normal distribution is said to be skewed. Skewness can further be of two types:

i. positive skewness

i. negative skewness.

Kurtosis

Kurtosis or K_u refer to the height of the curve, the height of a curve may be normal, may be higher than NC or may be shorter than NC. Hence, a symmetrical, non skewed curve may have $\overline{X}$ comparable to NC but the SD would differ i.e. SD will be smaller in case of leptokurtic and SD will be higher in the case of platy kurtic distribution.

't' Distribution for Small Samples

The sampling distribution of the statistics of small samples from a normally distributed population differs from the normal curve and often conforms with a theoretical model of sampling distribution called student's 't' distribution.

't' Distribution

't' distribution is comparable to NC. But when N is small the 't' distribution lies under the normal curve, but the tails or ends of the curve are higher than the corresponding parts of the NC. It is important to note that 't' distribution does not differ greatly from NC, unless N is quite small, i.e., as N increases the 't' distribution approximate with the NC.

1. The 't' distribution is in fact the theoretical sampling distribution of the statistics 't' is a ratio obtained by dividing the deviation of a statistic from its parameter, by the standard error of that statistics.

$$t = \frac{\overline{X} - m}{S_{\overline{x}}}$$

Again, t may often be the ratio with a numerator showing the deviation of the difference two sample statistics and a denominator consisting of the standard error of the differencc:

$$t = \frac{(\overline{X}_{1} - \overline{X}_2) - (\mu_1 - \mu_2)}{S_{\overline{X}_1 - \overline{X}_2}} = \frac{\overline{X}_1 - \overline{X}_2}{S_{\overline{X}_1 - \overline{X}_2}}$$

Where $\overline{X}_1$ and $\overline{X}_2$ are the means of two samples, μ_1 and μ_2 are the respective population parameters, $\mu_1 - \mu_2$ coincides with the mean difference between the sample means and amounts to 0 when the two samples come from the same population ($\mu_1 = \mu_2$), and $S_{\overline{X}_1 - \overline{X}_2}$ is the SE of the difference between $\overline{X}_1$ and $\overline{X}_2$. The frequency distribution of t, ccmputed by any such formula for each of many small samples of identical size and from the same population, forms a 't' distribution.

2. The 't' distribution forms a bilaterally symmetrical unimodal curve with its centre at the mean (t = 0) and with its tails extending from -a' to + a' (asymptotic curve). But its tails are thicker than those of the normal curve, indicating more numerous extreme deviations than in the normal curve. The peak of the 't' curve also differs from that of the normal curve with an identical mean (the 't' distribution is lepto kurtic its lepto kurtosis rising with a lowering of the degrees of freedom).

3. Relative frequencies and the values of 't' are scaled along the ordinate and abscissa; equation for the same given by:

Where, Y is the height of the ordinate representing the relative expected frequency of 't', df represents the degrees of freedom and depends on the sample size N, and Y_0 is a constant whose value is obtained from df by the following formula:

4. The total area under the 't' distribution curve representing the total frequency (N) and is taken as 1.00, all such sampling distributions are the distribution of relative frequencies.

5. There are different 't' distribution curves for different degrees of freedom. As the sample size increase, df also rises and this brings the 't' distribution closer to the normal distribution in shape, with negligible difference between the two when $N \geq 30$.

6. As 't' distributions vary in shape with df, the distances along the abscissa to include specific fractional areas also vary with the df.

7. The 't' distribution is the appropriate theoretical model of continuous probability distributions for small samples (i.e. for samples arbitrarily considered small, when $N < 30$), 't', therefore, serves as the basis for small-

sample statistics but it may also be used for large samples as the t-curves for large samples are almost identical with the normal distribution.

8. The fractional area of a t-curve between the ordinates at any two 't' values on the X axis gives the proportion of cases within the range $\overline{X} \pm t$. When the 't' value has been computed for an observed difference between the statistics of two samples, the sum of the fractional areas in the two tails of the t-curve beyond the ordinates at the positive and negative values of the computed 't' gives the probability 'p' of obtaining by mere chance a difference of that magnitude, irrespective of its sign. These fractional areas vary according to df. Critical values or confidence coefficient of 't' are tabulated according to df and p; each such critical value is the highest value of 't' upto which the observed differences has the specified probability 'p' of occurring by mere chance, provided the df conforms to that for the critical value C. Conventionally, the critical values of 't' are expressed in terms of 't' α (df) where α is the chosen level of 'p' and is called the level of significance. Thus, $t_{0.50(20)}$ indicates a critical value of 't' for giving 'p' of 0.05 when the data provides 20 degrees of freedom.

Degrees of Freedom

The degree of freedom (df) of a statistics is the number of independent values or scores of a variable that retain their freedom to change in magnitude and direction without alteration of the value of other statistics used in its computation. The computation of each statistic causes the loss of free movement of one of the independent values because the variation of the later value is so determined by the free variations of the other values or scores as to keep the statistic unchanged.

The df falls short of the sample size by one for each statistic computed. This lowers the df by one below the sample size for the use of each such statistics as an estimate of the parameter. Thus, the df of a statistic may also be defined as the sample size (N) less the number (m) of parameters i.e. (N-1) or (N-2) or (N-3) etc.

SD computed with the help of the mean has N-1 degree of freedom: $SD = \sqrt{\sum (X - \overline{X})^2 / (N-1)} = \sqrt{\sum x^2 / df}$. Similarly, μ is the only parameter used in computing 't' by the formula: $t = (\overline{X} - m)/^5 x$, so that 't' has N-1 degrees of freedom in the case. But the pooled SD of two small independent samples (of sizes N_1 and N_2) is computed using the two sample means ($\overline{X}_1$ and $\overline{X}_2$) as the point estimates of the corresponding parametric means:

$$\text{Pooled SD} = \sqrt{\frac{\sum (X_1 - \overline{X}_1)^2 + \sum (X_2 - \overline{X}_2)^2}{N_1 + N_2 - 2}}$$

hence, SD has $N_1 + N_2$ -2 degrees of freedom.

The statistics t, SD, X^2, F, s^3 and r are some of the statistics whose applications involve the consideration of df.

6

PHYSICAL EDUCATION AS A PROFESSION

We need to define a profession before looking specifically at physical education. A profession requires extensive period of training, has an intellectual component that must be mastered, offers opportunities for communication among its members, and provides an important service that is recognized by society. Physical educators usually have at least a bachelor's degree and frequently have advanced study and training in an extensive body of knowledge that takes considerable time and effort to learn. Colleagues in related careers share research findings and new ideas while serving people in all aspects of society. The following overview of the structure and activities of the American Alliance demonstrates that physical education qualifies as a profession.

NATIONAL ESTABLISHMENT AND SERVICES

The American Alliance for Health, Physical Education, Recreation and Dance (AAHPERD, or the Alliance) has enjoyed a century of service and growth (from 49 to more than 37,000 members). According to Executive Vice President Jack Razor, No other organization in America can match the scope of our efforts and the impact we are having.

We can be proud of all that we do. The breadth of our services and the many lives that we touch indirectly and directly serve together as an essential catalyst for our continuing viability and a foundation upon which to build. One reason for the widespread influence of the AAHPERD is the many professional groups that have merged into its structure. In 1937, as a department of the National Education Association, the former American Physical Education Association became the American Association for Health and Physical Education. (It became an alliance in 1974.) Recreation was added to its title in 1938, and dance was added in 1979.

The Alliance's missions are to improve the quality of school programs and to enhance positive life-style changes for all Americans. It is headquartered in Reston, Virginia. Its objectives are follows (AAHPERD By-laws):

1. Professional growth and development— to support, encourage, and provide guidance in the development and conduct of programs in health, leisure, and movement-related activities which are based on the needs, interests, and inherent capacities of the individual in today's society;
2. Communication— to facilitate public and professional understanding and appreciation of the importance and value of health, leisure, and movement-related activities as they contribute toward human well-being;
3. Research—to encourage and facilitate research

which will enrich the depth and scope of health, leisure and movement-related activities; and to disseminate the findings to the profession and other interested and concerned publics;

4. Standards and guidelines—to further the continuous development and evaluation of standards within the profession for personnel and program in health, leisure, and movement-related activities;
5. Public affairs— to coordinate and administer a planned program of professional, public, and governmental relations that will improve education in area of health, leisure, and movement-related activities.

The services provided by the Alliance are also varied. For example, in 1958 the Alliance developed the Youth Fitness Test, the first of its kind with national norms and fitness standards for boys and girl aged 10 to 17 years. In 1980, the Alliance launched its Health Related Physical Fitness Test, which measures cardiorespiratory function, body composition, strength, and flexibility.

Other services include holding an annual convention; publishing brochures, research abstracts, books, conference proceedings, and other information pertinent to its fields of interest; positively influencing public opinion and leg- isolation; and providing consultant services. Three periodicals are published by the Alliance. The *Journal of Physical Education, Recreation and Dance* includes articles of a broad and practical nature, while the *Research Quarterly for Exercise and Sports* reports research findings. Update, in newspaper format, keeps the membership apprised of current events and legislation.

The following discussion describes the six associations that constitute the Alliance.

The American Association for Leisure and Recreation promotes leisure services at the local and national levels and recreation education in the schools. Areas of concern and services include leisure education in higher education, the place of recreation in American society, continuing education workshops, bicycle education, and legislative support for outdoor recreation resources. Programs of health education in school, communities and colleges are the purview of the Association for the Advancement of Health Education Health issues are vigorously promoted by this association through position papers; leadership for projects such as the drinking/driving problem is provided; and health education legislation is actively supported.

The Association for Research, Administration, Professional Councils and societies is composed of 10 special-interest groups, including the Aquatics Council, the College and University Administrators Council, the Council of city and county Directors, the council on Outdoor Education, the Therapeutics Council, the Council on Facilities and Equipment, the International Relations Council, the Measurement and Evaluation Council, and the Physical Fitness Council. Among the varied professional services these groups provide is co-sponsorship of the FITNESSGRAM with the President's Council on Physical Fitness and sports, the Institute for Aerobics Research and the Campbell Soup Company. The project provides parents with a computerized fitness report card of their child's test results on the AAHPERD Youth Fitness Test or on the

Health Related Physical Fitness Test.

The student Action Council, the tenth special-interest group, has served student members of the Alliance and has worked with collegiate majors' clubs since 1969. Because the future of the profession and its organization depends on today's student, it is essential that student become actively involved in professional activities. The objectives of the student Action Council include improving local, state, district, and national student programs, providing opportunities for student leadership experiences, supporting and promoting youth service projects, and serving as an advocate for maximum involvement of student on all Alliance associations. This group also promotes the active involvement of student in local physical education majors' clubs as avenues for leadership and enhanced professional preparation. The National for girls and Women is sport seeks to improve and to expand sport opportunities for girls and women at all levels of competition. One major effort has been the training of officials through its Affiliated Boards of Official.

The National Association for Girls and Women in Sports and the National Association for Sports and Physical Education share leadership in the National Council of Athletic Training and the National Intramural Sports Council. The largest of the Alliance associations, the National Association for Sports and Physical Education, Promotes physical education and sports for all people through its numerous substructures and activities. Its Physical Education Justification Packet helps colleagues whose programs are threatened by economic cutbacks and lack of community support by providing materials such as documented research survey results and statements relative to the importance of physical education in the daily lives of students. Physical Education Public Information (PEPI) actively spreads the word about physical education through print ads, pamphlets, public service announcements, and the observance of the annual National Physical Education and sport Week. Ten academies (Adapted Physical Education, Curriculum, Exercise Physiology, History, Kinesiology, motor Development, philosophy, psychology, sociology, and sport Art) play an integral role in enhancing research. Five special-interest council are also a part of the National Association for sport and Physical Education; these are the council on Physical Education for Children, the Secondary School Physical Education Council, the college and University Physical Education Council, the College and University Physical Education Department Administrators Council, and the National Council of Secondary Athletic Directors.

The National Dance Association, the only association serving dance as education, promotes dance through conferences, workshops, publications, research, and realisations with numerous groups, such as the Kennedy Centre for the performing Arts' education program and the National Endowment for the Arts. It cooperates with Dance USA to promote National Dance Week.

The Alliance is divided into six district associations that share the goals and activities of the Alliance while providing leadership opportunities and services within each region. Memberships in the Alliance and in a district are combined, thus enabling professionals to attend their district's and the Alliance's annual conventions. Non-convention workshops, clinics, seminars, and other learning opportunities provide

Alliance members with the latest research findings, innovative activities, and teaching approaches and provide opportunities for personal enrichment and growth. Most state associations, state departments of education, and other physical education-related organizations also provide year-round programming.

Each state also provides professional the opportunity to learn different coaching techniques, to acquire new skills, and to interact and exchange information with other members at its annual convention. Students especially you, should take advantage of state conventions, because not only will you learn from these experiences, but you also may make contact with many individuals who later may hire you or help you to get a job. The aims of the North Carolina Alliance for Health, Physical Education, Recreation and Dance, like those of other state organization, are consistent with the purposes of general education and relate specifically to the areas of athletics, dance, health education, intramural programs, physical education, and recreation.

These aims include the following(constitution of the North Carolina Alliance):

1. To awaken and stimulate wide and intelligent interest in its areas of concern;
2. To acquire and disseminate accurate professional information.
3. To promote adequate programs in the areas of concern and to advance the standards of teaching and performance in these areas;
4. To cooperate with the American Alliance for Health, Physical Education Recreation and

Dance, the Southern District Association for Health, Physical Education and Recreation, and other state and national education associations interested in the growth and development of children and adults.

Physical education provides enrichment opportunities to its members as they prepare themselves to serve other. They are joined in their efforts by related groups who seek to share knowledge for the benefit of all.

AFFILIATED ORGANIZATIONS

While the AAHPERD is largest organization associated with physical education and its related fields, it shares its interests with numerous other groups. The discussion that follows briefly describes some of these organizations.

HIGHER EDUCATION

In 1978, the National Association for Physical Education in Higher Education (NAPEHE) was formed by a merger of National Association for Physical Education of College Women and the National College Physical Education Association for Men. Since the merger, NAPEHE has continued the publication of *Quest* and its conference proceedings. Since 1930 the American Academy of Physical Education has been the highest honorary group in health, physical education, and recreation. Its more than 100 members have contributed scholarship and professional service, especially in colleges and universities. Some of their research studies are published annually in *The Academy Papers*. Illustrative of its leadership the Academy, in

1981, identified the following contemporary social problems of import to the professional: that physical educators need to help their clientele in all sectors to discriminate between fact and myth in the developing of fitness, diets, exercise equipment, and health programs; that if moral and ethical values are to result from physical education and athletic programs, teachers and coaches must emphasize them; and that physical educators should share their knowledge with other involved in sport programs for youths to help ensure quality experiences.

HEALTH

Since 1926, the American School Health Association has sought to improve health instruction, healthful living, and health services in the school. Although originally only for physicians, membership is now open to anyone engaged in school health work. This association publishes the *Journal of School Health.*

RECREATION

Development and expansion of programs and services along with environmental concerns constitute the primary work of the National Recreation and Park Association. It is also dedicated to having trained personnel conduct community recreation programs. *The Journal of Leisure Research* and *Parks and Recreation* are its publications. The National Intramural-Recreational Sports Association was begun in 1950 to provide an opportunity for college intramural directors to meet annually to exchange ideas and information. With the expansion of college programs into recreational services of all kinds, the Association assumed its present name in 1975. Sharing innovative program ideas, reporting research, and discussing policy and procedures highlight its annual convention and the *NIRSA Journal.*

SPORTS MEDICINE

The need to establish professional standards and to disseminate information led to the establishment of the National Athletic Trainers' Association in 1950, which publishes *Athletic Training* for its membership. The American College of Sports Medicine was founded in 1954 by individuals drawn from medicine, physiology, and physical education. Among its objectives are advancing scientific studies dealing with the effects of physical activities in health and well-being; encouraging cooperation and professional exchange among physicians, scientists and educators; initiating promoting, and correlating research in sports medicine; and maintaining a sports medicine library. It encourages research publications in injury prevention and rehabilitation and in environmental effects of exercise, nutrition, and other factors through its *Medicine and Science in Sports and Exercise.*

PSYCHOLOGY, HISTORY, PHILOSOPHY, ANTHROPOLOGY, AND SOCIOLOGY

North American Society was founded by the psychologists, psychiatrists, and physical educators for the Psychology of Sport and Physical Activity in 1965 to promote this increasingly popular field of study. Since 1973, the North American Society for Sport History has encouraged scholarly research in all aspects of this discipline of sport, conducted an annual conference, and published the *Journal of Sport History.* The Philosophic society for the Study of sport, founded in 1972, encourages scholarly investigation of the philosophical aspects of sport through its *Journal of the Philosophy of Sport.* Other specialized association are the Association for the Anthropological Study of Play, the North American Society for the Sociology of sport, and the Association for the Advancement of Applied Sport Psychology.

FITNESS

Since 1974, the Association for Fitness in Business has led in the expansion of employee fitness programs through its approximately 2000 members. These exercise-testing technicians, exercise physiologists, recreation specialists, and program directors conduct exercise testing prescribe exercise programs, promote healthful lifestyle changes, and administer programs for corporate executives and employees.

ATHLETICS

In the realm of college athletics, the regulatory bodies include the National Collegiate Athletic Association (founded in 1906), the National Association of Intercollegiate Athletics (founded in 1952), and the National Junior college Athletic Association (founded in 1938). The National Collegiate Athletic Association, with 644 members, promotes competition through 22 championship in 12 sports for women and 42 championships in 19 sports for men. The 520 members of the National Association of Intercollegiate Athletics represent smaller institutions and provided 15 women's and 17 men's championships. The National Junior College Athletic Association conducts championships in 9 sports for women and 12 sports for men.

Other athletic organization that encourage the exchange of ideas include the college sports Information Directors of American, the College Athletics Business Manager, the National Association of Collegiate Directors of Athletics, and the National strength and Conditioning Association. The Amateur Athletic Union (AAU) was founded in 1888 to promote amateur sports and to check the spread of the problems associated with professional sports. Using more than 300,000 volunteers at the local, regional and national levels, this organization conducts sports events for competitors of all ages. The National Federation of State High School Associations (founded in 1920) and the 50 state high school athletic and/or activities associations work to protect the activity and athletic interests of high school, to promote the growth of educational interscholastic athletics, and to protect high school students from exploitation.

Many state also have coaches' associations that either are specific to one sport or have coaches from all sports in their memberships. These groups usually sponsor statewide or regional workshops or clinics about specific coaching techniques or strategies, rule changes, value and ethics in school athletics, and sport psychology.

YMCA—YWCA

The Young Men's Christian Association, since 1851, and the Young Women's Christian Association, since 1866, have promoted physical activities and sports as will as the development of values. Today, both groups offer a wide range of fitness and sports activities that target all skill and age levels. The basic objectives for all professional groups are to exchange information to learn, and to serve.

To enhance both you knowledge about and commitment to your chosen career, you should seek opportunities through these organization to grow professionally. By exchanging program ideas and instructional and motivational techniques, members can improve their abilities to serve others and to learn how to communicate their goals and activities to colleagues and to the general pupils. Through the sharing of experience and research, many ideas for further study are generated. Therefore, as a young professional, you are encouraged to join your college, state, and national associations and one or more of those in your interest area. You also should being to read physical education periodicals, as listed in to help you more fully understand your profession.

PROFESSIONAL PREPARATION FOR PHYSICAL EDUCATION PROGRAMS

Assuming that you are considering physical education as a career, the second section of this chapter introduces you to the various tracks or majors that exist in many colleges and universities. This will prepare you for chapter 5, which describes many careers related to physical education, and chapter 6, which explains many specific programs and certifications. Professional preparation programs in physical education traditionally have been oriented toward teacher education with a secondary track or option sometimes available for those interested in physical education in other settings.

Until demand for teachers decreased dramatically in the late 1970s most students completed the first option in case they ever wanted to teach. Seldom dose this occur today due to a surplus of teachers. The tight job market, however, is only one factor in this change. Colleges and universities, in response to the decreasing number of teaching positions, have revised their curricula to include non-traditional tracks. Simultaneously, the popularity of and resultant expansion in fitness, leisure, recreation, athletic, and sports-related activities have created a boom in diversity and availability of careers. Since qualified individuals are needed for these positions, several non-traditional tracks offer specialized course work, internship, and certifications.

TEACHING TRACK

Teacher certification following graduation from an accredited 4-year institution is the goal of the teaching track. This preparation may occur throughout the undergraduate years or may by concentrated in just 2 years or may be concentrated in just 2 years following the completion of general course work taken at a junior or community college or at a 4-year institution. Certification that can be obtained include those of physical education for kindergarten (K) through grade 6; grades 7 through 12; K through 12; health education ; and dance. The National Council for Accreditation of Teacher Education (NCATE) NOW ALLOWS "learned societies" such as the American Alliance for Health Physical Education, Recreation and Dance, to recommend guidelines for the professional studies component of its standards.

These guidelines, containing all the attitudes,

knowledge, and skill required of a physical education teacher have been subdivided into three elements: academic, professional and pedagogical. Aquatics, dance exercise, games, sports, and other leisure pursuits are components of the unique academic content of physical education. The applied sciences of motor development, sport management, sport pedagogy, motor learning, sport philosophy, sport biomechanics, adapted physical education, exercise physiology, sport psychology, spot sociology, and the humanities of art, literature, and music, as discussed earlier, provide the intellectual and theoretical base for studies in physical education aspect of the undergraduate program develops an awareness of and commitment to the various educational, research, and service activities of physical education. These include studies in curriculum models, organization structures, diagnostic and evaluative procedures, and problem solving. Knowledge about the teaching and learning of physical skills constitute the pedagogical element. Abilities to plan, implement and evaluate learning are observed in a supervised student teaching experience.

According to the Council on Physical Education for Children, the curriculum for prospective elementary physical educators should develop competence in:

1. Understanding child growth and development, with an emphasis on motor development;
2. A knowledge of and appreciation for the structure and function of human movement;
3. Observing and assessing children and their movement;
4. A knowledge of learning processes, teaching strategies, and factors that affect motor learning;

5. Developing curriculum with emphasis on curriculum designs and strategies appropriate for elementary school programs;
6. Assessing and working with children who have special needs;
7. Personal skills and teaching skills in the content areas of fundamental movement patterns, games/ sports, dance, gymnastics, and aquatics to meet the needs and interests of children in kindergarten through grade six.

Following completion of a program that includes learning and developing these competencies and a supervised student teaching experience in grades K through 6 student receive their certification. Similarly, all prospective work in academic, professional, and pedagogical areas, although specific requirements very by state as they do for elementary school certification.

Students often must complete fieldwork experiences, such as class observations, beginning as early as the first year in college in some programs. These are often used to help student decide whether they wish to pursue a teaching track.

A part of this commitment of teachers at all levels is the belief in and advocacy of the essentiality of physical education in the school. Health education and dance majors have similar requirements, but their academic bodies of knowledge differ from those of the physical education student.

NON-TRADITIONAL TRACKS

Non-traditional tracks or course work options very widely in colleges and universities as each seeks to meet the interests of its student. Six of the most common curricula are listed below.

ATHLETIC TRAINING

Athletic training is currently offered as a undergraduate major in 63 colleges and universities. The curriculum specifies 11 courses emphasizing the sciences and at least 800 hours of clinical experiences for completion.

SPORT OR EXERCISE SCIENCE

A sport or exercise sciences option focuses on courses in chemistry, biology or zoology, anatomy, physiology, biomechanics, and exercise physiology.

This background prepares graduates for advanced studies in one of these scientific fields as well as for careers in which understanding the scientific bases of exercise and sport is vital.

COACHING AND TRAINING

Coaching emphasis or certification program are becoming increasingly popular as junior and senior high school and youth sport leagues want individuals who are trained specifically to work with this population.

The need for coaches of interscholastic teams exceeds the supply due to increased numbers of girls' teams, the hiring of fewer new teachers, and the resignation of tenures physical educator from coaching but not from teaching.

Coaching curricula most often include first aid and care and prevention of athletic injuries, anatomy, physiology, coaching theory and techniques, human growth and development, sport administration or management, sport psychology, and sport pedagogy.

HEALTH AND FITNESS OR FITNESS SPECIALIST

A health and fitness or fitness specialist track combines a scientific foundation, such as in biomechanics and exercise physiology, with business and management courses for physical education-related careers in the public and private sectors. In this option, some emphasis is placed on the teaching of arious physical activities.

SPORT COMMUNICATION OR MANAGEMENT

Sport communication seeks to merge knowledge in physical education and sport with skills in English, speech, journalism, and broadcasting. Similarly, sport management combines business and management course work with selected physical education courses. A diversity of courses selected to meet each individual's interests and needs, combined with independent studies emphasizing practical application of knowledge, is the best preparation for careers in these two fields.

The six tracks are not the only ones available, but they are illustrative of the emphasis on professionally preparing yourself for a career.

CONCLUSIONS

A part of becoming a professional is the adherence to the highest ethical standards. This is especially essential for the educator because of the magnitude of the trust and responsibility inherent in the teaching process. Educators must believe in the worth and dignity of all students and must seek to held them realize their potential as effective members of society.

Students are encouraged to inquire, to acquire knowledge, and formulate and to achieve worthy goals. As a student aspiring to a particular career, you need to understand the significance of your commitment when you join a career. While physical education is characterized by extensive training in a body of knowledge and service, communication among colleagues is also essential.

The services provided by the Alliance will enhance development of each of these component parts; involvement starting while you are a student is important in this process, too Similarly, you need to participate in conferences, attend workshops, and read publications of physical education- related organizations to prepare for you chosen career. As a young professional, you can make a significant contribution to the quality of life of those you serve as either a teacher, a researcher, or a program leader.

7

MANAGING PHYSICAL EDUCATION PROGRAMMES AND POLICIES

Management has emerged as an essential activity since people began forming groups to accomplish goals they could not achieve as individuals, and also to mobilise and coordinate individual efforts which are recognised essential for the good of the society. Managing, like all other practices, is an art and craft. It encompasses action in the light of the realities of a situation. Managers can work better by using the organised knowledge. Knowledge may be primitive or advanced, exact or inexact, but when well-organised, clear and pertinent it becomes a science.

Thus, whereas managing as practice is art, the underlying organised knowledge may be referred to as a science. Science and art are not mutually exclusive but are complementary. As science improves, so should the art. Management takes into account the multitude of influences of internal and external factors in decision-making process. Managing is an open system that operates within the organisation and also interacts with the external environment. It is now quite obvious that provision of only money or technology does not bring development.

The limiting factor in almost every failure is mainly the lack of quality and vigour on the part of managers. Need of managing is not accepted universally. Certain critics of modern management feel that people together work better with more personal satisfaction if there were no managers. Such an ideal group operation is referred to as team effort. But the fact remains that in the most elementary form of even team-play, each individual member has clear group goals with specific assignments of positions, play patterns, rules and guidelines. Every effective group effort needs to have organised cooperation by putting in minimum of time, money, material and discomfort, besides adopting basic principles and techniques of management.

Management may differ in its purpose, definition and accomplishment in one situation than in another, but the basic managerial aim remains the same, that of having "surplus" in terms of performance, achievement and profits, economic use of input of resources, greater personal satisfaction and accelerated future advancement. Management in sport in an important consideration as in other of human endeavours. It involves important matters like personnel, programmes, facilities, budgets, and public relations. Management may be described as "the total of the process through which appropriate human and material resources are made available effectively for accomplishing the purpose." According to Zeigler and Bowie, "Management involves the execution of managerial acts, involving conceptual, technical and human skills, while combining varying degrees of planning, organising, staffing, directing and controlling within the management process to assist an organisation to achieve its goals." Halp in, after analysing management in education, industry and government, states that "management refers to a human activity involving a minimum of four components:

- The formal organisation to operate,
- The leader or leaders within the set-up,
- The functions or tasks to be performed, and
- The work-group or groups.

Management has also been defined as a means of bringing about effective cooperative activity to achieve the purpose of an enterprise. Parkhouse and Lapin, in The women in Athletic Administration, state that "successful management is working towards the achievement of objectives with and through people." Understanding of sports management for sports personnel is of great importance because most of them perform some type of management work to contribute towards better performance of individuals, teams, departments and institutions, health and happiness of society at large.

A clearer understanding of the elements of sports management is also desirable to ensure the cooperation of the members, produce greater efficiency and a better-ordered society. Through such an understanding, goals of sports world can be achieved faster, ideas be implemented clearly, policy-planning be facilitated on the basis of what proved good in the past.

Management in Sport

Although the systematic study of management as a separate branch of human knowledge has a recent origin, the practice of management in general is as old as human society. The history is replete with the evidence of organisational activity that implies knowledge of many ideas that has later been reflected in various writings. In this context, sport and physical education is no exception. Sports management is an emerging concept although the management in sports programmes at formal and non-formal levels has already been in existence, may be in a disjointed form. A considerable amount of attention has been given to an analysis of the present structure and function has been given to an analysis of the present structure and functions in sports programmes.

But, in view of the fact that things are changing evidently in sport, organised management support is needed to face new challenges. The opportunity is not to start from the scratch but to begin with the current situation as it is. Despite the availability of relevant literature on sport, an integrated approach to sports management is needed. As the sports technology is advancing, more people are needed to perform specific managerial duties in sports world. Besides the existing opportunitics, many morc avenues are emerging in sport, physical education, health, industry, governmental and non-governmental sectors.

Individuals are essentially expected to understand certain basic facts and acceptable management procedures. This is needed specially to avoid any loss of efficiency, low performance and health management, low morale of staff and poor human relations in sports organisations. Sports management and organisation have been existing for at least a century and a half, but until 1950's was learned by assimilation and through on-the-job experience. In the mid-fifties, Walter O'Malley, owner of Brookly Dodgers, advanced the idea for background academic knowledge and expertise to successfully administer modern sports programmes.

In 1966, the Department of Health, Physical Education and Recreation at Ohio University, initiated the first sports administration programme which generated considerable interest. Today almost all the universities all over the world offer programmes in administration and management in sport. Besides the existing available guidance, sports management as today needs to be understood in two distinct underlying dimensions, i.e. sport and management.

Historical Background

Until World war II, literature on management was rather scarce, although progress of industry was good in the earlier part of the century. Urwick and Breach have commented upon thirteen writers who have contributed to the development of management thought. Towards the end of first century Bultion and later watt in United Kingdom evolved procedures for employer-employee relationship, cost accountancy, payment, planning and book-keeping. Robert, as early as 1810, based his observations on personnel management, pioneering certain rules and regulations for maintenance of peaceful environment, and personnel relations within an enterprise.

In 1923, a comprehensive work on management by Oliver Sheldon entitled, The Philosophy of Management, laid the foundation of Taylor, the scientific management school put forward the fact that, presence or emergence of certain things is casually accompanied by other things to follow in due course. However, same was cautioned not to be mixed up with cause and effect theory by George R. Terry. In 1949, English translation by Henri Fayol of a French work based practical management on the component of functions of an organisation. Although a good deal of literature has appeared since World War II, yet the real boom in the management writing has followed after 1970.

In recent years, a greater emphasis has been laid on the evolution of management as a system. It has also named as "systems approach to management" with three essential characteristics that:

- Common purpose through inter-relationship,
- It has larger system besides sub-systems, and
- Communications and complex characteristics of change in one factor affecting the change on the whole.

The scientific principles were evolved through a process of thorough investigations, analyses and observations of the circumstances in the course of historical development. However, Henry Alberts argument that accumulated knowledge alone cannot help train an executive, is quite relevant. It provides sufficient scope for executive development through experiences in any professional pursuit, e.g. medicine, law, industry, military, sport and the like.

AREAS OF CONCERN

Sport today exists in one form or the other, in all walks of life. If some participate in it for gaining acceptance, others take to it for personal fitness. Some co-opt for character values and others for business, glamour and so on. Like any other human activity, sports management also changes with the propose of activity, ranging from fun-seeking to competitive; recreational to commercial and business; sports programmes to academic programmes in sport etc. It also deals basically with human resources with emphasis on participants and spectators, coaches and trainees, sports officials and sports agencies. An attempt has been made to list the areas in which extensive research may be conducted for effective management.

Organisational Aspects

Sports contests are the formal means for presentation of sports programmes. Management of sports contest comprises three phases:

- Duties after the game,
- Preparation before the game, and
- Game responsibilities.

Sports competitions are mainly of two types, i.e., local and outstation, and both have different bases of management. One cannot ignore the need for redesigning the wide range of management areas, which include invitation of officials, eligibility, physical examination, utilisation of equipment, publicity, exhibition games and fund raising. Management also involves looking into the other aspects, e.g., arrangements for police on duty, parking, usher, stadia, seating, interval or gap-time facilities, public address system, medical facilities and dressing rooms.

In view of the human support requirement, it also needs internal staff management for refreshments, accommodation, reports and records, filing of data, besides finances, reservations and travel arrangements. An effective sports contest arrangement also needs a probe in its educational phase, i.e., plans and enforcement procedures. The nature of management differs depending upon whether a program is obligatory or invitational, and also on the sponsors e.g., state association or national federation or being adopted by the private sector.

Personal Management

Although importance of selecting qualified personnel is beyond doubt, yet management is actually required essentially in the areas of selection process and post-selection elements of orientation, training and development. A perpetual research may be of good use to have right people-athlete, coach and staff, to provide equal employment opportunities. It may evolve a system to have a suitable person for a variety of jobs in sport dealing with finances, facilities, health care, travel, game management, public relations and so on. Appropriate management training methods should be developed for the staff aimed at promoting the professional and institutional growth.

Management of Physical Education Instructional Programmes

The instructional programmes in sport and physical education are the best way to teach skills and strategies. They also provide for understanding and essential knowledge concerning the relationship of physical activity to physical, mental, emotional and social development. These also provide a platform for the participants to achieve optimum state of physical fitness.

Thus the nature of physical education at pre-school, elementary, primary, secondary school and college level should be as per the status, maturity and performance objectives at different levels. Changing concepts of education needs of the society and approach towards ultimate objectives also influence such instructional programmes. Physical education as an institutional programme is a continuous process, therefore a constant effort should be made to have long-term, short-term and immediate plans.

Facilities and Equipment Management

Facilities and equipment management is usually the responsibility of specific incharges. Facilities include indoor and outdoor grounds along with additional necessities of change rooms, lockers, showers, refreshment counters, etc. Besides playing facilities, supplies and equipment need to be managed efficiently for overall success of any sports programmes. In view of the ever-increasing cost, high inflation, limited financial provision, there is continuous need to predetermine the supply and equipment required.

Therefore, a purchase system may be evolved in view of ever changing needs for maximum utilisation of the facilities and resources available to any sports organisation. As far as planning and construction of new facilities are concerned, concepts of convertibility, multipurpose utilisation and other similar needs should be identified for effectively managing a sports organisation.

Office Management

Successful management in sport to a great extent depends on the office management. It includes tasks like communication, correspondence, logistics support recording minutes and proceedings, report and budget preparation and policy implementation, etc. Office work handles the management of information to all concerning sport. In the process, manual assistance to automation and computerisation is of great utility as a routine. The point of managerial importance is how best and effectively the office can work. Dynamic principles and new techniques are being developed every day and need to be continually probed as their utility arises.

Organising Sports Programmes

Organising is a situation-based function influenced by various factors ranging from structure to positions to qualifications and resources. Since it is difficult to set forth a model for as-it-is adaptation in sports programmes, the need arises for identifying parameters to re-examine organising structure for a good spade-work for sound process of sports management.

Directing and Controlling

Sports management process has a vast scope for review and research in the mechanism of leadership and performance, evaluation standards and motivation, reporting and reward systems, etc. Such a review can hopefully lead to clues to effective directing and control of sports programmes.

Competitive Sport and Training Programme Management

Competitive sport and training programmes have probably peculiar difficulties attached to them. Some of these are the desire to win, participation in advance, university and inter-state level sports, pressures of admissions in educational institutions, academic balance, eligibility framework, awards and rewards, limited resources, etc. Such challenges can be met only if competitive programmes are well managed to draw attention of the administrators and general public.

Fiscal Management

Fiscal management has become an increasingly important dimension of sports management in the light of current financial trends of various societies. To prevent misuse and waste of funds, and to ensure maximum and appropriate utilisation, policies and procedures should be laid out to ensure sufficient inflow of finances, preparation of budgets and expenditure with accountability.

Theory of Sports Management

Sport and management, as two extensive human activities, provide a great potential for re-synthesis of theoretical bases for establishing a relationship between human ability and enhancement of sport. An examination of the nature of sport management is attempted here to maximise the performance within available resources and their optimum utilisation.

Coach

Athlete management is the core process of sports but management of coach, and quality services are of prime importance among other officials around the athlete. It is the coach who extends real training and competent coaching to the athlete to prove the test in actual game conditions. The coach initiates management concept while maintaining records, providing motivational force and evaluating personal performance of the athletes. Management is also needed on the personal front of a coach towards sense of personal betterment by virtue of improving qualifications, job security, position and status in society during the short span of glorified sports life.

Athlete

An athlete as a sports participant is the first unit of any sports programme. Of course, nothing really starts until the signal from officials, but it is the athlete who demonstrates and remains the focus of attention. It is the players who make the game, the competition and everything around the game. If the athlete is the central variable of management, the dependent variables include scheduling, officials, adequate facilities, equipment, spectators, besides appropriate preparation of the athlete. Management of the athlete is primarily needed to decide the channels for sportsmen to be identified and groomed, their academic, medical and health cover as well as placement in careers. Social, psychological, physical and emotional aspects of the athlete are also required to be managed properly.

The Press and Public Relation

Media plays a vital role in sport by reporting and commenting upon the conduct of sports programmes, performance of participants, technique and tactics of the game. Effect of television coverage and extensive reporting in newspapers, magazines and sport bulletins provide broad scope for any sports manager to redesign and evolve appropriate patterns to deal with various kinds of sports journalism. The kind of information to be furnished to press, selection of sports information and public relation officer, etc. are major staffing dimensions which need theoretical and practical support of management concepts.

Women and Sport

Sport, historically were designed for men, however, later, the same were adapted and modified for women. But today women participate in sport not only to prove the equality but for their satisfaction. Participation of women in sport should be encouraged in view of their changing needs. It also demands for new philosophy, change in policy perspective, and additional steps to enhance personality, and socio-cultural background of women in sport. The area of sports management by sportswomen has unlimited potential for establishing new patterns.

Spectators and Fans of Sport

Sport fans and spectators adapt to various sport on account of the need for strong identification with teams or athletes besides other educational, entertainment and recreational values. Thus, sport today potentially involves a large number of fans and spectators, giving various new dimensions to sports management. For example, spectators interested in watching games on TV and others on field have different requirements for management. Management structure also depends upon the climatic influences and varies from place to place and region to region.

Money and Business in Sport

Individuals and organisations without having any direct bearing on sport influence the complexion of sports management by investing money and giving it the direction of a kind of business.

Planning and Policy Development

Management requires planning before implementation of actions. Hence, further research is needed to identify specific requirements to forecast sports programmes based on various factors like resources, population, shifting trends of sports popularity, etc. It also requires proper understanding of complex factors like individual and institutional objectives, budget, critical analysis of policies and procedural consideration.

THEORETICAL PERSPECTIVES

Nature of Sport: A managerial Viewpoint

Paul Weiss in Sport: A philosophic Enquiry presents that the theme of pursuit of excellence in sport advances the dual hypothesis: First, the participants take part in sport to fulfil the desire to pursue excellence, and second, spectator is attracted to it as a result of identification need with the athletes. Another managerial view of sports from management is presented by Michael Noval in Joy of Sports. It emphasises that sport is centred around fans, who are just not casual spectators merely to be entertained.

But, such fans are a special kind of spectators, who really crave for the specific outcome of the contest because to their strong identification with teams or players, or both. Thus, sport as a medium to pursue excellence, and for identification of active participants from on and off the field, provides a wider base for management in sport. In the process of managing participants and spectators and to maximise the potential of sport, various reference points like suitable schedules, selection of competent officials, provision of facilities, equipment, attraction of spectators, appropriate training and coaching, records and standardisation are key considerations of sports management. School, college and university systems have acquired additional significance in the society.

Sports programmes at formal and non formal education level make a great contribution to the vitality, imagination and moral unity. The basis of sport serves as guideline for management of sports programmes. An overview of sport indicates additions of recreational sport, club sport, sports agencies, community programmes and mass-participation requiring specific management procedures. The nature of sport perhaps can be better understood through experience in sport than only through any theoretical explanation.

However, it is also impossible for anyone to generalise accurately only from one's experience. Differences in individual experiences are likely to affect contrasting conclusions regarding the nature of sport. However, a combination of practical experience and understanding of theoretical structure of sport is most desirable for management implication. It is also important to study deeply sports management for an insight into various areas such as structure of organisation, role of leadership and human relations that affect the achievement of goals.

Management in sport aims to help people achieve the goals, to fulfil their desire to live happy, productive, healthful and meaningful lives. Management in sport in not an end in itself, rather it is means to an end, i.e. welfare of people for whom organisations exist. To sum up, management in sport is for its participants and not that people are for management.

Parameters of Sports Management

The best way to learn about the management is to get involved with it, but that does not mean that management experience is necessary in becoming an effective manager. Many view management as a continuity of thought process. By and large management process is analysed through its functional activities. Harold and Vander have identified the following functions of management:

- Organising
- Planning
- Directing
- Evaluating
- Decision-making
- Staffing
- Communicating, and
- Controlling

Organising

Organising as a word is often used in common terms. For some, it is coordinating behaviour of all participants, to others it is equivalent to the entire system of social and cultural relationships. Some others refer to it as structuring an enterprise, corporation or a department. For most managers, the term implies formalised intentional structure of roles or positions that people working together must fill. The roles people are asked to fill often are intentionally designed to make sure that abilities and activities fit together, so that people can work smoothly, effectively and efficiently in groups.

In simple terms, organising consists of identifying and grouping of activities, assigning of authority to managers, and providing for coordination. Formal organisation is the intentional structure of roles and informal organisation is the joint activity of people without a conscious common purpose. Possibly both types of organisations contribute to achieve results. For example, university basketball team and morning joggers respectively are true forms of formal and informal organisation.

The formal organisation must be flexible to channel-lies creative talents of individuals for attaining group goals. It is also important to understand the patterns and dynamics of interpersonal relations existing in informal organisations. The term organisation has been defined by a number of authors; given below are some of the representative definitions: "Purposive bodies which get a pay off from multiple contributions by coordinating them towards a common end ".

"Two or more people, specialised in the functions, each performing and working together toward some common goal, and governed by formal rules of behaviour". A social system deliberately to carry out some definite purpose". The given definitions for an organisation essentially incorporate four elements:

- The members' contribution is specialised;
- There is a common end/goal which is being sought.
- These specialised functions are coordinated;
- More than one person is needed;

A logical overlapping of elements can also be noted since the concept of management relates only to an organisation. A clearer understanding of a sports organisation involves the following characteristics:

1. Instrumentality: Instrumentality of a sports organisation in the achievement of goals of its members is quite obvious. For example, a local sports club provides facilities, instructions and opportunities to people of

similar interest and skill.

2. Identity: The identity of a sports organisation is separate and independent of the identity of its constituent members such as managers, coaches, players or other office-bearers. The identity of the members is independent of that acquired by them in a collective capacity in an organisation.

3. Membership: Individuals in a sports organisation shall have skills or expertise to carry out programmes and activities.

4. Permanency: It is essential to override the transfers, resignations, etc. of individual members, so as to avoid the functional breakdowns.

5. Hierarchy of authority: Chain of commands is required for specified purpose, to schedule the activities, to allocate funds and to monitor in general.

6. Clear boundaries: The area and scope of operation shall be delimited. For example, a department of physical education is to carry out teaching, coaching and research, placement service, intramurals and extra-murals by its teachers and office staff members for the enrolled students.

7. Division of labour: Division of labour and particularly the resultant specialisation characterise the smooth and efficient running of a sports organisation.

8. Formal rules and procedures: These are formed to ensure the consistency of work performed to the expected target standards.

Sport as an organisational set-up at various levels of school, college, university, club, private industry, team, state or nation possesses all the attributes of an organisation. Ball points out that sports organisations are also unique in terms of the constant roster size of members in various sport/same sport/public or private club, etc. These establish a strong underlying need for facilitating organisational analyses of sport, catering to society in consumer and professional service programmes in a very unique way. Keeping in view the understanding and the functions of the organisation as a unit, organising sport management involves breaking down the planning process into smaller specific jobs to establish a relationship among the individuals assigned to carry them out.

While the planning process specifies what, when and how a work is to be done, the organising process details as to who should do it in the absence of a distinct dividing line between the various overlapping functions of management. The organisational structure is necessary to provide base for the proper functioning of the organisation. It should be represented by an organisation.

It is an essential tool in the management process. Osgood makes the following comments about the necessity of an organisational. "It is not only extremely helpful but a practical necessity to have organisation structure formalised functions of each of key personnel. These duties must then be described and related to the resume of each person's background and the date they will or did join the set-up. The organisation plan will specify who is going to do what.

The total need of the organisation and the people in the organisation who will be performing the different required functions or activities must be identified." While preparing the, besides listing a complete statement of the objectives, jobs, functions, it needs to be determined whether each job is considered a line or a staff position. A line job is expected to be the one that has a direct bearing or relationship with the attainment of the primary objectives. A staff position is one that has a secondary or indirect effect on achievement. All staff positions originate from the line and report to a superior line manager. Staff people do not have authority over line people.

The line positions derive their powers from the chief. Positions should be grouped according to other functions and/or physical location in the organisation. A simple organisation helps in clear understanding of whom to report to avoid confusion over priorities and loyalties. Such a concept may enhance the effectiveness of management establishing a formal hierarchy of authority specifying the chain of command within the organisation. For example, a university team coach needs to assign the available players to the offensive, defensive and special talent/positions in team as per the ability/talent criteria. He must be clear of the expectations of different game situations.

The plan document of play providing minute details should serve as a model of coordination, which may also specify hierarchy of authority, e.g. manager, coach, assistant coach, technical assistant, captain, vice-captain, etc. Organising process follows classical principles, which have also been called "cornerstones of organising" by Robbins. They include:

• Span of control should depend upon the type of work done. Competence and expertise for doing the job must aim for high performance and better results.

• Unit of command needs to be clearly specified to protect against the possibility of conflicting commands by different superiors.

• Specialisation to contribute to efficiency by increasing the skill and ability to perform.

• Responsibility and authority must also be extended in balanced manner to individuals for deciding the task for themselves.

• Departmentalisations is essentially needed, since individually one cannot administer unlimited number of subordinates and manage diverse activities. Thus, departmentalisation should be on the basis of function, programme and goal orientation.

However, over-emphasis on organisational structure is also not desirable, because it creates the gap among the members of the work force.

Planning

To plan is to decide or to select the course of action from amongst the available alternatives that are futuristic in nature. Planning is a basic function of management, but it also reflects in other parameters of management. Planning is a rational approach to selected objectives. The basic function of the planning is to make sure for members of a group know as to what are they expected to accomplish to reach selected realistic goals. Planning is deciding in advance what to do, how to do, when to do and who is to do it. Many types of plans can be arranged in a hierarchy.

It may include purposes of missions, defining the basic tasks, objectives towards which the activity is aimed at, and strategies to determine its achievement.

These plans must bring in clarity on the kind of operation and policies for guidance of thought, action and non-actions to achieve the aim. Plans must have minute details of planning supported by a budget to be carried out during the course of action. Planning in an overview is important for its major four goals:

• Focus attention on objectives, since they are the end points of the sports management programme.

• Facilitate control and check the progress during the process. While planning is looking ahead, controlling is looking back to lay sub-plans for future within the framework of the already laid out plans. Planning to control and check is also necessary for not letting the planning fail, but also to make it more effective.

• Offset uncertainty and chance since the future is seldom certain. Even if the future is highly certain, some planning is necessary. For example, while planning a sports programme, consideration of financial constraints, societal trends, competitive value, professionalism over the next few years cannot be overlooked.

• Make an operation possible by way of planning a coordinated and even flow of work with deliberate decisions.

The planning process must have enough flexibility to allow retention of control of the direction. Higher the flexibility built into plans, lesser the danger of mismanagement on account of unexpected events. Flexibility is possible only within limits, first, no decision can be put off for a long to ensure its rightness; second, it may not be worth; and third, sometimes it is impracticable. Hence, flexibility should be weighed against its advantages, and policy development might be viewed as the capstone of the entire planning process.

The policy is considered an essential link between objectives and implementation and as integral in complete planning. That is why policy development is a continuous process. Today, in our setup, policy development of sports programmes have shown a number of deficiencies. Policies are needed to be guided with a clear focus on the needs of the society, programme structure and resource mobilisation for better direction. To have a clear idea a planning in sports management, an example of a coach of the university team may be considered. He sets the goal for his team in terms of a number of victories or series of tournaments.

While planning to undertake the project, certain constraints such as finance, quality of players and opposition are taken into account. Further, the means adopted to achieve the goals must be within rules of the sport. The coach then transforms it into strategies and tactics to be adopted. During the game and after every match, the coach tries out evaluation, introduces changes in plans toward complete control of achievement of the objectives.

The plan may take into account one match or one championship or may encompass whole season or series of tournaments. Planning is an ongoing process surely to be the beginning of the management. Planning may be guided by certain principles, for example:

1. The objectives are to be meaningful, clear, attainable, actionable and verifiable,

2. Major plans must have supporting plans or sub-

plans in total harmony,

3. The process of planning should be accomplished by choosing favourable alternatives from amongst the available ones, commitment towards series of actions, flexibility to review the plans from time to time so as to redraw them, if required.

4. Purpose of each plan is to be the promotion of the set objectives,

5. Planning logically must precede the execution of all other managerial functions, and

6. A clear concept and understanding of strategies and policies for effective framework of plans must be among the staff.

However, over-emphasis on planning of a project is always harmful. One does not have to be a scholar or a researcher to have good ideas; it does not need any particular skill but calls for just conscious thinking. Improvement in a plan comes with its purpose and design, and not by accident. If once a problem or a project is taken charge of, attitudes develop, environment is built around, and ideas pour in to chisel leadership. The method of planning may range from following autocratic to democratic means. Autocratic managers plan on their own, whereas in a democratic way subordinates are delegated to plan in consultation with their staff.

Directing

Directing may sound authoritarian, but an essential component of management is directing. It involves getting the job done from the perspective of management. Probably one shows the leadership ability while directing. Leading is the process of influencing people so that they will strive willingly and enthusiastically toward the achievement of organisational goals. However, they is necessity of understanding complexity and individuality of people. Dignity of people should never be violated, they need to be treated with respect irrespective of their position in the set-up as they all contribute towards achieving the aim of the organisation.

Individuals should be treated as humans with weaknesses and strengths. They have characteristics of knowledge, attitudes, skills and personality traits to varying degrees, and also get influenced by the external factors. Planning and organising can be carried out without great deal of interpersonal interaction but considerable face to face interaction is required in the directing process. Thus, an understanding of the human motivation factor is essential for directing any effective management. Motivation in the context of leading have been defined by Hoy and Miskal as "the complex forces, drives, needs, tension states or other mechanism that start and maintain voluntary activity towards the achievement of personal goals" It is further stated that "activating forces are assumed to exist within individuals.

Examples of such internal force include memory, effective response and pleasure-seeking tendencies. Motivation also directs and channels behaviour, that is, it provides a goal-orientation and direct human behaviour towards something." Though numerous theories of motivation have been researched and advanced, but in general, it has been realised that motivation can come from within the individual by way of satisfaction and from outside in the form of rewards, money, appreciation, etc. obtained from the performance.

For example, in case of sports programmes, personnel gets internally motivated by the built-in appeal of activity itself besides secondary factors of money, award, reward, etc. as external factors. It is not enough to simply motivate and then expect a congenial situation on its own. Sports management presents dramatic evidence of professionally exhausted coaches, professors and teachers. In fact, relationship between motivation and satisfaction of various needs of an individual towards goal-directed behaviour cannot be undermined. Maslow's hierarchy of needs explains to some extent the emphasis placed on needs for motivation from managerial perspective. The practical implication of the need theories is that job must be designed to trigger as well as satisfy the higher order needs of the worker. Hackman and Oldman's "Job Characteristics Model" of motivation is also based upon the notion that "motivating potential of jobs is a function of job characteristics like task identity, task significance, autonomy and feedback, etc." An important point is that a satisfied need does not mark the end of the motivational concern.

The healthy individual is in a continuous state of motivation. After satisfying a particular need, one is always motivated towards new horizons. Sports programmes are real examples of motivational drive. After achieving a particular standard of performance, one desires and attempts for the next higher and complex stage of excellence. In sports management, opportunity for personal advancement has to be considered as a prime motivator. It may be in the form of pay rise, promotion or assumptions of new responsibilities or upgrading of academic ranks, and accompanying responsibilities for teaching, research and service.

In the more traditional sense, programme development is next closely related motivator in sports management. Generally personnel and programme development are interlinked, unless insufficient resources and support result in situational factor affecting the total development. In a way it is an administrative challenge providing motivation to staff members and mobilisation of resources and support to make the programme a success. Further, programme development is directly tied up with professional development.

Sport enterprise is an extensive and highly significant cultural factor which can achieve its potential only if all working members are directed to the focus of the advancement of sport. Sport management have certain special concerns and challenges motivating the staff. For example, the desire to win or the evident nature of results of sport; the in-built appeal of intra-mural and extra-mural programmes; facilities existing in an organisation; structure of sports programme and its popularity, attitude that is established within the organisation towards academic and non-academic appointments, play a big role in affecting motivational levels for staff. Reference to the theories of motivation "Content" , and "Process" theories, as well as job characteristic model of Hackman, put forward a concept that job must be enriched enough for workers to find it challenging and satisfying.

However, organisations differ in purposes, processes and environmental conditions which affect matching of jobs, individuals and organisational characteristics. Understanding of the various behaviour patterns of the manager and the subordinates may be of great help in harmonising objectives. Such an understanding is probably the key to effective leading. However, besides "motivation", other prime considerations of "delegation", "coordination", "managing differences" and "managing change" are of considerable significance in the area of directing a sports programme.

A brief description of various above mentioned concepts of directing is given below. Delegation is to entrust the responsibility and authority to another person. The entire process of delegation, according to Broyles and Hay, shall be supported by:

• Authority along with responsibility to take immediate action on routine matters,

• Responsibility is fixed and delineated as carefully as possible,

• Clarity of delegation between delegator and subordinate regarding as to what is being delegated,

• Feedback usually in the form of written reports or actual observation of results to assess the delegated responsibility, and

• A clearly defined chain of commands to establish the unity of command.

Generally, delegation in sports management is in the areas of budgetary control, facilities, game management, promotion and information of sport, academic affairs, conferences and seminars, travel arrangement, organisation of sport, etc. Degree and kind of delegation is also affected by the size, highlights and special circumstances of sports programmes, and by the strength and weakness of the director. Coordination is the process of briefing a group into common action.

Coordination must necessarily be strengthened with appropriate model of communication, assessment of group atmosphere and tasks of sports programme. Managing differences of people with different backgrounds, abilities and attitudes, along with a variety of tasks to be performed is another significant dimension in directing. Differences in sports management due to the variety of programmes has its own mode of operation. Demands of each sport are different and thus necessary adjustment should be made for the benefit of overall sports programme. Managing change is largely external in its origin but results in internal changes in the organisation. Such needs can be mainly due to financial limitations, promotions, the part-time sports services, and shift and objectives of sports programmes.

Staffing

All the efforts put in planning and organising may be of no avail if the staffing procedures are inefficient and ineffective. The function of staffing is defined as filling positions in the organizational structure through identifying work force requirements, creating an inventory of the work force, recruitments, selection, placement, promotion, appraisal, compensation and training of people. Some view staffing as a part of organising. It has an independent function to perform.

It requires specialised knowledge and approach for effective functioning and a greater emphasis on the human element in selection, appraisal and managerial development. Staffing may be the responsibility of the manager and not the personnel department, which otherwise provides valuable assistance. The policy-making group of executives ascertains staffing policy and pattern, its proper execution by subordinates with regard to interviews of candidates and selection procedures, later to be followed by appraisal programmes, promotion and retirement policies. Situational factors in staffing are directly and indirectly affected by environmental factors.

External factors include the level of education and prevailing attitudes in society, low and regulations, political and economic conditions, supply and demand of personnel. The internal factors also affect staffing by way of goals, tasks, the kind of people employed, the reward system and attitude towards subordinates, etc. A system approach shall ideally be used to staffing. According to the organisation plan, after determining the number of staff required, it shall be double-checked against the areas and needs established. Sources should be best explored from with and outside the organisation for recruitment, selection, placement and promotion. Staffing as a process goes through various critical and refined phases.

Even if position, qualifications and pool of talent are carefully established, the element of human factor in selection process plays a crucial role. Various personal and political considerations tend to work at cross-purposes while selecting staff. However, after the selection is made, formal and informal orientation in the form of written material or oral instructions should include information regarding objectives of organisation, strategies, policies, working relationship and responsibilities of staff, etc. As compared to orientation, training should be job-centred with focus on in-depth instruction on practice in the work.

Development, in a way, also entails extension of training for improvement of knowledge, attitudes and skills to advance beyond the immediate situation for growth. Widening the scope of growth and development can save staff and the organisation from many future problems. Appraisal is another essential function closely linked to selection, placement and promotion. Appraisal truly serves as a basis for identifying persons within the set-up who are ready for promotion. It should certainly deal with:

- Performance in accomplishing goals and plans, besides
- Performance of functions and activities,
- Focus on the personality traits.

Well-selected and well-trained staff provide good leadership and create an environment in which people are motivated and communicate effectively.

Controlling

The term control has different meanings in different situations. But, in general, it revolves around checking or keeping within specified limits. In sports management controlling is the measurement and correction of performance to ensure the ultimate accomplishment of desired objectives. Feedback is the essence of controlling, hence evaluation emerges to be the key concept. Control as a process involves various steps. To have a clear indication of job performance, performance standards need to be designed. According to Deegan and Fritz, such fixation of objectives helps in providing a framework of good teaching and coaching appraisal methodology, interactive relationship and motivation.

It also provides clarity with regard to authorities and

responsibilities, measurement of performance and level of satisfaction of the performer. Specific performance standards in sports organisations must be developed for teachers, coaches, athletes, directors, finance officers, public relation officers, coordinators, facilities managers and various others who all contribute significantly in the effective management. Though performance standards are specific to situation, and it is difficult to have a clear idea of specific expectations, yet some specification of expected standards on the basis of territorial responsibility of result areas must be remarked.

CLASS MANAGEMENT

Good management does not just happen. It requires careful thought, good judgment, and planning before the calls begins to have a group of participants act in an orderly manner, accomplish the tasks that have been established, and have an enjoyable, satisfying, and worthwhile experience. The leader who is in charge of a class where these optimal conditions exist has spent considerable time planning the details of the class from start to finish. The following reasons for good organization should be recognized by every teacher and administrator:

1. It gives meaning and purpose to instruction and to the activities.

2. It more fully ensures that the needs and interests of the participants will be satisfied.

3. It provides for measurement and progress toward objectives.

4. It encourages program adaptations to each

individual's needs and interests.

5. It helps to conserve the instructor's time and strength and aids in giving the instructor a sense of accomplishment.

6. It helps to eliminate discipline problems.

7. It results in efficiency, the right emphasis, and the best use of the time available.

8. It more fully ensures progression and continuity in the program.

9. It ensures a participants' health and safety.

10. It reduces errors and omissions.

Management guidelines

1. A definite time schedule should be planned for each period, considering time to be devoted to showering and dressing, taking roll, class activity, and other essentials.

2. The classroom environment should be one of safety. The equipment should be in good condition, and line markings, arrangements for activities, and other essential details should be attended to.

3. Long-term planning for the semester and the year, as well as daily, weekly, and seasonal planning, should be done.

4. The activity should be carefully planned so that it proceeds with precision and dispatch, with a minimum amount of standing around and a maximum amount of activity for each student.

5. Procedures to be followed in the locker room should be established to provide for traffic, valuables,

clothes, and dressing and showering.

6. Participants should be encouraged and motivated to do their best.

7. The instructor should wear suitable clothing.

8. Desirable attitudes and understandings toward physical fitness, skill learning, good sportsmanship, and other concepts inherent in physical education should be stressed at all times.

9. The instructor should always be punctual for class meetings.

10. The instructor should have a good command of the subject, recognizing the values of demonstrations, visual aids, and other techniques to promote learning.

11. A planned program of measurement and evaluation should be provided to determine progress being made by participants and the effectiveness of teaching.

SCHOOL AND COLLEGE PHYSICAL EDUCATION PROGRAMS

Physical education programs in schools and colleges have had a prominent place in educational systems since the turn of the century. These programs exist at the preschool, elementary school, junior high school, senior high school, and college and university educational levels.

Preschool physical education programs

The concept of early schooling is no longer regarded as a custodial or compensatory undertaking. Instead it is viewed as a necessary provision for the normal growth and development of children. This change has come about because of research on the growth and development of children from birth to 6 years, as well as the change in family life, as indicated by such developments as more mothers entering the work force. Research by such professionals as psychologists and sociologists has indicated that the early years are crucial for the child intellectually, physically, and socially.

In light of such developments, play schools and nursery schools have gained wide popularity. Preschool educational programs involve indoor and outdoor play-learning activities. Physical education activities include the development of fundamental movement skills, fitness and self-testing activities, music and rhythmic activities, and rhymes and story plays. The program of selected physical activities helps the child develop a positive self-concept, develop social skills, enhance physical fitness, and improve cognitive and sensorimotor skills. Research maintains that a relationship exists between perception and motor development and that perception is related to cognition; therefore physical movement experiences play a part in cognitive development. Preschool programs are becoming an important part of educational systems in this country, and physical education is playing an important role in such programs.

Management guidelines for elementary school physical education programs

Elementary schools stress perceptual motor development and, in addition, an interdisciplinary approach whereby the subject matter of physical education is integrated with certain other subjects such as music, science, and art. Some management guidelines that should be recognized in elementary school physical education programs follow. The program should meet the needs of all children, including the handicapped, slow learner, culturally deprived, gifted, and normal.

The program should stress movement education, perceptual-motor development, and interdisciplinary analysis. It should include a variety of experiences that will help the child form a sound foundation on which to build more complex skills, strategies, and techniques. It should provide developmental and progressive experiences. The program should stress such factors as creativity, self-expression, positive self-concept, social development, and safety.

Elementary school physical education programs

The elementary schools of the nation are stressing movement education. Experts do not agree on a single definition for movement education. They do agree, however, that movement education depends on physical factors in the environment and on the individual's ability to react intellectually and physically to these factors. Movement education attempts to help the student become mentally and physically aware of his or her bodily movements. It is based on a conceptual approach to human movement.

Through movement education, the individual develops his or her own techniques for dealing with the environmental factors of force, time, space, and flow as they relate to various movement problems. Movement education employs the problem-solving approach. Each skill to be explored presents a challenge to the student. Learning results as the student accepts and solves increasingly more difficult problems. For this reason, the natural movements of childhood are considered to be the first challenges that should be presented to student. Traditional physical education emphasizes the learning of specific skills through demonstration, drill, and practice.

Movement education emphasizes learning skill patterns through individual exploration of the body's movement potential. Traditional physical education stresses the teacher's standard of performance. Movement education stresses the individual child's standard of performance.

Innovative ideas in secondary school physical education

Many innovative instructional programs are being used in physical education at the secondary school level. These include programs stressing personalized and individualized learning; those emphasizing performance objectives, competency packages, and goal setting; those concerning themselves with career and leadership opportunities; those including electives; those stressing flexibility in scheduling; and those concentrating on such specialized types of experiences as cycling, exercise physiology, and the environment.

Secondary school physical education programs

The junior high and senior high schools of the nation should build on the physical education provided at the elementary school level. Some management guidelines that represent important considerations in secondary school physical education programs follow. Most of the guidelines set for the elementary school also have merit in developing programs for secondary schools. The program should be based on the developmental tasks of secondary school students.

The program should consist of a variety of activities, including gymnastics, self-testing activities, rhythm and dance, aquatics, dual and individual sports, team sports, movement skills, and physical fitness activities. The program should provide an understanding of the human body and the impact of physical activity on its various organic systems. Basic Stuff Series I and II that include concepts, principles, and developmental ideas extracted from the body of knowledge for physical education and sports should be used. The program should teach skills progressively and eliminate excessive repetition of activities. Title IX regulations should be adhered to. Handicapped students should be provided a program in the least restrictive environment.

The program should encourage vigorous physical activity and develop an optimum state of physical fitness. In addition to the management guidelines above the following points should be stressed: The physical education class is a place to teach the skills, strategy, appreciation, understanding, knowledge, rules, regulations, and other material and information that are part of the program. It is not a place for free play, intramurals, and varsity competition. It is a place for instruction. Every minute of the class period should devoted to teaching boys and girls the skills and subject matter of physical education.

Instruction should be basic and interesting. Skills should be broken down into simple components and taught so that each individual may understand clearly what he or she is expected to accomplish and how it should be done. Use of demonstrations, loop films, models, slide films, posters, and other visual aids and materials can help to make the instruction more meaningful and interesting.

Instruction should involve definite standards. Students should be expected to reach individualized standards of achievement in the class program. A reasonable amount of skill—whether it is in swimming, tennis, or another activity—should be mastered, depending on individual differences. Laxity and indifference to achievement should not be tolerated any more in physical education than in any other subject area in the curriculum. When boys and girls graduate from high school they should have met definite standards that indicate that they are physically educated.

Instruction should be progressive. There should be a definite progression from simple to complex skills. Just as a student progresses in mathematics from simple arithmetic to algebra, geometry, and calculus, so the pupil should progress in physical education from basic skills and materials to more complex and involved skills and strategies.

Instruction should involve more than physical activity. All physical education classes do not have to be held in the gymnasium where physical activity predominates. A reasonable proportion of class, time, perhaps as much as 10% to 20%, can be devoted to discussions, lectures, independent study, Basic Stuff Series I and II, working on learning packages, and meaningful classroom activity. Outstanding coaches often have chalk talks for their players, in which they study rules and regulations, strategies, execution of skills, and other materials essential to playing the game effectively. This same principle can be applied to the physical education class period.

Physical activity should not be conducted in a vacuum; if it is, it has no meaning and will not be applied when the student leaves the class and school. As the student understands more fully the importance of sports and activities in life, what happens to the body during exercise, the history of the various activities in which he or she engages, and the role of physical activity in the culture of the world, the class takes on new meaning and physical education takes on new respect and prestige.

There should be homework. It is just as reasonable to assign homework in physical education as in general science. Much subject matter is to be learned, and many skills are to be mastered. If teachers would require their students to work on various activity skills and knowledge outside of class, there would be more time in class for meaningful teaching.

There should be records. The instructor should keep adequate records to provide tangible evidence of the degree to which objectives are being met by the students. This means that data on physical fitness, skill achievement, knowledge of rules and other information, and social conduct—such as sportsmanship—should be a part of the record.

The teaching load of physical educators should be determined not only by the number of instructional class periods assigned but also by the total number of activities handled by the teacher both in class and outside of class. To do efficient work a teacher should have a normal work load—not an overload. Some professional standards have established that class instruction should not exceed 5 hours, or the equivalent of five class periods each day.

Each student should have a health examination before participating in the physical education program. An annual health examination should be regarded as a minimum essential to determining the amount and nature of physical activity that best meets each student's needs.

Management guidelines for college and university physical education programs

Colleges and universities should provide instruction in physical education that meets the following management criteria: The program should be available to all students. The program should not be a repetition of the high school program but should offer more advanced work in physical education. The program should include innovative features to meet the needs of students and at the same time be interesting and challenging to them. The program should not allow ROTC, band, athletics, or other activities to be a substitute for physical education.

The program should provide electives. The program should stress knowledge and understanding of the value of physical activity. The program should stress the study and practice of the science and art of movement. The program should stress lifetime skills. The program should be conducted by qualified faculty members. A survey of the status of required physical education in colleges and universities in the United States indicates that many institutions require physical education for students. Also, many institutions have made physical education voluntary for students. A few have a requirement for students only in certain departments or schools. The majority of the institutions requirement is for a 2-year period.

The survey indicates the trend is toward more emphasis on recreation and fitness activities and on coeducational classes. The college and university physical education program is the end of formal physical education for many students. The age range of individuals in colleges and universities is wide, incorporating those from 16 to 60 years of age. However, most college students are in their late teens or early twenties. These individuals have matured in many ways. They are entering the period of greatest physical efficiency. They have developed the various organ systems of the body. They possess strength, stamina, and co-ordination. College and university students have many interests.

They want to prepare themselves for successful vocations, an objective that requires the physical educator to show how the physical education program can contribute to success in their work. College students are interested in the opposite sex. They want to develop socially. This has implications for a broad coeducational program, as does Title IX. They are interested in developing skills that they can use and enjoy throughout life. They are interested in becoming physically fit. In formulating a program at the college and university level, one needs to remember that many students enter with limited activity background.

Therefore the program should be broad and varied at the start, with opportunities to elect activities later. Considerable opportunity should exist for instruction and practice in those activities in which a student desires to specialize. As much individual attention as possible should be given to ensure necessary skill and fitness development. Most colleges offer physical education twice a week for 2 years. Some colleges and universities have few requirements, whereas others state that certain physical standards of achievement must be met. The program of activities should be based on the interests and needs of students and the facilities and staff available.

Some colleges have introduced "Foundations" courses, getting at the subject matter of physical education. An important place for coeducation exists at the college level in activities such as tennis, dancing, swimming, badminton, volleyball, golf, softball, racquetball, aquatics, dance, bowling, table tennis, skating, archery, horseback riding, mountaineering, orienteering, snow skiing, skydiving, judo, hiking, tumbling, and camping. In college physical education programs physical achievement tests should be used to asses student needs and assure progress. Special help and prescribed programs should be offered to help physically underdeveloped students.

Another suggestion has been made to institute a requirement that all students demonstrate proficiency in swimming and physical fitness. The growth of the 2-year college has been significant. In many respects the activities for the 2-year college are the same as those for the 4-year institution. However, because many community college students end their education after 2 years of study, the need to develop skills to enrich their leisure time and to stimulate a desire to keep themselves fit throughout their lifetime. Most of the 2-year colleges require students to take physical education both years.

Most of the programs require 2 hours each week and stress the successful completion of the service program as a requirement for graduation. Activities required in one California junior college include aquatics, archery, badminton, bowling, fencing, folk and square dance, golf, ice skating, modern dance, sailing, social dance, tennis, tumbling, gymnastics, trampoline, and volleyball.

Interrelationships of elementary, secondary, and college and university programs

The physical education programs at the elementary, secondary, and college levels should be interrelated. Continuity and progression should characterize the program from the time the student enters school until graduation. Overall planning is essential to ensure that each student becomes physically educated and to guarantee that duplication of effort, waste of time, omissions, and shortages do not occur. Continuity and progression do not exist today in many of the school systems of the United States. To a great degree each institutional level is autonomous, setting up its own program with little regard for what has preceded and what will follow. If the focus of attention is on the student—the consumer of the product—then program planning will provide the student with a continuous program, developed in light of his or her needs and interests, from the time he or she starts school until graduation. Consideration also should be given to adult years.

Directors of physical education for the entire community should shoulder this responsibility and ensure that such a program exists. Some communities have directors of school and community physical education and recreation programs, ensuring a continuous program for the entire population.

Management factors relating to one or more educational levels

Certain factors relate to one or more educational levels. Some of the more pertinent factors include interrelationships of elementary, secondary, and college and university programs; teaching aids and materials; class management; implications of Title IX for instructional strategies; and implications of Public Law 94-142 for instructional strategies.

MANAGEMENT MATTERS RELATED TO PHYSICAL EDUCATION INSTRUCTIONAL PROGRAMS

Flexible scheduling

The introduction of flexible scheduling into school programs has implications for the administration of school physical education programs. Flexible scheduling assumes that the traditional system of having all subjects meet the same number of times each week for the same amount of time each period is passe. Flexible scheduling provides class periods of varying lengths, depending on the type of work being covered by the students, methods of instruction, and other factors pertinent to such a system.

Whereas the traditional master plan makes it difficult to have flexible scheduling, the advent of the computer has made such an innovation practical and common. Flexible scheduling also makes it possible to schedule activities for students of differing abilities differently so that all are not required to have a similar schedule based on a standard format of the school day. Under the traditional system, all students who were the slowest, for example, took as many courses as the brightest. Under flexible scheduling, some students may take as few as four courses and some as many as eight. Modular scheduling breaks the school day into periods of time called modules.

In a high school in Illinois the school day is composed of 20-minute modules, and classes may vary from one to five modules, depending on the purpose of the course. The school is on a 6-day cycle and operates by day one, two, or three rather than the traditional days of the week. In physical education, each grade level meets for three modules per day, 4 days each week. Each grade level also has a two-module group meeting once every cycle.

In this meeting students hear guest speakers and lectures concerned with physical education concepts. In other schools using modular scheduling, students frequently have unscheduled modules that can be used for swimming pool or gymnasium activities. Intramurals, open lab sessions, sport clubs, and demonstrations also provide incentives for students to use the skills they have learned.

Scheduling

The manner in which physical education is scheduled reflects the physical education leadership and the attitude of the central administration. Physical education is more meaningful for participants when the schedule reflects their interests, rather than administrative convenience. Scheduling should be done according to definite plan. Physical education should not be inserted in the overall master scheduling plan whenever there is time left over after all the other subjects have been provided for.

This important responsibility cannot be handled on

a hit-and-miss basis because that disregards the interests and needs of the students. Instead, physical education should be scheduled first on the master plan, along with subjects such as English and science that are required of all students most of the time they are in school. This allows for progression and for grouping according to the interests and needs of the individual participants. The three important items to consider in scheduling classes are (1) the number of teachers available, (2) the number of teaching stations available, and (3) the number of students who must be scheduled. This formula should be applied to most subjects in the school offering.

Physical education will normally be scheduled correctly, as will other subjects, if this formula is followed. All students should be scheduled, with no exceptions. If the student can go to school or college, he or she should be enrolled in physical education. Special attention should be given, however, to the handicapped or gifted individual to ensure that he or she is placed in a program suited to his or her individual needs. Also, special attention should be given to the weak student who needs extra help developing physical skills. Special attention should be given to the availability of facilities, equipment, and supplies, and the weather.

Planned units of work usually become increasingly longer as the student progresses to the next grade level, because of the student's longer interest span and greater maturity, and the increased complexity of the activities. Every physical educator should make a point of presenting to the central administration his or her plans for scheduling physical education classes. The need for special consideration should be discussed with the principal and the scheduling committee. Through persistent action, progress will be made. The logic and reasoning behind the formula of scheduling classes according to the number of teachers and teaching stations available and the number of students who must be scheduled cannot be denied. It must be planned this way to ensure progression in instruction.

Class size

Some school and college administrators feel that physical education classes can accommodate more students than the so-called academic classes. This is a misconception that has developed over the years and needs to be corrected. The problem of class size seems to be more pertinent at the secondary level than at other educational levels. At the elementary level, for example, the classroom situation represents a unit for activity, and the number of students in this teaching unit is usually reasonable. However, some schools combine various classrooms for physical education, resulting in large classes that are not desirable. Classes in physical education should be approximately the same size as classes in other subjects in the school or college offering.

This is must as essential for effective teaching, individualized instruction, for effective teaching, individualized instruction, and progression in physical education as it is in other subjects. Physical education contributes to educational objectives on an equal basis with other subjects in the curriculum. Therefore the size of the class should be comparable so that an effective teaching job can be accomplished and the objectives of education attained. After much research, many committees established a standard for an acceptable size of physical education classes.

They recommend not more than 35 students as the suitable size for activity classes. Normal classes should never exceed 45 for one instructor. Of course, if there is a lecture or other activity scheduled adaptable to greater numbers, it may be possible to have more persons in the class. For remedial work, the suitable class size is from one-on-one to 20 to 25 and should never exceed 30. With flexible scheduling, the size of classes can be varied to meet the needs of the teacher, facilities, and type of activity being offered.

Area of student leadership in involvement

In recent years students have been demanding greater involvement in the educational process, and in most cases this increased involvement has been satisfactory to both students and administrators. Some of these areas of involvement are discussed briefly here.

1. Curriculum planning

Student surveys reveal the extent of curriculum changes desired by the student body. Administrators, teachers, and students should carefully weight this information in light of the current literature, research studies, and actual curriculum changes in other schools and colleges. Student participation and feedback and essential; however, students do have limited experience in educational matters, and this must also be considered. Frequently the use of experimental programs on a limited basis can test the change before implementing it on a larger scale. In a high school in Massachusetts students take an active role in curriculum planning.

Students plan what they are going to learn and how they would like to learn the gymnastics unit of the physical education class. Several days are set aside for students to set goals, plan the steps needed to reach a specific goal, and make a commitment to learning and improvement. The students put their goals in writing and then set about to achieve them. Instruction is provided, and grading is a cooperative venture between students and teachers.

2. General planning

Students should be involved in planning meetings that discuss schedule changes, curriculum innovations, and recent changes in educational methods. Students might be invited to attend school board meetings and parent association meetings and could also accompany teachers and administrators to other schools where certain innovations may be directly observed. Some schools and colleges have instituted student advisory boards that meet with staff members to discuss problems, changes, and future planning ideas.

3. Selecting student leaders

Several methods are used by physical educators to select student leaders. Some advocate appointing temporary leaders during the first few sessions of a class until the students become better known to their classmates and instructor. Some selection methods are discussed in the following paragraphs.

Appointment by the instructor. The physical education instructor may appoint the student leader. One of the limitations of this procedure is that it is not democratic because it does not involve the students who are going to be exposed to the student leader. However, if the teacher's objective is to let each student in the class have a student leadership experience, this limitation can be overcome.

Volunteers. Students are asked to volunteer to become a student leader. It may happen that the least qualified persons are the ones who volunteer. If this method is used, it should be with the understanding that the student leader will serve for only a relatively short time.

Selection based on test results. A battery of tests is sometimes used by physical educators to select student leaders. Tests of physical fitness, motor ability, sports skills, and leadership and personality characteristics yield useful information. They provide tangible evidence that a person has some of the desirable qualifications needed by a student leader in a physical education class. In addition, if the physical educator desires to have the entire class participate in the student leadership program, the test results may also be valuable to the teacher in helping each student identify weaknesses that need to be overcome during the training period.

Election by the class. The students in the class may elect the persons they would like to have as leaders. A limitation of this method is that the persons selected are often the most popular students as a result of participation in sports or student government. Being the most popular does not mean that they are qualified to be leaders. This is a democratic procedure, however, and if the guidelines for selecting leaders are established and if the proper climate prevails, it can be effective.

Selection by Leaders' Club. Physical educators sometimes organize Leaders' Clubs to provide a continuing process for selecting student leaders. The members of the Leaders' Club, under the supervision of a faculty advisor, select new students to participate as leaders-in-training. Then, after a period of training, these students in turn become full-fledged student leaders.

4. Using the student leader

Student leaders may be used in the physical education program in several capacities.

Committee members. Many committee assignments should be filled by student leaders so that they gain valuable experience. These include being a member of a rules committee, where rules are established and interpreted for games and sports, serving on an equipment and grounds committee, where standards are established for the storage, maintenance, and use of these facilities and equipment, and participating on a committee for planning special events in the physical education program, such as play, sports, or field days.

Class leaders. There are many opportunities in the basic physical education instructional class period where student leaders can be effective. These include duties such as: acting as squad leader; being a leader for warm-up exercises; demonstrating how skills, games, and strategies are to be performed; taking attendance; supervising the locker room; and providing safety measures for class participating, such as acting as a spotter, checking equipment and play areas, and providing supervision.

Program planner. Various aspects of the physical education program need to be planned, and students should be involved. Student leaders, because of their special qualifications and interest, are logical choices to participate in such planning and curriculum development. Their knowledge and advice can ensure that the program meets the needs and interests of the students who participate in the program.

Officials, captains, and other positions. Student leaders can gain valuable experience by serving as officials within the class and intramural program, being captains of all-star or other teams, coaching intramural or club teams, and acting as scorers and timekeepers.

Supply and equipment manager. Supplies and special equipment including basketballs, archery, golf, and hockey equipment, and audiovisual aids, are needed in the physical education program. The equipment must be taken from the storage areas, transferred to the place where the activity will be conducted, and then returned to the storage area. The student leader can help in this process and profit from such an experience.

Special events coordinator. A multitude of details always are involved in play days, sports day, demonstrations, and exhibitions. Student leaders should be involved in planning and conducting these events.

Record keeper and officer manager. Attendance records and inventories must be taken, filing and recording done, bulletin boards kept up to date, visitors met, and other responsibilities attended to. These necessary functions provide worthwhile experiences for the student leader and benefit the program.

5. Leadership training programs

An innovative student leadership program is the Physical Education Leadership Training Program sponsored by a school in Virginia. As part of an elective course in the physiology of exercise, juniors and seniors can relate their learning experiences to leadership inexperience in elementary schools. The program has as its primary objectives (1) to assist in instruction, particularly when the physical education teacher is absent; (2) to provide in-depth study of health and physical education for students who want to teach as a career; (3) to provide students with leadership opportunities; and (4) to provide individualized instruction.

The content and leadership experiences are developed and coordinated by the eleventh and twelfth grade classes. Supervision of the program is provided by the elementary physical education teacher, elementary classroom teacher, senior high school physical education teacher, head of the senior high school physical education department, and supervisor of physical education. The four phases of the program are (1) in-service training, (2) observation, (3) teaching, and (4) teaching without supervision. This program is valuable to both teachers and students and helps the elementary grade teachers provide individualized help for cach student.

6. The role of the Leaders' Club in training student leaders

One method of training student leaders is through a Leaders' Club. These clubs commonly have their own constitution, governing body, faculty advisor, and training sessions. The written constitution of a Leaders' Club usually states the purpose of the club, requirements for membership, qualifications and duties of officers, financial stipulations, qualifications and duties of officers, financial stipulations, procedures for giving awards and honours, and other rules governing the organization. The governing body of the Leaders' Club may consist of a president, vice-president, treasurer, and secretary, all of whom are elected by the members of the club. The faculty advisor works closely with the leaders to ensure that the objectives of the Leaders' Club are accomplished.

The faculty advisor supervises the affairs of the club and provides inspiration and motivation to the leaders, encouraging creativity and helping the students achieve their goals. The Leaders' Club usually has regular meetings weekly, biweekly, or monthly. The students who are interested in becoming student leaders apply for membership in the leaders' Club. Certain eligibility requirements are usually established for membership in the club.

7. Evaluating the program

The student leadership program should be evaluated periodically to determine the degree to which the program is achieving its stated goals. Students should be involved in this evaluation. Questions such as the following might be asked: "Are the experiences provided worthwhile?" "Are the experiences provided worthwhile?" "Are the students developing leadership qualities?" "Is the teacher providing the necessary leadership to make the program effective?" "Are any of the assigned tasks incompatible with the objectives sought?" "Is the Leaders' Club helping to create a better leaders' program?"

Time allotment

Just as scheduling practices vary from school to school, college to college, and state to state, so does the time allotment. In some states there are mandatory laws that require that a certain amount of time each day or week be devoted to physical education, whereas in others permissive legislation exists. For grades one to twelve the requirement varies in different states from none, or very little, to a daily 1-hour program. Some require 20 minutes daily and other 30 minutes daily. Other states specify the time by the week, ranging from 50 minutes to 300 minutes. Colleges and universities do not usually require as much time in physical education as do grades one to twelve.

One practice in higher education is to require physical education two times a week for 2 years. The general consensus among physical education leaders is that for physical education to be of value, it must be given with regularity. For most individuals this means daily periods. Health experts also agree that exercise is essential to everyone throughout life. Some individuals feel that, especially in the elementary schools, a program cannot be adapted to a fixed time schedule.

However, as a standard, there seems to be agreement that a daily experience in such a program is needed. Such a recommendation is made and should always be justified on the basis of value and contribution to the student's needs. There should be regular instructional class periods and, in addition, laboratory periods where the skills may be put to use. On the secondary level especially, it is recommended that sufficient time be allotted for dressing and showering in addition to the time needed for participation in physical education activities. Some leaders in physical education have suggested a double period every other day rather than a single period each day.

This might be feasible if the daily class periods are too short. However, the importance of daily periods should be recognized and achieved wherever possible. Administrators should work toward providing adequate staff members and facilities to allow for a daily period. The amount of time suggested for adults to spend in exercise programs is a minimum of three times a week. However, a daily exercise period is considered best.

Dress

Dress does not have to be elaborate. An important concern is that the uniform ensure safety when students are engaged in physical activity. For girls and women simple washable shorts and blouses or one piece suits are suitable. For boys and men white cotton jerseys and trunks suffice. Of course, appropriate footwear also should be worn. An important consideration is to keep the uniform clean. The instructor should establish a policy on clean uniforms and work diligently to see that hygienic standards are met by all.

Instructional loads and staffing

The load of the physical educator should be of prime concern to the administrator. To maintain a top level of enthusiasm and strength, it is important that the load be adjusted so that the physical educator is not overworked. A few years ago one state recommended that one full-time physical education teacher should be provided for every 240 elementary pupils and one for every 190 secondary pupils enrolled. If such a requirement is implemented, it would provide adequate staff members in this field and avoid and overload for many of the teachers. Professional recommendations regarding teaching load at pre-college educational levels have been made that would limit class instruction per teacher to 5 hours or the equivalent in class periods per day, or 1500 minute per week.

The maximum would be 6 hours per day or 1800 minutes a week, including after school responsibilities. A daily load of 200 students per teacher is recommended and never should exceed 250. Finally, each teacher should have at least one free period daily for consultation and conferences with students. It is generally agreed that the normal teaching load in colleges and universities should not exceed 15 hours per week. The work load in a health spa or industrial physical fitness centre is usually an 8 hour or 9 am to 5 pm shift 5 days each week. Many stay open at night so the staff may have other work hours.

Grouping participants

Homogeneous grouping in physical education classes is desirable. To render the most valuable contribution to participants, factors influencing performance must be considered when organizing physical education groups. The lack of scientific knowledge and measuring techniques to obtain such information and the management problems of scheduling have handicapped the achievement of this goal in many programs. The reasons for grouping are sound. Placing individuals with similar capacities and characteristics in the same class make is possible to better meet the needs of each makes it possible to better meet the needs of each individual.

Grouping individuals with similar skill, ability, and other factors aids in equalizing competition. This helps the student realize more satisfaction and benefit from playing. Grouping promotes more effective teaching.

Instruction can be better organized and adapted to the level of the student. Grouping facilitates progression and continuity in the program. Furthermore, grouping creates a better learning situation. Being in a group with persons of similar physical characteristics and skills ensures some success, a chance to excel, recognition, a feeling of belonging, and security.

Consequently, this helps the social and personality development of the individual. Finally, homogeneous grouping helps protect the participant physically, emotionally, and socially. The problem of grouping is not so pertinent in the elementary school, especially in the lower grades, as it is in the junior high school and upper levels. At the lower levels the grade classification serves the needs of most children. As children grow older, the complexity of the program increases, social growth becomes more diversified, competition becomes more intense, and consequently, a greater need for homogeneous grouping exists. At present students are grouped on such bases as grade, health, physical fitness, multiples of age height-weight, abilities, physical capacity, motor ability, interests, educability speed, skill, and previous experience.

Techniques such as the following are used to obtain the needed information: health examinations; tests of motor ability, physical capacity, achievement, and social efficiency; conferences with participants; and determination of physiological age. The ideal grouping organization would consider all factors that affect performance—intelligence, capacity, interest, knowledge, age, height, weight, and so on. To apply all these factors, however, is not administratively feasible at the present time. Some form of grouping is essential to provide a program that promotes educational objectives and protects the students.

On the secondary and college levels, the most feasible procedure is to organize subgroups within the regular physical education class. Classification within the physical education class. Classification within the physical education class should be based on age, height, weight, and other factors, such as interest and skill, which are developed after observing the activity. For those individuals who desire greater refinement in respect to grouping, motor capacity, motor ability, attitude, appreciation, and sports-skills tests may be used. To abide by Title IX regulations, physical educators should not group by sex.

Some physical education departments have adopted a non-graded curriculum that places students in learning situations according to present levels of skill achievement and physical maturity. A child's chronological age or grade level attainment is not a factor in the non-graded physical education curriculum. This allows for individual student differences and interests.

Taking roll

There are many methods of taking roll. If a method satisfies the following three criteria, it is usually satisfactory. (1) It is efficient—roll taking should not consume too much time. (2) It is accurate—after the class has been held, it is important to know who was present and who was not and who came late or left early. (3) It should be uncomplicated—any system that is used should be easy to administer. Some methods for roll taking follow:

• Reciting numbers orally—each member of the class is assigned a number that he or she must say out loud at the time the signal for "fall in" is given. The person taking attendance then records the numbers not given.

• Delaney system—a special system developed by Delaney involves using a folder with cards that are turned over when a person is absent. It is a cumulative system that records the attendance of pupils over time. Adaptation of this system are used elsewhere.

• Having numbers on the floor—each member of the class is assigned a number that he or she must stand on at the time the signal for "fall in" is given. The person taking attendance records the numbers not given.

• Issuing towels and equipment—the roll is taken when a towel is issued to each student or when it is turned in, or when a basket with uniform is issued or returned.

• Tag board—each member of the class has a number recorded on a cardboard or metal tag that hangs on a peg on a board in a central place. Each member of the class who is present removes his or her tag from the board and places it in a box. The person taking attendance records the absentees from the board.

• Signing a book or register—students are required to write their names in a book or register at the beginning of the class. Some systems require the writing of a name at the beginning of a period and crossing it out at the end of a period. The person taking attendance records the names not entered.

• Squad system—the calls is undivided into squads and the squad leader takes the roll for his or her squad and in turn reports to the instructor.

Criteria for selection

Activities should be selected in terms of the values they have in achieving the objectives of physical education. This means they should develop not only body awareness, movement fundamentals, and physical fitness, but also the cognitive, affective, and social make-up of the individual. Activities should be interesting and challenging. They should appeal to the participants and present them with problem-solving activities and situations that challenge their skill and ability.

For example, golf always presents the challenge of getting a lower score. They should be adaptable to the growth and developmental needs and interests of children, youth, and adults. The needs of individuals vary from age to age. Consequently, movement activities and the pattern of organization must also change to meet these needs. The activity must be suited to the person, not the person to the activity. Wherever possible, participants should be allowed some choice in their activities. Activities should be modifications of fundamental movements such as running, jumping, throwing, walking, and climbing. Activities must be selected in light of the facilities, supplies, equipment, and other resources available in the school, college, or community.

One cannot plan an extensive tennis program if only one court is available. Activities should be selected not only with a view to their present value while the child is in school but also with a view to post school and adult living. Skills learned during school and college days can be used throughout life, thus contributing to enriched living. Patterns for many skills used in adult leisure hours are developed while the individual is in the formative years of childhood. Health and safety factors must be considered when selecting activities.

An activity such as boxing has been questioned because of its effect on the health and safety of individuals. The local education philosophy, policies, and school or college organization must be considered. School activities should provide situations similar to those that children experience in natural play situations outside school. Activities should provide the participant with opportunities for creative self-expression. Activities selected should elicit the correct social and moral responses through high-quality leadership. Activities should reflect the democratic way of life. One survey produced a list of physical education activities offered throughout the country, here classified into various categories. These do not necessarily meet criteria that have been listed. They merely indicate current offerings in physical education programs in the United States:

Other activities

Camping and outdoor activities, Combatives, Correctives, Fly-tying, Games of low organization, Jogging, Kayaking, Mountaineering, Movement education, Orienteering, Relays, Self-testing activities, Yoga.

Team games

Baseball, Basketball, Codeball, Field hockey, Flag football, Football, Soccer, Softball, Speedball, Touch football, Volleyball.

Rhythms and dancing

Folk dancing, Gymnastic dancing, Modern dancing, Movement fundamentals, Rhythms, Square dancing, Social dancing, Tap dancing.

Outdoor winter sports

Ice hockey, Roller skating, Skating, Skiing, Snow games, Snowshoeing, Tobogganing.

Formal activities

Calisthenics, Marching

Gymnastics

Acrobatics, Apparatus, Obstacle course, Pyramid building, Rope climbing, Stunts, Trampoline, Tumbling.

Water activities

Canoeing, Diving, Life-saving, Rowing, Sailing, Scuba diving Surfing, Swimming, Water games, Water skiing.

Dual and individual sports

Archery, Badminton, Bait and fly casting, Bowling, Checkers, Cycling, Darts, Deck tennis, Fencing, Fishing, Golf, Handball, Horseback riding, Horseshoes, Paddle tennis, Racquet-ball, Rifle, Rope skipping, Shuffleboard, Skeet shooting, Table tennis, Tether ball, Track and field, Trap shooting, Wrestling.

TITLE IX

Today's relevant physical education program must take into account the passage of in important law by the national government, namely, Title IX. On may 27, 1975, the president of the United States signed into law Title IX of the Education Amendments Act of 1972, which prohibits sex discrimination in educational programs that are federally assisted. The effective date of the regulation was July 21, 1975. Title IX affects nearly all public elementary, secondary, and post secondary educational institutions. This includes the nation's 16,000 public school systems and nearly 2700 post secondary institutions. As a first step the regulations provide that educators should perform a searching self-examination of policies and practices in their institutions and take whatever remedial action is needed to bring their institutions into compliance with the federal law.

Reason for Title IX. The main reason for the enactment of Title IX was such testimony before Congressional and other committees as the following: Girls were frequently denied the opportunity to enrolle in traditionally male courses and activities, and girls and women were frequently denied equal opportunity. A national survey conducted by the National Education Association showed that although women constituted a majority of all public school teachers, they accounted for only 3.5% of the junior high school principals and 3% of the senior high school principals.

Interpretation of Title IX regulations

Some interpretations of Title IX regulations that affect physical education instructional programs are listed here. Interpretations such as the following have come from various sources. Sex designations associated with class schedules, activities, and budgets are not permitted. The term girls' gymnasium can be used; however, the scheduling of this facility must be nondiscriminatory in respect to each sex. Policies and procedures in regard to items such as uniforms and attendance must apply to both sexes. Sex-segregated administrative units, such as departments, do not necessarily have to be merged, although having faculty of men and women in integrated offices in newly combined administrative units is encouraged.

If a significantly greater number of one sex is enrolled in a particular physical education class, the administration, if called on, should be prepared to provide the rationale for such organization. Supervision of locker rooms may be assigned to teacher aides, paraprofessionals, or teachers in other departments. Marks or grades given in physical education classes should reflect individual growth and performance and not compare sexes with one another. Standards of performance that provide an unfair comparison for one sex should not be used. In some cases separate standards might be used for each sex; for example, on a physical fitness rating, where boys may be taller and stronger than girls, separate standards may be used.

1. Compliance with Title IX

Title IX is being enforced by the Office for Civil Rights of the federal government. The first step seeks to have voluntary compliance. If violations are found, federal financial support may be cut off and other legal measures taken, such as referring the violation to the Department of Justice for appropriate court action. The Office of Civil Rights is trying to approach Title IX constructively. It wishes to achieve the goals of Title IX, that is, to end discrimination against women, in the shortest time possible. Opportunity for women is the law of the land and must be enforced.

The aim will be to use the Department's enforcement machinery by giving priority to systemic forms of discrimination rather than following an approach whereby individual complaints assume priority. This means that the total picture of noncompliance will be assessed, taking into consideration information received from individuals and groups, as a means of determining enforcement priorities and compliance reviews. Title IX regulations have been evolving for a long time.

They should result in increased physical education opportunities for all students. The question whether Title IX applies to all programs in an educational institution or whether it applies only to programs that get direct federal aid has been referred to the courts. The Grove decision ruled that Title IX applies only to programs that get direct federal aid. Although the courts favour the latter, many institutions impose Title IX regulations on all programs within their jurisdiction.

2. Coeducational physical education classes

Because the provision for coeducational classes is one of the key implications of Title IX regulations, this topic is discussed further here. Problems in physical education classes have been cited in the professional literature. Weber indicates that problems such as the following have developed as a result of Title IX: the teacher is not professionally prepared to teach various activities in a coeducational setting; male and female teachers who traditionally made decisions on their own are finding it difficult to function as a team with the other sex and share the decision-making process; students are also finding problems such as being unable in some activities to perform satisfactorily in front of members of the opposite sex, and thus lose face; and girls with poor skills are excluded from participation on highly skilled coeducational teams.

Weber also points out how many of these problems can be solved by such means as teachers getting rid of their personal sex biases, using new techniques, seeking a balance between female teachers' and male teachers' instructional methods, and re-examining philosophies regarding the teaching of physical education. Other problems that have arisen in physical education classes as a result of Title IX include assignment of office space, scheduling a gymnasium for various activities, teaching certain activities such as wrestling, the danger of being accused of making sexual advances against students, supervision of locker rooms, and dressing standards. The main consideration in establishing coeducational sports programs is to respond to the interests and ability levels of the participants.

Because of their level of skill and other reasons, some males and females will not wish to participate in coeducational sports programs, even on an intramural or recreational level. Opportunities should be provided for these individuals to participate on separate teams. When conducting sports on a coeducational basis, appropriate modifications should be made in the rules and conduct of the activities to equalize competition between the sexes.

Implications of Title IX for physical education instructional programs

Physical education classes must be organized on a coeducational basis. This regulation does not mean that activities must be taught co-educationally. Within classes, students may be grouped by sex for such contact sports as wrestling, basketball, and football. Also, within physical education classes, students may be grouped on an ability basis even though such grouping results in single-sex grouping. However, sex must not be the criterion for grouping. It must be something other than sex.

Furthermore, if an evaluation standard has an adverse impact on one sex, such as a standard of accomplishment in a physical fitness test, different evaluation requirements must be used. Schools and colleges must provide equal opportunities for both sexes. This is true in respect to such items as facilities, equipment and supplies, practice and games, medical and training services, coaching and academic tutoring opportunities, travel allowances, and housing and dining facilities. Equal opportunity means that the activities offered must reflect the interests and abilities of students of both sexes. Adequate facilities and equipment must be available for both sexes in every sport.

Furthermore, one sex cannot dominate the facilities or the new equipment. Also, adequate time for practice and games must be provided for both sexes. Again, one sex cannot dominate. Schools and colleges must spend funds in an equitable manner. Although equal aggregate expenditures are not required, an educational institution cannot discriminate on the basis of sex in providing proper equipment and supplies. Title IX takes precedence over all state and local lows and conference regulations that might be in conflict with this federal regulation.

If an institution receives federal aid, it must be in compliance with Title IX, even though its athletic or physical education program does not directly receive any of this aid. The Grove decision overturned this ruling. There can be no discrimination in respect to personnel standards. No discrimination can exist in respect to personnel standard by sex, including parental status, for employment, promotion, salary, recruitment, job classification, or fringe benefits. Scholarships must be awarded equitably. The regulations require an institution to select students to be awarded financial aid on the basis of criteria other than a student's sex.

MANAGEMENT GUIDELINES FOR SELECTING TEACHING AIDS AND MATERIALS

When selecting audiovisual aids or other resources and materials, physical educators should consider the following principles that make using these aids effective and valuable:

Materials should be carefully selected and screened. The teacher should preview the materials to make sure they are appropriate for the unit and age level of the students and that they present information in an interesting and stimulating manner. Proper preparation of materials should be made. The teacher should check all equipment that may be necessary for the presentation of materials to make sure that it is in operating condition. Record players and movie projectors, in particular, need to be carefully checked before they are used.

Materials should be varied. Different types of materials should be chosen for presentation to stimulate the varying interest of the students. A teacher using films or slide films exclusively does not take full advantage of supplementary materials available for widespread appeal. Use of supplementary materials should be limited. The teacher should place a reasonable limit on the use of extra teaching materials to maintain a balance between supplementary learnings and those gained from regular instructional materials.

The presentation of materials should be planned and integrated into the lesson. Students should be properly introduced to the materials so that they know what to expect and so that they understand their relationship to the unit of study. Materials should be presented to the students in a proper learning situation. Students should be located so that all may hear, see, and learn from the material being presented to them. They should realize that they will be held responsible for the information being presented.

Care should be taken to avoid excessive expenses. A reasonable part of the instructional budget should be set aside for supplementary materials. This amount should be in accordance with the emphasis placed on this phase of the teaching program. Records and evaluations of materials should be maintained. All supplementary materials should be carefully evaluated and records kept on file for future reference. This should save the unnecessary expense involved in recording or duplicating materials and in maintaining outdated materials.

By following these principles the teacher is able to supplement learnings with materials that are valuable and interesting to the students. Various types of materials, activities, and personnel that can be used in the instructional process include the following:

1. Audiovisual aids: motion pictures, slide films,

learning loops, television, video-tape, phonographs and audio-tape records, records.

2. Professional personnel: from professional associations and organizations

3. Reading materials: textbooks, magazines, booklets, pamphlets

4. Clinics: special games and programs put on by visiting teams, teaching organizations, community organizations.

5. Special aids: photographic materials, bulletin boards, magnetic boards

6. Community activities: recreational activities, PTA-sponsored events.

SELECTED MANAGEMENT PROBLEMS IN INSTRUCTIONAL PROGRAMS

The manager of any physical education program is perennially confronted with questions such as: Should physical education be required or elective? How much credit should be given? It possible to substitute some other activity for physical education? What should be the policy on class attendance? How should an instructor deal with excuses? These and other questions are answered in the following discussion.

Required

Physical education is a basic need of every student. The student is compelled to take so many required courses that the choice of electives is limited, if not entirely eliminated, in some cases. The student considers required subjects most important and most necessary for success. Various subjects in the curriculum would not be provided unless they were required. This is probably true of physical education. Until state legislatures passed laws requiring physical education, this subject was ignored by many school administrators.

If physical education were elective, the course of some administrative action would be obvious. Either the subject would not be offered at all or the administrative philosophy would so dampen its value that it would have to be eliminated because of low enrolment. Even under a required program, physical education is not meeting the physical, social, and cognitive needs of students. If an elective program were instituted, deficiencies and shortages would increase, further handicapping the attempt to meet the needs of the student.

Should physical education be required or elective?

General agreement that physical education should be required at the elementary level exists. However, there are many advocates on both sides of the question of whether it should be required or elective on the secondary and college levels. Both groups are sincere and feel their beliefs represent what is best for the student. Probably most specialists feel the program should be required. Some school administrators feel it should be elective. Following are some of the arguments presented by each.

What about excuses?

The principal, nurse, or physical educator frequently receives a note from a parent or family physician asking that a student be excused from physical education. Many abuses develop if all such requests are granted. Many times for minor reasons the student does not want to participate and obtains the parent's or family physician's support. Once survey showed that high schools permitted a student to be excused on the basis of a parental note, a memorandum from the family physician, or the discretion of the physical education teacher. Although some schools would accept the recommendation of any of these three persons, other schools would accept only an excuse from the school physician.

At the college level most programs accept the college physician's excuse or permit the instructor of each class to use his or her own discretion in granting excuses to students. Those surveyed listed reasons for granting excuses in physical education. Secondary schools grant most of their excuses for participation in athletics and for being in the school band. Some schools permit their athletes to be excused only on the day of the game, whereas others grant a blanket excuse of the entire sports season. Other reasons for excuses on the secondary level included make-up tests, driver training, counselling, a too-heavy extracurricular load, and medical reasons.

At the college level excuses were granted to athletes, veterans, students who could pass physical fitness tests, honour students, and older students, for medical reasons, in "hardship cases," and so on. The survey also reported what was done with the students who were excused. Students in secondary schools were required to attend study halls; to score, officiate, or help around the physical education department; to write reports; to remain on the sidelines; or to report after school. At the college level most colleges did nothing except follow a pattern of failing a student in some cases if he or she exceeded the legal number of excused absences each semester.

A few either required the student to observe the class, substitute a health class, or study in the gymnasium; some left it up to the instructor's direction. Some school systems have controlled the indiscriminate granting of requests for excuses from physical education. Policies have been established, sometimes through conferences and rulings of the board of education, requiring that all excuses be reviewed and approved by the school physician before they are granted. Furthermore, family physicians have been asked to state specific reasons for requesting excuses from physical education. This procedure has worked satisfactorily in some communities. In other places physical educators have taken particular pains to work closely with physicians.

They have established a physical education program in collaboration with the school physician so the needs of each individual are met, regardless of his or her physical condition. They have met with the local medical society in an attempt to clear up misunderstandings about the purpose and conduct of the program. Family physicians have been brought into the planning. As a result of such planning, problems with excuses from physical education have been considerably reduced. It has been found that in those communities where parents, family physicians, and the lay public in general understand physical education, the number of requests for excuses is relatively small. In such communities the values derived from participation in the program are clearly recognized, and because most parents and physicians want children to have worthwhile experiences, they encourage rather than limit such participation. A few years ago, a conference concerned with close cooperation between physical education and medical doctors drew up this list of statements in respect to the problem under discussion.

1. Discard permanent and blanket excuses. Instead of being categorically excused, boys and girls can be given an activity in keeping with their special needs.

2. Conferences between the school physicians and the head of the physical education department on the local level need to be emphasized.

3. Orient the student, parent, and physician at an early date in regard to the objectives of the physical education program.

4. The problem of excuse from physical education should be tied in with the total guidance program of the school.

5. Route all requests for excuse through the school physician. In the absence of the physician, the school nurse should have this responsibility.

6. Students involved in the excuse request should have a periodic re-check on the need for excuse.

Elective

Physical education "carries its own drive." If a good basic program is developed in the elementary school, with students acquiring the necessary skills and attitudes, the drive for such activity will carry through in the secondary school and college. There will be no need to require such a course, because students will want to take it voluntarily. Objectives of physical education are focused on developing skills and learning activities that have carry-over value, living a healthful life, and recognizing the importance of developing and maintaining one's body in its best possible condition. These goals cannot be legislated.

They must become a part of each individual's attitudes and desires if they are to be realized. Some children and young adults do not like physical education. This is indicated in their manner, attitude, and desire to get excused from the program and to substitute something else for the course. Under such circumstances the values that accrue to these individuals are not great. Therefore it would be best to place physical education on the elective basis where only those students who participate actually desire to do so.

What policy should be established on class attendance?

It is important for every department of physical education to have a definite policy on class attendance that covers absenteeism and tardiness. Because it is felt that students should attend school and college regularly, it follows that they should also attend physical education classes regularly. However, time for independent study should be included in the schedule. Regular participation in physical education is essential to the value of the program; therefore every physical education department should have a clear-cut policy on attendance regulations.

These regulations should be few and clearly stated in writing so that they are recognized, understood, and strictly enforced by teachers and students. They should allow a reasonable number of absences and tardiness. Perfect attendance at school or college should not be stressed. Many harmful results can develop if students feel obligated to attend classes when they are ill and should be at home.

There should probably be some provision for make-up work when important experiences are missed. However, make-up work should be planned and conducted so that the student derives essential values from such participation, rather than enduring it as a disciplinary measure. There should also be provision for the readmission of students who have been ill. A final point to remember is importance of keeping accurate, up-to-date attendance records to minimize administrative problems.

Should substitutions be allowed for physical education?

A practice exists in some school and college systems that allows students to substitute some other activity for their physical education requirement. This practice should be scrutinized and resisted aggressively by every administrator. Some of the activities used as substitutions for physical education are athletic participation, Reserve Officers' Training Corps, and band. No substitute for a sound program of physical education exists. In addition to healthful physical activity, it is concerned also with developing an individual socially, emotionally, and mentally. The individual develops many skills that can be applied throughout life. These essentials are lost if a student is permitted to take some other activity in place of physical education.

Who should conduct the elementary school physical education class?

The question of who should conduct the elementary school physical education class has been continually discussed for many years. Some educators advocate that the classroom teacher handle physical education classes, and many supporters want a specialist to take over this responsibility. The classroom teacher has limited professional education in physical education.

Some classroom teachers are not interested in teaching physical education. Furthermore, there is increased interest in physical education today, which implies that qualified and interested persons should handle these classes. The trend is toward more emphasis on movement education, perceptual motor development, physical fitness, skills, and other aspects of education with which physical education is concerned. More research is needed on physical education programs as they relate to the learning and growth of children. There is an increased emphasis on looking to the specialist in physical education for help and advice in planning and conducting the elementary school program.

These developments have implications for a sound in-service program to help the classroom teacher do a better job in physical education. In light of the present status of physical education in the elementary schools of this country, such recommendations as the following should be very carefully considered. Each elementary school should be staffed with a specialist in physical education. The class from teacher may find his or her best contribution to physical education programs in kindergarten to grade three, but to do the best job he or she needs preparation in this special field and the advice and help of a physical education specialist. Although the classroom teacher can contribute much to the physical education program in grades four to six, factors such as the growth changes and interests taking place in boys and girls and the more specialized program that exists at this level make it imperative to seek the help of a specialist who processes the ability, experience, and training required to meet the needs of growing boys and girls and to gain their respect and interest. The specialist and the classroom teacher should pool their experience to provide the most desirable learning experience. Each teacher has much to contribute and should be encouraged to do so.

Should credit be given for physical education?

Whether credit should be given for physical education is another controversial problem with which the profession is continually confronted. Here again advocates can be found on both sides. Some feel the joy of the activity and the values derived from participation are sufficient in themselves without giving credit. On the other hand, some feel that physical education is the same as any other subject in the curriculum and also should be granted credit. The general consensus among physical education leaders is that if physical education is required for graduation and if it enriches a person's education, credit should be given, just as for other subjects.

Dressing and showering

Such factors as the age of the participant, time allowed, grade participating, and type of activity should be considered in a discussion of dressing and showering for physical education classes. The problem of showering and dressing is not so pertinent at the lower elementary level where the age of the participants and type of activities as a general rule do not require special dress and showering. Also the time allotted is too short in many cases. In the upper elementary and at the junior and senior high school and college levels, however, it is a problem. Physical education embodies activities that require considerable movement, resulting in perspiration.

In the interests of comfort and good hygiene practices, provisions should be made for special clothing and showering. The unpleasantness of a student's returning to class after participating in a physical education activity, with clothes malodorous and wet from perspiration, does not establish habits of personal cleanliness and good grooming. Therefore all schools should make special provisions for places to dress in comfortable uniforms and for showering. Such places should be convenient to the physical education areas, be comfortable, and afford privacy. Although boys and girls are increasingly becoming accustomed to using a group shower, many still prefer private showers.

In the interests of these individuals, such facilities should be provided. There should also be a towel service. Many schools have facilities for laundering towels that have proved satisfactory.

Providing for the health of the participant

Physical education staff members must safeguard the health of all individuals in the program. To accomplish this objective, the staff members in the health program must have a close working relationship. Every participant should have periodic health examinations with the results of these examinations scrutinized by the physical educator. A physical education program must be adapted to the needs and interests of each person. The physical educator is responsible for health guidance and health supervision in the physical education activities. The physician should be consulted when persons return after periods of illness, when accidents occur, and at any other time that such qualified advice is needed.

Records

Records are essential in keeping valuable information regarding the participants' welfare. They also are essential to efficient program planning and administration. They should, however, be kept to a minimum and should be practical and functional. They should not be maintained merely as busy work and for the sake of filling files. Some of the records should be concerned directly with the welfare of the participant and others with certain administrative factors. Records that concern the welfare of the participant are the health records, the cumulative physical education form, attendance reports, grades, and accident reports. Health records are essential.

They contain information on the health examination and other appraisal techniques, health counselling, and any other data pertaining to the person's health. The cumulative physical education record should contain information about activities engaged in, after-school play, tests, interests, needs, and other pertinent information about the student's participation in the physical education program. There should be special records for attendance, grades, and any special occurrences with a bearing on the participant that are not recorded in other records. If a student is involved in an accident, a full account of the circumstances surrounding the accident should be recorded.

Usually special forms are provided for such purposes. Management records provide general information and equipment records, including a list of the year's events, activities, records of teams, play days, sports days, intramurals, events of special interest, techniques that have been helpful, budget information, and any other data that would be helpful in planning for succeeding years. Memory often fails over time, with the result that many good ideas are lost and many activities and techniques of special value are not used because they are forgotten. There should be records of equipment, facilities, and supplies that show the material needing repair, new materials needed, and the location of various materials, so that they can be found easily. Records of such items as locker or basket assignments are essential to the efficient running of physical education program.

THE ADAPTED PROGRAM AND PHYSICAL EDUCATION FOR HANDICAPPED PERSONS

The adapted program refers to the phase of physical education that meets the needs of the individual who, because of some physical inadequacy, functional defect capable of being improved through physical activity, or other deficiency, is temporarily or permanently unable to take part in the regular physical education program or in which special provisions are made for handicapped students in regular physical education program or in which special provisions are made for handicapped students in regular physical education classes. It also refers to students of a school or college student population who do not fall into the "average" or "normal" classification for their age or grade.

These students deviate from their peers in physical, mental, emotional, or social characteristics or in a combination of these traits. The principle of individual differences that applies to education as a whole applies to physical education. Most administrators believe that as long as a student can attend school or college, he or she should be required to participate in physical education. If this tenet is adhered to, it means that programs must be adapted to individual needs. Many children and young adults who are recuperating from long illnesses or operations or who are suffering from other physical or emotional conditions require special consideration in their programs. It cannot be assumed that all individuals in physical education classes are not handicapped.

Unfortunately, many programs are administered on this basis. One estimate has been made that one out of every eight students in our schools is handicapped to the extent that special provision should be made in the educational program. Schools and colleges will always have students who, because of many factors such as heredity, environment, disease, accident, or some other reason, have physical or other impairments. Many of these students have difficulty adjusting to the demands society places on them. The responsibility of physical education programs is to help each individual who comes into class.

8

PHYSICAL ATTRIBUTIONS AND CHARACTERISTICS IN PHYSICAL EDUCATION AND SPORTS

Dr. Roger Bannister, the world's first four-minute miller, acted for a few years as chairman of the British Sports Council. During that time, he launched a campaign entitled Sport for All. There are well over a hundred different sports which all require various skills and body types.

One finds in humans a similar spectrum of attributes as are found in nature. The physiology of athletes, such as sprinters is that they are capable of explosive effort. As with a jet fuel, they ignite and burn up their energy sources very rapidly.

After a few seconds effort, a sprinter often needs to put his hands on his knees to recover from the rapid depletion of oxygen from his system. The middle-distance runners are the wood burners; they are exciting to watch as they flame for several minutes. At the far end of this spectrum are the coal and cock-burning endurance athletes, who glow for two hours or so. Even with a flame-thrower, one cannot hope to make coal react like jet fuel. The system may be modified to some extent, but the general percentage of fast and slow-twitch fibre types is born in the athlete.

A simple test of fibre types is through the sergeant jump. Standing beside a wall, with heels to the ground, the athlete stretches a hand straight up, making a mark on the wall with chalk dust to indicate the height reached. Then the athlete with no rup up, crouches and springs straight up in the air, touching as high on the wall as possible. The endurance runners, having little explosive capacity, usually get 12 to 18 in off the ground.

However, some exceptional sprinters, jumpers and basketball players have sergeant jumps measuring over 40 in. The well-trained endurance event athlete will have a greater cardiovascular efficiency that the average athlete or the untrained individual. This means that the athlete is able to breathe more efficiently by absorbing more oxygen per breath.

During 1969 twenty road racing cyclists were tested physiologically and given some mental-state variable tests. The conclusion was quite predictably, that the more genetically-gifted and physically-conditioned athlete will produce the better result. Without a fair amount of natural attributes, the competitor will not be vying for the very top. The fundamental question is, given adequate physiology to be in with a chance, what are the factors which will determine the winners. The Salford findings on the mental state of the competitor showed that during intense effort, the threshold level of discomfort varied between individual riders. This difference, they believed, could be accounted for by what their researchers referred to as selective attention. Various physical attributes can assist performance, for instance, large hands and long fingers helped the basketball player, as does wide peripheral vision. Throwers with long arms have an advantage because this allows them to exert force over a longer time on whatever is being thrown. Bulk helps some players as the need solid force behind the effort which helps them to throw further.

Most top class male discus throwers and shot putters would be 6ft 3in to 6ft 6in, and between 200 and 300lb. The confining element on speed and size for both these throwers is the requirement of staying within the relatively small circle. Speed is common factor in most physical sports. Team games require the application of speed many times over a short distance.

Several sports require a greater percentage of mental effort and concentration. In the case of yachtsman, it may take five minutes to inch past another vessel, gaining perhaps a foot each wave. A sudden burst of adrenaline and physical effort will not necessarily be helpful. The calm control of the yachtsman can be paralleled in the worlds of motor racing, equestrian events, bowls, shooting, darts, and snooker. The requirement is to lower the heart rate and where possible bring down the excitement level.

Another physical requirement is the need for good hand-eye coordination in ball sports. The brain calculates rapidly the speed and direction of the ball, puck or whatever is the target object, then instructions are sent to the muscles via the brain to place the body, hands or racket in the right position and at the right time, to intercept and make perfect contact.

If we did calculations to work out how this is achieved, it would fill pages. Most of us take this sort of skill for granted and simply focus our eye on the object and the subconscious mind does the rest. Yet another variable between the different sports is the degree of body contact. In sports such as rugby, the confrontation is not only highly physical but mental as well.

In some sports, there is a moderate level of body contact, basketball and soccer being examples. In most sports, direct physical contact is rare. For some, the opponents are on opposite sides of a net as in tennis, volleyball and badminton. Many sports require competitors to share space and the athletes react to the moves of the other competitors. In addition to the contact sports, other examples are squash, bowls, baseball, cricket etc.

In golf and sprint events, the competitors will usually be aware of each other but rarely impede another's progress. Swimming is probably the closest to the isolated effort which exists in downhill skiing, shooting and archery.

Physical Development

Do you consider that you were early, late or average in physical development. It may have been imagined that most of the high sporting achievers matured early and gained adult size soon after puberty, but research showed this was not the case. Exactly two thirds of the athletes were late developers.

A good example of successful handling of early talent development is the case of Chris Evert Llyod. Although she was good enough to embark on the circuit when she was fourteen years old, her father held her tournament play down to a minimum until she had completed high school. A section of the early developers achieved astonishing levels of performance very early on in their lives. Shane Innes started breaking world swimming records at 13 and only a month after her fifteenth birthday, she held every freestyle record from 100m to 1500m.

Statistics can be misleading especially. However, it is worth noting a few of the sports where early developers were common, swimming had 75 per cent, cricket 50 per cent, and tennis 40 per cent. Alternatively, of the twenty-one track and field athletes, 71.5 per cent classed themselves as late developers, 19 per cent average and 9.5 per cent as early developers. That fact that so many high achievers are late developers should underline the need to allow young athletes the alternative of specializing as late as possible. This should encourage those who are not winning constantly to.

Left-Handedness and Cross-Dominance

This phenomena is being raised because there are a disproportionate number of highly successful athletes who are left-handed or cross-dominant. When you consider that approximately one in ten of the population is left-handed, then this area should not left out of the discussion. In Feb. 1985, Robin Brightwell of the BBC produced a Horizon programme based on the research of the Norman Geschwind, head of the Neurology Unit at Beth Israel Hospital in Boston and a professor at Harvard. In 1968, Geschwind had shown that the two hemispheres of the brain are physically different. The left hemisphere, for most people, controls language, writing and calculations; for right-handers, it controls the dominant hand. The right hemisphere is more special and comprehension-oriented. For the left-handers, this right side of the brain controls their dominant hand.

Geschwind showed a strong connection between dyslexia, handedness and language. Dyslexia occurs ten times more frequently in left-handed people. He identified that if testosterone, the male hormone, had seeped into the embryo before birth, growth of the left hemisphere slowed, allowing the right hemisphere to take control. This hormone is produced by the mother as a by-product in making female hormones. The negative result for these individuals is that they often have allergies and because of their left-eye dominance, they frequently have learning difficulties.

On the other side, the advantage gained by these individuals is that they have a greater three-dimensional skill level. Several gifted individual have great difficulty in learning to read. Within this study of sports personalities, both Jackie Stewart and Duncan Goodhew have severe dyslexia. Both have learned to compensate and have become exceptionally articulate. The advantage for thc ball players is clear. The better the special awareness, the clearer the perspective.

Several top tennis players are left-handed including Martina Navratilova, John McEnroe. Many of those interviewed were either left-handed or cross-dominant. Of significance is that several have taught themselves to be ambidextrous, basketball players Bob Cousy and John Havlicek, and baseball player Pete Rose can all play equally well with either hand. Rugby players Barry John and Gareth Edwards can kick with either foot.

It is found that the left and right sides of the brain, although serving different primary functions, are not totally separate. A certain amount of skill transfer can be learned and should be encouraged, the object being to enhance and integrate the whole brain. For example, if a youngster is right-handed and is primarily a logical, linear-thinking person, then he or she could benefit from doing something to enhance their creativity.

In the case of the sportsperson, encouragement should be extended to spend at least some time and effort practising with the other hand or foot. Apart from some transfer of learning, there is also the advantage of building up a more balanced musculature system. In several sports, the option of striking the ball with either foot or shooting with either hand provides a double threat to the opposition and enhances the player's chances of success.

Courage and Risk-Taking

It is a point for debate whether courage and risk-taking is an inherent part of one's physical make-up or something that one has to adjust to psychologically. The following examples are taken from what can be termed contact sports. These sports lend themselves to the vision of courage and risk-taking through their speed or physical contact.

Several sports can endanger limbs and, at times, life itself. Examples of these sports are motor racing, downhill skiing, boxing, ice hockey. There is also a more subtle element of courage and risk-taking that involves choices which often determine the outcome of a contest. Individuals need courage to take chances in life. For instance, should you give up a secure but boring job to try and make it in your own business.

In sport, a certain amount of courage is needed from the start, trying out for a place on the team, competing for the first time in front of family, friends and public and within the event itself, the courage to take a risk and make a decision to go for it, to leave the pack and make a break on your own.

Many individuals do not have the courage to become the front runner or the highest goal-scorer because they fear being different. They may also fear public failure. The question was whether the high achievers ever saw this as a threat or only as an opportunity to challenge and to prove themselves.

Now the question arises whether the courage or risk-taking played any role in the sport. Different world class players gave their views. 22 per cent saw no risk involved. Even Bryan Robson, who is known for diving to head a ball at boot-kicking height said, No, it is just a natural part of the game. A very similar response came from Pete Rose. He said A lot of people think I take a risk because I slide into base head first, but I do not. I just think it is fastest and safest way to survive.

More than three-quarters of the athletes interviewed were aware of the courage and risk-taking involved in their sport, but for these athletes, it was not a source of concern, in their minds, they had already dealt with these factors. American football provides an obvious example of visible violence. Gene Upshaw said, You have to have courage to take the risk, because you are only one play away from ending your career at any point in time, but you cannot worry about it either. In the same sport and as his team's primary ball carrier, O.J. Simpson was a certain target, It is simply the nature of the game, in my position carrying the ball, and the men on the opposing side are mostly bigger than me and most have a lot more aggressive dispositions, which is the nature of a defensive player, all wanting to get me because of my status in the game. They would like to injure me and put me out of the football game, not just stop me on the play, but to get me out of the game. I never really focused on it because I have always approached the game as a game and I have always enjoyed it as a game. I have had conversations with the defensive players during the course of the game, but I do realize that at the core of one's personality, there must be a certain courage to play the game with passion.

Rugby union and rugby league are also physically demanding contact sports. Peter Sterling commented on the latter, Yes, you have to have a bit of courage to dive on a loose ball when there are boots flying around. It is a physical sport and you just cannot survive if you are not courageous to a fair degree. As with most of these athletes, the risk-taking was a calculated factor. Peter continued, Our game is getting very disciplined with less and less risk-taking. The game is becoming one of controlling the football and not trying to get in the extra pass, which might be a risk. That is the point where you have to weigh up quickly whether the risk is worth it and a try could be on. A bad neck injury was the reason for Billy Beaumont's decision to stop playing rugby, but in spite of his awareness of the risks, he said, If you do not fall on the ball someone has to. As captain you have to do it because you could never ask them to do anything you would not do. I had never chicken out of anything, even if I knew I had not chance, I had give it a go.

Bill epitomized the blind overpowering element in the make up of forwards. A more cautious, less risk-taking approach was held by Gareth Edwards, whose job it was to get the ball from the forwards to the backs. He said that he was told, never be a hero for anyone. Never go down on a ball in a position that you cannot get back up. He said, I never forgot that but I never thought about it. It is a case of putting ability above recklessness. Also from the sport of rugby is J.P.R. Williams who spoke of the risks being calculated and learning how to avoid injury. You know what you can get away with. In a contact sport, it is very important to know how to fall. Fall the wrong way and you get injured. You learn to fall as you would from a judo throw. I suffered a few injuries and was involved in tremendous collisions. I think the harder you go in the less likely, you are to get injured.

John Havlicek referred to his playing the part of the hero in high-school and learning a lesson. He said that he has pulled a muscle and was persuaded to have a shot of novocaine. It was probably the worst thing I ever did because after the football game, I could barely walk and for the next week, movement was severely limited. Even though John allowed this to happen, one onus seems to be even more on those who used John as a scoring threat, placing the outcome of the game as a higher priority than the well-being of the player.

Jackie Stewart made the point that even in potentially lethal sports, courage involved self-mastery. Courage does play a part, but risk-taking does not. I think there is a difference between courage and bravery. Bravery is usually a blind instinctive reaction, which is sometimes more dangerous, whereas courage is the control of fear and being able to channel and manipulate it, still with the full knowledge of the calculated risk. There has to be a very clear analytical evaluation of risk. Ken Read is another travelling at awesome speed. He said that courage was definitely needed. To press yourself when travelling up to 90 m.p.h. on skis, you have to handle the risks mentally within yourself. You are exposing yourself to danger. You realize the course is safe, but there are very high risks there. You have to be able to take a realistic view and deal with your emotions and channel them because they are right there on the surface. You have to know your limits, what you have trained yourself to do but you must be prepared to take risks. You have to know when it is worth taking a risk to win a race.

West Indies cricket player Viv Richards laughed as he said, I do treasure my teeth a lot. He want on to explain that he does not wear a helmet while playing cricket, it takes some courage to face fast bowlers sending down four bouncers in an over.

Former Australian captain Greg Chappell said that he was never frightened of getting hit during a cricket match, any fear was caused by the fact that they might get him out. Although it is a non-contact sport, Steele Bishop referred to the risk of cycling at 55 to 60 m.p.h. downhill on his way to training every morning, I do not wear a helmet and if a tyre blew on the bottom bend, I had be gone.

In the other non-contact sports, courage and risk-taking were still seen a part of what makes achievement. US golf legend Arnold Palmer wrote a book called Go For Broke. People used to say that I took chances and went for broke every time. I never really felt that was the case. I always thought the winners had to play aggressively and that they had to go and get it. It is an inner thought as much as anything. But gambling and not laying up was one of the things that I was known for and I suppose it was just a natural part of my game.

Herb Elliott referred to the psychological barrier of fear. If courage is beating your own fears and your uncertainties, then there was a lot of courage.

Heather McKay pointed out that it took courage to push yourself past your previous limit, giving yourself that extra push when you thought you could not do it.

Specialization

The natural movement of some of the runners will be apparent to anyone who has an eye for rhythm and flow; the variety of styles and forms has to be seen to be believed. Some are simply better suited to running faster than others. It does not mean that they are any better people, but their physiological blueprint enables them to start out with a physical advantage in that particular movement.

Here we have tried to analyse the question that how much the physical characteristics help a player in his performance and what are the views of some world class players about this. All players have different opinions relating to the fact whether their natural physique made them winners or not.

Double Olympic sprint champion Valeriy Borzov said that his innate speed was the biggest single factor in his success, whereas baseball star Pete Rose said that the only physical advantage he had was that he was not born with a handicapped body. The age old question as to which is more important, nature or nurture, will not be answered fully here but there is evidence to support both points of view. One cannot underestimate the substantial abilities born into these very high achievers. However, it is apparent that a great deal more than physical gift does into the making of a champion.

When the question was asked by different world class players that at what age did you start any type of competitive sport, it is found that most athletes started competitive sports while at school, generally this was between the ages of 6 and 13 with the average starting age being at around nine.

Barry John and J.P.R. Williams of rugby union, Bob Tisdall, Olympic 400m hurdle champion, and Ian Botham, the all-round cricketer, who have never, in their opinion, specialized in one sport or at least not for more than a few months in any one year, the average age is still over 16. Most of those interviewed were happy that they had not specialized until quite late on in their sporting life. They had fun in a variety of sports and had only started to make a push when they decided that they wanted to exclude the other options in order to see just how far they could go in their chosen speciality. Certain sports had a definite bias towards a younger starting age.

Duncan Goodhew led the swimmers in at seven years old, Chris Evert Lloyd the tennis players at nine years old. The majority of achievers seem to have delayed their decision until the end of school days, for some, this meant they were 15 or 16 years old, and for others 17 or 18.

Those pressing the top end were squash champion Johan Barrington and racing driver Jackie Stewart, both not starting until they were twenty-three, although it should be pointed out that Jackie won international recognition in shooting before getting behind the wheel of a car. At the extreme end is John Gilmour, who started his long continuing track athletics career after the Second World War at the age of 26, and at the same age Pat O'Callaghan who decided to specialize after he had won his second Olympic hammer title in 1932. His aim was the 1936 Games but unfortunately Ireland did not compete.

It seems that several of the athletes were always good at sport or could have been, highly successful in other areas of sport. The rugby men Gareth Edwards and Barry John were offered trial with good football clubs, and J.P.R. Williams won junior Wimbledon when he was nineteen. With almost no exception, these achievers played a variety of sports.

Olympic track athlete Peter Snell recalled that at school, he played in the top rugby and cricket teams. I was tenning champion, I was a handicap at golf. I had a good background at field hockey, and played badminton and table tennis. I did gymnastics and, when running schools steeplechase, I usually won. Peter was a world record sprint relay team while at University of Southern California and John Havlicek, basketball star with the Boston Celtics, was, during his high school days, an All-State football, basketball and baseball player.

Marathon runner Joan Benoit Samuelson was a state skier, and ice hockey scoring star Wayne Gretzky was the Ontario schools champion at eleven years old in 800m, 1500m and cross-country. Heather McKay, multiple worlds squash champion, started out as the local tennis champion and a member of the local softball team, and was twice named to the All-Australian hockey team, and she became world racketball champion following her exceptional squash career.

Track athletes Carl Lewis, Lynn Davies, Daley Thompson, Seb Coe were all good at soccer. The list could be very much more extensive, pointing out the variety of sports in which everyone has competed, but the main point of interest is that there was opportunity for a diversity of sports. A definite pattern emerged in the development phase of sport in the lives of these high achievers. The first step was that they were introduced to sport as fun and that it was enjoyed for its own sake.

Often the games were created to suit the environment. For example, Gareth Edwards talked of using a local lane for his own England v West Indies cricket match, where the placement of the ball over walls and past certain trees had special scoring significance. Lynn Davies and his friends had challenges as to who could jump the stream further down the valley where it gradually became wider. The games usually had a competitive element whether they were soccer, basketball or whatever, but they were informal teams and the children enjoyed themselves so much that they would stay out until darkness forced them home. The second step in their development was the introduction of fundamental skills. Quite often these fundamentals were introduced by their father or school teacher, but it was done in a clear-cut manner without pressure. The basics of good sound technique were invaluable because, under pressure, people tend to revert to what is their own natural, fundamental way of doing things. The final step was the introduction of pushing. The push did not come from the parents, it came from within the individual and in several cases, it was assisted by a coach after the individual had made the commitment.

Training

In many cases, the time spent in training did not alter significant from the start of specialization right up to top level. The rugby players rarely practised more than three times per week, unless they were on tour. Olympic swimmer Shane Innes was training seriously from the age of 13 with nine or ten sessions per weak. The aspect which changed with most athletes over the years was the level of intensity. There was a gradual recognition of the requirement to make it to the top.

It was like stepping stones with the athlete taking the first step, and doing what was needed to reach the next one. The total time commitment varied considerably in each sport. For a distance runner, an hour at either end of the day may well mean covering over twenty miles, and if more miles are then thrown in, the body simply will not recover in time to do the same distance on the following day. It seems astonishing, but often the time commitment did not change whether the individual was working, studying or playing sport full-time.

There were extensive hardships endured by those such as the swimmers, who had to get up in the middle of night to start swimming in order to get the required practice hours in before school or work. In case of ice dance champions Torvill and Dean, it was the restriction of the available time on ice in Great Britain which inhibited the hours put in. They were limited to a maximum of 6 hours per week and those were either after 11 p.m. or before 6 a.m. On these limited hours, the duo reached fourth in the world and came fifth at the Olympics. They were subsequently granted the opportunity to train overseas which enabled them to spend six hours on the ice every day, perfect scores of 6, gold medals and a new standard of excellence were the ultimate result. Another athlete whose training commitment was changed dramatically through sponsorship was world pursuit cycling champion Steele Bishop. Between the ages of fifteen and nineteen, he trained for thirty to fort-five minutes every day of the week. On the same seven-day schedule, he increased his workouts to more than 6 hours. The days went as follows, two hours on the road in the morning just taking it easy, rolling along at 20 m.p.h., which is training pace, then on to the track at the velodrome for starts and sprints, two hours solid and really hard work. Ride back to the hotel, twenty minutes and shower; a bite to eat for lunch and put my feet up for twenty minutes if I was lucky. Then two more hours on the track behind a motorbike, followed by a full body massage. That was the daily routine.

How often do you give 100 per cent in training. The response to this question of Jonah's was that he gave it too often. Training was pretty haphazard. I did not know about half-effort and three-quarters effort. I was putting in too many long sessions back to back. I called them total reduction sessions. I would start again far too close to eating, and feel ill and get a cold sweat which would disappear after 45 minutes. I would crawl through day after day and was terribly lucky not to have more injury. So little knowledge was available. Nobody stretched or warmed up before they played. More than half of those interviewed felt that they gave 100 per cent every time they went out.

Sometimes the effort was in terms of mental concentration, more often it meant that at some point, if not in the whole session, they were giving their all both physically and mentally. Heather McKay said that she would rather do one hour at 100 per cent and be finished than stay on court for an hour and a half and given only 75 per cent.

The old adage as you train so will you compete seems

to be borne out. Additionally, the volume of training always exceeded the competition time. After very intense training, Heather often said if she ever felt that in a match, she would give up the sport. But once in the match, she would say to herself Come on, if you are tired, the other person has to be just as tired and that is when I would push and that extra little bit of training would pay off. The notion that it takes hard work to improve one's standard was accepted by all athletes.

Rugby league's Peter Sterling said, The only thing that makes you successful is hard work as there are always going to be others with similar ability. The only thing that is going to make you more successful is the amount of work you put in.

Twice Grand Slam winner Rod Laver believed that the reason he was able to go successfully through any five-set tennis match was the intensity of his practice. He would go full out for three to four hours on court, enjoying the effort, and not just playing sets but rallying two-against-one. Another reason for giving 100 per cent to their sport came from Gene Upshaw in American football, Ian Botham and Clive Lloyd in cricket, and Billy Beaumont in rugby union. Each felt that their role as captain demanded setting an example.

Clive had turned around the thinking in the West Indies team and with it came a new determination to succeed. In the old days, when under pressure, we were seen to be unable to fight our way out of it. I saw that if you were physically fit, it helped you to think straighter. It meant that your mind and body were alert and that to me was the most important thing in being a top class sportsman. It is interesting to find some top runners do not train to 100 per cent. Sprint-king and long jumper

Carl Lewis said that he would give 100 per cent on starts and jumping, but not running.

Middle-distance star Seb Coe would give it his all in conditioning sessions, but again, not in running. The same was echoed by world 1500m champion Steve Cram. Steve Ovett, 800m Olympic champion, world marathon champion Rob de Castella and Ed Moses, Olympic 400m hurdles champion, said that they hardly ever gave 100 per cent in the training sessions. Peter Snell, another Olympic middle-distance winner, pointed out that it was not always appropriate, with multiple repetitions, and steady long hard runs, the work load could be enormous and it was important not to get to a state of complete depletion with the resulting risk of injury or sickness. There were several exceptions to this track rule.

Herb Elliott, unbeaten over a mile, pushed himself to the limit on one of the two daily Joan Benoit Samuelson pushes herself to the limit on one of her two daily sessions. Long jumper Lynn Davies, sprinter Shirley de la Hunty and 800m champion Ralph Doubell were part of the majority who replied most of the time. Those who did not push themselves to 100 per cent in training did not see this factor as being necessary. Steve Ovette's view was that consistency was better than quality. On a long run, feeling a bit tired, there would be the option to stay on the flat or go up a hill. He would go up the hill, and it would hurt but it would not be 100 per cent flat out. You have to endure a bit of pain in training for our sport. It is not the name of the game, but to a certain extent it is an acceptance of pain. It does not have to be severe, it can be gradual This is not masochism where one is seeking pain, rather it is an understanding that it is productive pain. The body is being positively modified in its strength and efficiency.

Duration

The question of the natural process of the ageing of the body was raised by soccer captain Bryan Robson. He said that he had always had the will to train hard and was a glutton for punishment. He had never been one to pack it in when it started to hurt. Most of the athletes were prepared to stick it out and in a sense, discover that the discomfort was not quite as bad as they had first feared or thought, or at least that it was quite possible to learn how to cope with it. Bryan went on to relate that at the end of a practice session when they were quite tired, they sometimes had a timed run, twice around the field. He would try to see if he could beat the times he had done when younger. When others pointed out that as you get older the legs go, Bryan enjoyed proving that with age one can improve strength and endurance. One of the classic examples of durability is Al Oerter who was challenging for another Olympic discus place in 1984, having won the first of his four successive Olympic titles in 1956. At fifty years old, Reg Harris came out of retirement and won yet another world sprint cycle title.

With greater sponsorship of amateur and professional sportsmen and sportswomen, it will be interesting to see whether the average age increases. Certainly in track and field athletics, the world records established by Jamila Kratochvilova in 400m and 800m at thirty-one, and the marathon world best by Carlos Lopes at thirty-eight, suggest that the college and university representatives of the last generation were several short of their ultimate best performances. It underlines the need to allow youngsters to enjoy a variety of sports for as long as possible, having the fundamental of several sports given them when young with continuing opportunities to play and compete after school days.

Intensity

How much do you think that your training intensity made a difference to your level of success, when this question was asked, the words differed from one player to another, but the answer was virtually unanimous. All the difference, totally, enormously, terribly, vital, tremendously important, it was the root of everything.

Lynn Davies pointed out that the mind has a significant part in setting sights and tolerating the level of training and stress. He recalled the story of the woman who lifted the side of a car when her child was trapped underneath. Many of our limits are self-imposed. Duncan Goodhew believed that an athlete was only as good as his worst day. 2 to 3 days each week he would not be feeling up to par and those were the days that he would push himself. I found that 95 per cent of the time it was psychological. I would get in and forty five minutes or an hour later. I was knocking out amazing times. I was doing broken competition distance, with five seconds' rest every 50 m. I would come in with uncontrollable shakes and still maintain the times on each 50m. My body was actually shuddering with the strain and I used to take it to that point two to three times each week.

Herb Elliott explained In retrospect my training was not to improve my physical strength or stamina, those came along as a secondary result, but the primary purpose of every training session was to toughen up mentally. A training session was totally useless until it started to hurt. That was the point when it started to be worthwhile. The best is only bought at the cost of great pain.

While training, Steele Bishop's thought was, if I do not suffer I am not going to win. Ralph Doubell did not like the term pain. He saw it more as a willingness to push oneself and that was both a mental and a physical exercise. He referred to the classic comment of the Oxford University coach who spoke to an athlete who was sweating while running round the track, Do not worry, it is only pain.

Ralph would say, My legs are killing me, and Franz would reply, Well that is fine as long as your chest is okay. He would try the next time and says, My chest's caving in. Franz would reply, How are the legs, fine? This was strongly reminiscent of a session I had with my coach Billy Smith. My legs were painfully tired and I told Billy that they hurt. Billy put his hand on his own leg and said, I cannot feel a thing, let us get on with the next repetition.

Gareth Edwards pointed out that in a physical game like rugby, a player may be carrying an injury or may have been hit and be dazed, feeling physically and emotionally drained. This is the time when you have to be emotionally stronger-willed, to maintain and hang on when it is hurting. One key is not to be afraid of pain.

O.J. Simpson would get hit during a game and say, that is going to hurt tonight, then it was dismissed from his mind. Also from Gene Upshaw said, if you do not push yourself that way, you are never ever going to move higher than you are. Ian Botham believes that one can or cannot deal with apin, but being able to cope with it distinguishes the top sportsman from the good sportsman. In many cases, it was the blood, sweat and tears given by these top athletes, which made them individual record breakers; they chose to make such efforts and it was done once they had reached maturity.

Peter Snell reckoned that a top athlete could only push hard at the international level for about six years. It would be a waste if a youngster was encouraged to push like this and left sport with a feeling of disaster rather than a sense of accomplishment. In spite of the need for intensity, it must be remembered that these athletes are still enjoying what they are doing. It is their choice to push themselves.

Fitness and Diet

Another area which has changed over the last time is the awareness that would you eat can seriously affect performance. Most of the world class players said that they never gave their diet much though, it was just Mum's home cooking. When asked if they though it was a balanced diet, they said yes.

In most cases, it included meat and fish and poultry, green vegetables, and potatoes, and fruit. Several of the track athletes claimed to be junk food addicts. Daley Thompson said that he gave up so much in so many other areas that he could not face giving up his McDonald's diet, which he really enjoys.

Steve Cram was addicted to fish and chips. Ed Moses believed that we all eat far too much food and, on several occasions, has continued training hard while fasting. Although, it is a sad extreme, John Gilmour virtually lost his eyesight as a result of malnutrition while a POW for three and a half years with the Japanese during World War Two. His diet was rice, occasionally seaweed as a vegetable, pickled horseradish and sometimes the tops of sweet potatoes boiled into a type of soup. Surviving on this diet, with a very heavy manual workload, made him aware of the infinite powers of the body when there is a will to live and will to win. That learning has, in no small way, contributed to his phenomenal succession of world records and wins in veteran track athletics. Many laymen have been made aware of the difficulty the body has in digesting meat, and that for endurance events, which last for a couple of hours, pasta and other high carbohydrate foods are the best answer.

Rob de Castella said that he had moved away from the commercial interest areas of high fat, high sugar, high salt and low fibre, and was back on fresh fruit, fresh vegetables and no red meat. This is the enlightened view but it was surprising just how many referred to the fact that as training increases, so did their apparent need for chocolate or similar sugary items.

There is a need for a fast-burning energy source and the quick fix of chocolate or sugary items was a popular remedy. However, the problem with this solution is that it produces a roller-coaster effect as the blood sugar level rises quickly then drops, with the result that there is once more, a craving for another sugar fix.

Carbohydrates break down more slowly in the body, providing a constant natural source of glycogen which the body needs for energy. There was a time when Herb Elliott was in the media's spotlight for living on nuts and raisins. In fact, he was on a balanced diet but breakfast was a mixture of nuts, raisins and rolled oats, which today is commonly known as muesli. Now many athletes were taking multi-vitamin pills, but one person who did say he occasionally took them was Lester Piggott. As a large framed jockey, he had to limit himself to one main meal a day. He did not go very long without food but never ate much.

Reaction to Injury

When the question was asked by the top players that how they read their bodies, five per cent had given it no thought. Billey Beamount said, I am not bothered, I just get stuck in. Basketball's Bob Cousy had the same reaction, I never thought about it, I was so healthy. Another 5 per cent felt that their assessment was better further on in their careers.

Donwhill skier Ken Read, I overdid it when I was young. Tennis star Margaret Court, Better yours later. And Seb Coe, I do now.

A further 8 per cent did not feel that they were very good at assessing themselves. Duncan Goodhew found it difficult, as did fellow swimmer Mike Wenden, while J.P.R. Williams added, I competed too often. The day after an international I had be out playing flat out in a fun game, in a different position, but that is just me. The other 82 per cent said that they could read their bodies very well. Steve Ovett said, I did not in L.A., but normally I do perfectly. It is part of the tools of trade, of being honest with yourself and respecting your body.

Snooker champion Steve Davis referred to his high degree of sensitivity, I do a lot of practice on my own and I can detect a fault without having anyone to tell them. Soccer legend Bobby Charlton commented, if I ate too much pre-match or if I had not slept well on the night before or may be gone to bed an hour later, than I should have done. I could sense it.

John Newcombe, Tennis player, gave an illustration of body awareness during a Wimbledon final against Stan Smith in 1971, I won the first set and it was four all in the second, when I dived for a ball at the net, landed on my gut and blew the wind right out of myself. We went on to five all, then he beat me 7-5. At 4-2 to him in the third, I suddenly realized that my energy level was very low. My first thought was panic. Then I realized that after the fall, I had not spent my time recovering, so I thought to myself, I have got about ten minutes before I have lost this set, so I have got about ten minutes to get myself back again. So I just spent ten minutes trying to get inside myself, taking deep breaths and relaxing and summoning the andrenalin to go again. I lost the third set 6-2. I did not lose a point on my serve in the fourth until I was serving for the set. John went on to win in the fifth and final set. He said, It is funny hearing the other guy's story. Stan thought at two sets to one, he lost concentration because he started thinking of his victory speech, while on my side of the net I had recharged my batteries and came out in the fourth changed up a gear and had another gear ready for the fifth set when we got into it.

Many a champion knows that a game is never lost until the last point is decided, the last ball bowled or pitched, or the final whistle blown. Being in tune with one's body is vital to remaining healthy. One of the most difficult aspects to judge for both the athlete and the coach is when a stress-induced injury starts hurtling. It is very difficult to distinguish the normal aches and pains associated with improving the condition of your body from the pain which might be signalling potential damage to the body's structure.

Often it seems that the right thing to do is to press ahead and the discomfort disappears during the training session. However, Mary Decker Slaney is an example of an athlete who was not correctly diagnosed and the result was years of pain. She was continually told that she had shin splints, but in later years, a bone scan showed that she had a series of stress fractures.

Most paediatricians are now strongly advocating that children are not introduced to either heavy weightlifting or long-distance running until they are fully mature and the bones have stopped growing. Another aspect of reading one's body involves a sense of its position in space. Certainly, some people have a more advanced sense than others.

For instance, Gareth Edwards, could simply see someone doing back somersaults and with little practice, could duplicate the action. Jayne Torvill and Christopher Dean increased their body awareness through ballet classes and by skating in an area surrounded by mirrors. The visual picture enabled them to define a mood in bodily art form.

Billie Jean King took this one stage further than physical awareness, she felt that self-awareness was probably the most important thing in fulfilling yourself because then you can set proper goals. Champions have an unbelievable level of self-awareness. The talent is conception. Some are born with talent and either do not do anything with it or do not even recognize it, but those who develop their potential, they are really talented.

A concise response on injury came from Joan Benoit Samuleson. She said that injuries were frustrating but when she recovered from them, she felt stronger and hungrier than ever for success. Several of the top athletes have had the good fortune of not being injured, but who were often competed with it if they could, or else worked around the problem.

At 13, Bob Cousy fell out of a tree and broke his right arm, I had it in a cast but I was soon out practising, shooting with the other hand and within the year, I could shoot left-handed almost as well as I could right-handed.

Lester Piggott accepted the possible prospect of injury, Well, we all get injured, that is inevitable. This attitude exemplifies the acceptance of injury or sickness as a slight inconvenience, not as something which would stop work or the individual's desire for progress or achievement. In their eyes, it is merely a frustration and an interruption to plans.

9

PHYSICAL EDUCATION AND SPORTS PSYCHOLOGY

Most of the early sport psychology research focused on attempts to link personality or character with participation in athletics. As such, the majority of those early investigations were designed to compare the personalities of athletes with those of non-athletes. When few definitive trends emerged from personality-based research, sport psychologists became disheartened with that approach and began to argue that a better avenue for understanding psychological aspects of individual sport behaviour might be theory testing. Throughout most of the 1970s sport psychologists searched the literature for theories in the parent discipline of psychology that might also be applicable to motor skills.

A good example of such theory borrowing is the use of social facilitation theory, which provided testable predictions of how the presence of other people should affect both initial skill acquisition and later skill performance. The most fundamental prediction was that the presence of other persons should be disruptive to early skill acquisition but facilitative to later performance. Much of this theory testing took place in laboratory settings, and the early laboratory-based results were promising in terms of developing sport psychology as a scientific field. Unfortunately, when those same predictions were taken to field settings for reality testing, little was uncovered in terms of practical applications to sport behaviour. As a result of the difficulties in applying theories such as social facilitation to sport, theory testing of this nature was almost totally abandoned by sport psychologists in the late 1970s and early 1980s.

Researchers began to ask more clinical questions such as "How does mental practice or imagery affect sport performance?" "How can relaxation or biofeedback assist in the management of sport-related stress?" Many researchers also studied coach-athlete compatibility and the relationship between team cohesion and team outcome. As a consequence of this more clinical approach to sport psychology, the field has moved closer to answering the questions posed most frequently by coaches.

This is certainly desirable; however, a distinct vacuum in sport psychology theory still exists. When sport psychologist rejected theory testing in favour of more humanistic concerns they also almost eliminated any systematic attempts at building theoretical understanding of sport-related behaviour. Such theory building is critical to providing a sound basis on which to draw the methods and strategies used to intervene or change behaviour within sport settings. On the other hand, many of today's leading researchers in the field are again arguing for and actively engaging in research that can lead to development of new theories that are unique to individual sport behaviour.

Research is taking place on the playing field, in the gymnasium, and in the laboratory . Questions are being answered for both practical and theoretical reasons. It is hoped that the next decade will continue to see much more sport-specific theory building as the discipline of sport psychology matures as a science in its own right, ultimately complete with its own theories and its own sound clinical principles.

BASIC SCIENTIFIC CONCEPTS AND VOCABULARY

Ways of Knowing

To more fully understand sport psychology as a science, it is necessary to understand the basic concepts and vocabulary of scientific inquiry. In this first section we will discuss various ways in which scientist answer questions such as "How do we know that is truth?" "What is reality or fact?"

Phenomenology

How does a scientific know that something is true, that an observed event is real and factual? One way is to call on personal experience, or phenomenology. Many of the beliefs we all hold are based on our own experiences. In the field of sport psychology, much of what takes place when coaches attempt to apply psychological principles to improve the performance of athletes is based on their own past experiences. They reason that "if it worked for me, then it should work for the other person." However, this is not necessarily true; people differ too much from one another. Therefore the phenomenological method is not considered adequate in a scientific sense. For a method to be adequate scientifically, it must allow for the generation of cause-and-effect relationships or laws that can be applied to large numbers of persons or events.

Authority

Another method of "knowing" that is used with great frequency in sport psychology is that of authority. From this perspective, one look to a major authority in the field to provide the answers or facts. For instance, many basketball coaches have looked to John Wooden, former UCLA basketball coach, for advice on how to best coach basketball. What's wrong with this approach? On the surface it seems logical to look to outstanding coaches for ideas on how to coach. But think for a moment: would Wooden's approach work equally well with high school students in a small low town? Would Pat Head Summit, coach of the U.S. Women's Olympic basketball team, be as successful as she was with the 1984 Olympic team if she used the same methods with a junior varsity basketball team? Is there a single, best approach to the coaching of all basketball teams, regardless of factors such as skill level, personality of the head coach, or gender of the players? Probably not. Thus the method of authority lacks sufficient scientific credibility because it fails to provide principles that can be generally applied.

Theory Building

The fourth method of knowing is theory building. A theory is developed by pulling together the known facts relative to a certain phenomenon and establishing predictions concerning how each may be related to the others. Those predictions are then subjected to testing through studies that follow the steps of the scientific method. Therefore, although the basic scientific procedures are identical to those followed by the empirical method, the purpose differs. In theory testing the hypothesis is derived directly from the theory, and the conclusion derived from the data analysis feeds back to the theory. In other words the conclusion indicates whether the prediction made by the theory was accurate. Therefore both the development and the eventual testing of theories is an efficient, ongoing process.

Developing a field of scientific inquiry requires both the method of empiricism and the method of theory building. Obviously, empirically based investigations must precede theoretically founded studies. A researcher needs a collection of facts before he or she can speculate on the interrelationships among those facts. Without empiricism there would be less possibility of generating fresh and innovative ideas. As you saw earlier in our example of what a coach would need to know about anxiety and athletic performance, without attempts at theory building a researcher would have only a cumbersome group of facts.

Theories, Models, and Paradigms

Frequently the three terms, model and paradigm are used synonymously. Actually they are quite different. A theory attempts to synthesize what is known about a collection of facts and to make predictions concerning the relationships among those facts. A theory can be conceived of as a collection of hypotheses that attempts to predict or explain the relationships between multiple independent and dependent variables.

Therefore a theoretical frâmework provides testable predictions concerning the interrelationships among the variables associated with a particular phenomenon. Although we realize that such a description of theory may leave you puzzled at this point, the concept will become clearer as we discuss several theories later in the text, such as theories concerning how anxiety should affect motor performance in predictable ways and conflicting theories concerning phenomena such as observational learning, imagery effects, and personality.

As you will see, all these theories have certain commonalities. They all identify independent and dependent variables of interest and they all propose specific hypotheses concerning the interrelationships among those variables. A model is an analogy that is devised to help you conceptualize something about the interrelationships between a set of variables. It is usually visual or graphic. When coaches use Xs and Os, that is a model of the play to be executed. The Xs and Os represent, or are analogous to, the actual players. When architects develop blueprints to represent the structure of a building or when pharmaceutical companies design plastic human figures to show how certain drugs such as aspiring move through the body, they have constructed models.

Scientists interested in the relationship between psychology and sport and motor behaviour have developed several models of their own. One of the earliest of those models was developed by Lewin. As shown below

$$B = f(P \times S)$$

this model simply indicates that behaviour is a function of the interaction between some characteristic of the person and some event in the situation. From this perspective, behaviour is seen as being determined by the interrelationships among elements contained within a certain person and the circumstances that are observable in the social situation. An alternative explanation for human behaviour is that proposed by the external causation model:

Stimulus—Response—Positive Reinforcement

It states that a human response is caused by some observable, antencedent environmental condition called a stimulus. Is such a response is followed by some pleasurable consequence labelled positive reinforcement, then that same or a highly similar response will tend to recur under those same stimulus conditions. The underlying notions of this model are that responses are generated on the basis of some external factor in the first place and are maintained by some other external. To better understand the external causation model, suppose that a Little League player is at bat with a single runner on third base. With no previous instructions or experience, the player bunts the ball. The coach is ecstatic and praises the athlete profusely. The external causation model would predict that the next time this player is at bat under those same stimulus conditions, the same response will most likely recur.

In this model the term stimulus is used to describe the sensory input into the human system, whereas cognition is used to describe how information is processed before eliciting a response. Therefore this model portrays humans as thinking beings who process environmental information before deciding on an appropriate behavioural response. For instance, this model would predict that an athlete would mentally process feedback or information from a coach before attempting to changes in those skills. Once a model is developed, it influences how a research experiment is designed.

The manner in which such an investigation is carried out is called a paradigm. A paradigm describes the experimental protocol or methodological procedures used in a particular investigation. These procedures are drawn logically from the theoretical framework, or model, on which the study is based.

We will use the external causation model and the internal mediational model to help clarify this definition. Suppose that two scholars were both interested in understanding how a person learns motor skills. If you were to walk unannounced into each of their laboratories, you would probably not find the same experiment underway because they probably would not have selected the same motor task or the same subjects.

However, for the sake of our argument, assume that they were both assessing motor skill acquisition on the same task by highly similar subjects. Would they be following identical procedures? Probably not. However, it is certain that each would be setting up an experimental arrangement that would be consistent with the theoretical model that each experimenter believed best explains the acquisition of motor skills.

If the first experimenter believed that such behaviours are acquired as a function of some external factor he or she would then logically design an experiment in which some factor in the environment was varied, such as whether positive reinforcement was provided after each response.

On the other hand, if the second scientific took the perspective that motor skills are learned primarily through cognitive processing then it would follow that he or she would construct an experimental protocol in which some aspect of cognition was varied.

Thus it is clear that the paradigm employed by each

of the two scientific is drawn logically from the different theoretical perspectives they hold. Teachers and coaches follow the same pattern as scientific. If coach A believes that players can improve athletic performance primarily through means such as awarding letters or posting track times, then that coach is following the principles of the external causation model. If Coach B attempts to improve athletes' sport performance by pointing out errors and video-taping plays, then Coach B is trying to enhance performance by providing information to the players and is therefore applying the principles of the internal mediational model. Although the examples of experiments cited earlier both took place in a laboratory setting, there is no reason why similar studies cannot be conducted in field situations. The type and location of research studies in sport psychology are quite flexible.

Empiricism

The third approach to knowing is empiricism, which simple means " based on observation." Thus it is similar to the phenomenological method, which is based on personal experience. However, it differs from phenomenology in that empiricism refers to observations that are made under strictly controlled experimental conditions. From this perspective, a "fact" is generated by following the steps of the scientific method. The scientific method is common to all scientific inquiries, regardless of whether the question concerns physics, biology, sociology, or sport psychology. These are four basic steps in the scientific method.

First, a statement of the problem must be formulated. This simply means that the scientific must state exactly what the question is that he or she is attempting to answer, such as "What are the effects of failure on future tasks persistence?" or "Is there any cause-and-effect relationship between the coach's leadership style and team success?"

Second, one or more hypotheses must be posed. A hypothesis is a prediction of the answer to a previously identified question. In the first question above, the hypothesis might state that failure will cause a decrease in duration of task persistence. The hypothesis posed for the second question might be that a task-oriented coach should be more successful as compared with a socioemotionally oriented coach.

Third, an experiment is designed in which data are collected and analysed. The method of data collection varies according to the nature of the question asked. If, as in the first question above, task persistence was to be observed, then time of duration at the task would be measured.

However, if the study were designed to determine differences between leadership styles of coaches, then the data would most likely be collected through the assessment of personality by means of a standardized instrument. In sport psychology research, data are collected in a wide variety of settings, ranging from the playing field to the ski slopes to the laboratory situation. However, the analysis of those data is almost always accomplished by the use of statistical procedures. Given that the data must eventually be subjected to statistical analysis, it must be capable of taking on numerical values; it must be quantifiable. For instance, task persistence could be quantified on the basis of some unit of time such as seconds or minutes, whereas personality would take on some numerical value associated with a person's score on a particular personality scale.

Fourth, after the data are collected and analysed, the scientist draws a conclusion the basis of what the data analysis has shown. Recall that the purpose of the third step is to design an investigation that will allow the scientist derived on the basis of the data analysis tell the experimenter whether the hypothesis can be accepted or must be rejected. In our examples, the data analysis would indicate whether a failure outcome did indeed have a negative effect on subsequent task persistence and whether differences in coaching style had nay measurable effect on team outcome. The scientific method is elegant in its simplicity, yet rigorous in a scientific sense because of its inherent checks and balances.

Give the latter, and given that the scientific empiricism is the best or should be the only acceptable method of "scientifically" knowing. What could be lacking? One difficulty is that the method of empiricism has as its goal only the identification of facts. More specifically, the generates fact for their own sake, regardless of any connection or relationship to other existing facts.

In the early stages of scientific inquiry the identification of such facts is crucial. However, as more and more facts are generated, if they are allowed to remain in insolation from one another, adequate understanding of a phenomenon becomes almost impossible. Look at this problem from the point of view of a coach and consider the array of seemingly unrelated information that a coach would need to know about psychology to work effectively with just one athlete in a single-event.

The coach would need to understand why some

athletes are anxious in competitive settings whereas others are not; why people with different levels of anxiety perform differently within competitive sport settings; and how an athlete's anxiety reaction can be raised or lowered. Certainly it would be inefficient to require that every coach attempt to identify and synthesis all of the known facts about each of the notions just mentioned. What is the alternative?

Variables

A variable is an entity capable of being measured, or quantified; that is, it can be assigned numerical value. In the early stages of the development of a science, much energy is put into identifying and measuring variables thought to be important to that particular domain. However, the individual variables themselves provide little information of real value; it is the interrelationships that occur between the variables that are of most concern. For instance, it is of small value to be able to say that it is possible to measure whether an athlete tends to be an extrovert or an introvert. Of more importance is the ability to specify exactly how the level of introversion or extroversion relates to successful performance on a team sport such as water polo.

Thus in the first case one variable, the degree of extroversion versus introversion, was measured. In the second case the interrelationship between the psychological variable of introversion versus extroversion and sport team performance was identified. Clearly, the second case provides more valuable information.

At its most fundamental level, research in the area of sport psychology consist of the study of two variables in an effort to establish if any relationship exists between those variables. These important relationships are called causal relationships because a change in one of the variable causes a systematic change in the other. These cause-and-effect relationships relative to individual behaviour in sport or movement settings formulate the research domain of sport psychology.

Independent variables are those thought to the cause of an observed effect. They are the variables that are usually manipulated across experimental groups in a study. For instance, suppose that you designed an investigation in which you predicted that athletes who mentally practised would perform better than similarly skilled athletes who did not. The study was then designed so that one group mentally practised basketball free throws and the other group did not. If you then measured the actual free throw performance of both groups and found that the group that had practised mentally had better free throw performance than the group that did not, you could conclude that practising mentally caused the effect of enhancing basketball free throw performance. In this example the causative, or independent variable was mental practice.

Control variables are any other variables that could effect changes in the dependent variable. In the example above, because you obviously wanted to establish a cause-and-effect relationship between mental practice and effectiveness of basketball free throw shooting, you would not want a situation in which you could not be sure that the observed effect was a result of mental practice alone. Therefore when designing your study you must eliminate or control any variable, other than the independent variable, that could effect changes in the dependent variable. In our basketball example, control variables might be variables such as initial differences in skill level or initial differences in free throw percentage between the two groups of free throw shooters.

Dependent variables are those variables that are affected systematically by a change in the independent variable. The dependent variable is measured or assessed during the collection of data. In the basketball free throw example described above, the dependent variable would be free throw performance.

PRINCIPLES OF SCIENTIFIC INQUIRY

To more clearly understand how a science develops and why theory development is so important, it is necessary to understand certain aspects of science and scientific inquiry. If sport psychology is to be considered a legitimate science, then it must use the methods and vocabulary common to all sciences. Throughout the text you will encounter common scientific vocabulary. We hope that by explaining the vocabulary, methods, and strategies of scientific inquiry, you will be free to concentrate on the pertinent topics and issues presented in the rest of this text. The unit of analysis in sport psychology is individual behaviour as it occurs in sport situations. To achieve an understanding of that behaviour, four steps must be followed.

Prediction and Intervention

The third step is a prediction. A primary goal of the science of sport psychology is the ability to predict individual sport behaviour under identifiable conditions. Returning to our tennis example, if nothing changes, you can reasonably predict that any time this tennis player attempts to play in the presence of spectators, his or her performance will be hindered. Should you simply stop at that point? Certainly not! Once you are able to make fairly definitive predictions, you can then apply principles of psychology so that behaviour can be changed or controlled. This is the process of intervention, the use of psychological principles to enhance individual sport performance. In the case of the tennis player, performance can be enhanced by applying any one of several intervention strategies. For example, the athlete can be instructed in the use of relaxation procedures so that control over muscular tension is increased. Or attentional control can be gained by teaching the performer to use verbal cues such as "bounce" and "hit" at the appropriate time. Sport psychology has the same goals as does any other behavioural science—the description, explanation, prediction, and change of individual behaviour.

Its uniqueness lies in its attempt to achieve those goals within the framework of sport and motor performance situations. The attainment of those goals allows you to apply strategies to assist the performer in enhancing sport performance.

Description and Explanation

First, you must attempt to describe exactly how a person behaves in an indefectible situation. For instance, you might observe that when other people are watching, the strokes of a particular tennis player become stiff and erratic. Once you see that this behaviour is rather consistent, the second step is to try to explain why such effects occur.

Therefore, once you are able to describe behaviour, you then try to explain the causes underlying that behaviour. Although the latter may seem relatively easy, in reality it is often most difficult. In our tennis example it is not enough to say that presence of spectators causes the negative effects on the tennis player's strokes. That merely describes what take place.

To explain more fully the relationship between the presence of spectators and negative effects on tennis performance, you can then test other hypotheses. For instance, instead of measuring the patterns of muscle activity, you can assess what is happening to the person's processing of environmental cues. Perhaps the tennis player is distracted by the presence of other persons and therefore splits his or her attention between watching the tennis ball and assessing what is happening among the spectators. It seems reasonable that such attentional scanning or switching can cause performance problems. Perhaps the player cannot see the oncoming ball soon enough and therefore hurries the stroke. It is through this process of testing alternative hypotheses to determine their "fit" that you can ultimately construct a sound explanation of the relationship between the presence of other persons and its effects on one person's tennis strokes.

FUNDAMENTAL TYPES OF RESEARCH

The research undertaken in the field of sport psychology involves (1) the relative applicability of the findings and (2) the origin of the hypothesis.

Applied Research versus Basic Research

Research that is completed with an eye toward directly applying the results to a real-life situation is called applied research. Evidence obtained from such investigations is applicable to athletes in actual sport settings. Obviously, this is the type of research that most coaches and teachers want sport psychologists to do. They want answers to questions about psychological aspects of athlete behaviour. Thus applied research hold an extremely important position within the research efforts of many sport psychologists. Other researchers are more interested in basic research, in which they gather information concerning individual psychology in movement settings simply for the sake of increasing knowledge; they are not interested in the immediate application of their results.

Often students, teachers, and coaches do not understand why basic research is important because it has not clear-cut relationship to real-life behaviours or situations. Perhaps a contemporary example will help you understand why basic research is necessary. Few of us could deny the impact that contemporary high-technology information and applications have on our daily life.

What any persons do not realize, however, is that the fundamental mathematical principles and theoretical notions associated with those technological advances were generated from basic research; that is, the information was generated simply for the sake of the information itself. It was only later that other researchers took the basic information and applied it for various technological purposes. For instance, in the field of biomechanics, much of the research uses computer-assisted techniques. However, when those techniques were first developed, no thought was given to their application to movement analysis.

Quasi-Experimental Research versus True Experimental Research

To conclude our discussion of the scientific

dimensions of the psychology of sport behaviour, one final notion needs to be addressed: the distinction between quasi-experimental research and true experimental research. Earlier we said that the independent variable in an investigations was considered to be the cause of some effect on a dependent variable. One example was the possible effect of failure on subsequent persistence behaviour at the same task. In that example, failure would be categorized as the independent variable and persistence would be classified as the dependent variable.

The distinction between quasi-and true experimental research rests on two criteria. The first is whether an independent variable is actually varied or manipulated in that particular study. The second criterion is whether there is a control group. A control group is a group of subjects who are not exposed to the independent variable. If the independent variable is not manipulated and there is no control group, the study is called a quasi-experiment.

If an independent variable is manipulated and there is a control group, then the study is considered a true-experiment. It is important to note that in either case some measurement is made on the dependent variable. Consider a situation in which an experiment notices that highly skilled gymnasts appear to exhibit lower degree of anxiety as compared with less-skilled participants. An anxiety test is then administered to both groups of gymnasts, and the data analysis reveals that the experimenter's hypothesis was correct.

On the average the more highly skilled athletes had lower levels of anxiety as compared with the less-skilled gymnasts. In this example a dependent variable was assessed. However, the independent variable was not actually varied by the investigator; the athletes possessed that skill before the study. In addition, there was no control group, such as a comparison group of non-athletes.

Therefore even though the study proposed a hypothesis, systematically collected data, and used appropriate statistical analysis, it would not be considered a true experimental design but rather a quasi-experiment. Suppose that another person observed that beginning tennis player seemed to perform better or worse as a consequence of the information that was provided to them after a response.

In terms of the content of the feedback, it appeared that beginners performed better after positive feedback and worse after negative feedback. An experiment was then designed in which half of the players performed and always received negative feedback, whereas the other half performed an identical task but always received positive feedback. After the collection and analysis of the data, no differences between the groups were shown. Was this a true or a quasi-experiment? Could it be considered to be a true experiment in that the independent variable was manipulated? Half the players were provided with negative feedback, whereas the other half received positive feedback.

However, something is missing from the experiment the design did not include a control group. In this case, to be a true experiment, a third group should have been included, one to which no feedback was provided. There are some very real advantages to designing true experiments.

The inclusion of a manipulated independent variable

and a control group allows researchers to show cause - and-effect relationships. Those cause-and-effect relationships allows a science to move toward adequate explanations and eventually to the point at which genuine theory building can begin.

However, good quasi-experiments or descriptions of variables must usually precede the design and implementation of true experiments. The science of sport psychology is young and exciting. It is not limited to one experimental site or to a single research approach. It is equally appropriate to conduct studies in locations such as a swimming pool, a baseball diamond, or an experimental laboratory. Scientific inquiries are limited only by the creativity and imagination of the researcher, who can be a full-time researcher, a teacher, a coach, or an athlete.

Empirical Research versus Theoretical Research

The second dimension along which research in sport psychology can be conceptualized is the origin of the hypothesis to be tested. We used the term empiricism earlier to refer to the method of observation. Many research hypotheses are generated on the basis of the observations or experiences of the scientist. For example, a scientist might observe that there appears to be something different about the personalities of athletes who prefer team sports to individual sports.

This observation could lead to the development of a study designed to test the validity of that empirically based hypothesis. At the other end of the empirical dimension lies the element of the theoretically based hypothesis. In that instance, the hypothesis is derived directly from an existing theory depicts the two dimensions along which research can be classified. To better understand the interrelationships among the elements of applied, basic, empirical, and theoretical research, suppose that a particular scientist was interested in the question of how images are stored in memory.

Suppose further this interest was purely to gain new knowledge and that there was no available theory to guide the investigator. This investigation would be classified as being from the basic-empirical perspective. If, on the other hand, there was a theory available that predicted that images are stored in analog form the same study should be categorized as being within the domain of basic-theoretical research.

Ethics in a Highly Visible Environment: Consultation and Intervention with Athletes and Athletic Teams

On November 15, 1975 an athlete at Colorado State University established a new NCAA major college football record by kicking a 63-yard field goal. I had been serving in a consultative role with the football program at CSU and my work included assisting this particular athlete through the application of a muscle relaxation and imagery rehearsal technique based on learning theory and behaviour modification principles. Following the game, a number of reporters were interviewing the athlete about his recordsetting feat when he revealed to them that I had helped him in his training program.

Local and state newspapers, and later national wire-service release, mentioned the athlete's acknowledgement of my deliver of psychology assistance. Unfortunately, some reports were incomplete or misleading as to the nature of the assistance rendered. For example, one article state I had "counselled" the young man after he had become "despondent' over having missed kicks in key situation in earlier games. The incompleteness and inaccuracies probably were due to the athlete not knowing quite how to explain how I had helped him, my reticence about giving information to the reporters, and misconceptions which journalists and others have about forms of intervention used by psychologists. The highly publicized event, albeit a happy one for the athlete pointed up the need for guidelines for the psychologist who consults with athletes and athletic teams-individuals and groups who alternately suffer and enjoy the unique vagaries of high visibility and public exposure. Athletic coaches and athletes who seek psychological assistance and entitled to the full protection of the psychologist's principles and standards of ethics, the same degree of protection guaranteed any other client.

This holds whether a coach wants advice on coaching methods, staff relationships, team morale, or the colour of the locker room walls. This also holds whether a given individual athlete is sent for help by a coach, as opposed to a self-referral, and whether the intervention consists of simple advice, counselling, or psychotherapy or if it involves training the athlete in a behavior modification technique designed to improve motor performance. The fact that the organization and the participating athletes are in the public eye directly or via the media should not override any of the principles of confidentiality or any other ethical considerations. By way of contrast, it seems customary in the sports world for certain medical information, at least medical information which relates to an athlete's current ability to perform, to be released one's medical or physical condition. But should psychologists publicly reveal psychological information about teams or athletes? I believe not, and for reason alluded to above. The general public is not familiar with the kinds of services a psychologist might render a sports team or an athlete. For example, many people might automatically assume that if an athlete is being seen by a psychologist, it must be a "head" problem, and negative attributions and attitudes toward the athlete might result.

Nevertheless, there should be no gray area in psychology even in sports-as in any other setting the client's rights and the psychologist's responsibility must be sustained. Yet, certain realities and problems exist in the consulting and intervention role of the sports psychologist. The psychologist involved with a team or with certain athletes may have other, and sometimes conflicting, roles in the same general setting or location, e.g. a university. Athletes have other dimensions to their lives, and they may seek psychological help unrelated to their existence as athletes.

Coaches are inevitably interested in the outcome of psychological intervention with athletes in their charge, for their own welfare may be directly at stake. Should the goals of intervention be the goals of the athlete, or the goals the coach has for the athlete, i.e., who is the client if the coach is the one who has "hired" the psychologist? Are behaviour modification procedures designed merely to improve a specific normal motor behaviour exempt from those rules of confidentiality governing personal counselling or psychotherapy? What about working with an athlete at the practice or game site in view of others? What constitutes a "public revelation" of the relationship by the athlete? Are certain case histories or search studies precluded from publication because any description of the problem and the outcome would immediately make the identify of the athlete known-via his or her publicized accomplishments and notoriety?

Although these problems and question are related to general and specific ethical and professional standards applicable to all psychologist-client contacts, they illustrate certain aspects somewhat unique to the psychologist-athlete or psychologist-athlete-team relationship. Following are some suggested guidelines pertaining to these unique aspects.

THE COACH AS THIRD PARTY

Coaches, especially in the collegiate ranks, appear to have a tradition-based authority to send players to see whomever they want them to see- a rather mandatory referral process. According to my experience, their motive generally seems to be a compromise between a genuine interest in the athlete's welfare and an equally genuine interest in their own welfare, i.e., winning. In situation wherein a psychologist has contracted to serve an athletic program and the participating athletes, it should be the responsibility of the psychologist to inform the coaches in the organization as to the condition under which an athlete will be seen and what information stemming from the contacts can and cannot be revealed to the coaching staff.

The athlete should be given clear information at the outset as to the principles and guidelines of confidentiality and an agreement reached as to what kinds of information; if any, the athlete wants conveyed to the coaches. Regarding referral, the psychologist should insist that athletes not feel forced into approaching the psychologist. Ideally, contacts should be by mutual agreement among the coach, the athlete, and the psychologist, when the athlete is a candidate for assistance directly related to his or her performance.

WHO IS THE CLIENT? WHO SETS THE GOALS

The psychologist who has contracted as a consultant and deliverer of services to a program may be serving, on occasion, two clients-the coaches responsible for the program and the athletes. Psychologists so involved should determine-first in an overall sense and subsequently in each specific case-whether the goals of the coaches and the athletes are congruent.

These goals should also be congruent with the values and ethics of the psychologist. In some cases the psychologist might wish to avoid service or input to the organization or an athlete when an unresolvable incongruency appears to exist. However, in most cases congruence can be achieved and/or incongruencies resolved through mutual discussions.

THE DUAL ROLE PROBLEM

In some settings, the sports psychologist may be in more than one set of dual roles with athletes. In the college or university setting, for example, the psychologist may be on the staff of the counselling centre and also a classroom teacher. A student who happens to be an athlete may come to the psychologist for assistance as an athlete, but may seek from the same person help with a personal matter unrelated to sports.

In the same semester the psychologist as teacher might look up from the podium and see the same student-athlete in the front row of the classroom. In each case of psychologist-client contact, the role of both the psychologist and the athlete should be clarified through mutual discussion at the outset of the involvements.

PSYCHOLOGICAL TESTING, PSYCHOTHERAPY, AND BEHAVIOUR MODIFICATION: DIFFERENT RULES?

The current wide application of behavior modification techniques used in various settings and the alleged non-personal nature of these modes, especially in their application to normal behaviours in normal people, can lead to laxity in certain ethical measures. Stolz, Wienckowski, and Brown emphasize the need for careful attention to such issues as voluntary and informed consent, goal setting, and other professional and ethical standards in the use of behaviour modification techniques. Deeply emotional, cognitive, historical, or personal material is usually not involved in behaviour modification, especially when the alteration or enhancement of a normal behavior in a normal person in the focus of treatment.

Nevertheless, any client, including an athlete, receiving behaviour modification should be afforded the same degree of ethical and professional considerations as the consumer of psychodynamic therapies or other services. If behaviouristic procedures are used with an entire team in a group setting, those who do not wish to participate should be allowed to so choose, and the psychologist should insist that the coaches accept this without retribution toward those who decline.

Further, it is as much the responsibility of the sports psychologist to help coaches understand why some athletes reject psychological assistance as it is to help them understand why other athletes want and accept such help. Additionally, the same ethics applicable to group or individual psychological testing should be adhered to in the use of tests with individual athletes or entire athletic teams. There is nothing about the world of sport which justifies any departure from these principles.

CONTACT IN THE PUBLIC SETTING

Unique to the psychologist-athlete relationship is that the psychologist might recommend, as part of the service, observation or even direct intervention at the practice site or contest setting. An example would be a behaviour modification method such as the imaged motor rehearsal I utilize with some football players. In addition to training sessions in the confidential confines of my office, I believe that some on-the-field observation and instruction enhances the effectiveness of the method.

As a consultant to a football program I have the privilege of unrestricted access to practice sessions, the locker room, and the sidelines during games, and I travel with the team. They have become accustomed to and accept my presence, even though it makes some of my work visible. This is in marked contrast to my other clinical practice- I do not observe, follow around, eat with, treat, or train any of my other clients in their natural habitats.

When public setting contact seems justified as part of the service, the athlete and coaches should be apprised of this, and their consent obtained. However, even though the sports psychologist may be seem working in the practice, pre-game, or game settings and consent of the client has been obtained, there is no consent implied that permits the psychologist to announce publicly to anyone that a particular person or unit is the client, to describe the process being used, or to reveal any privileged information about a particular athlete or the team.

PUBLICATION OF CASE HISTORIES OR RESEARCH REPORTS

Case histories and research findings are an important part of the professional literature in psychology, athletics, and physical education. It is an accepted ethical practice to conceal the identity of the clients or subjects in publications, but a contrary and unique situation often arises in sports psychology. It is different to publish a case history on an athlete who broke a NCAA football record and conceal his identity. Or to mention only that the subject was a collegiate athlete and mention the sport speciality narrows it down considerably, especially if the author's institutional or organizational affiliation is known. When a psychologist believes a case history should be part of the professional literature, permission should be obtained from the athlete and he or she should read and approves the manuscript prior to its submission for publication.

If any aspect of psychological work with an identified or identifiable athletic organization or team is described in published material, permission for publication from those in charge of the program, whether or not they are mentioned by name in the publication, should be secured. The authorized publication of work with identified or identifiable athletes or athletic organization does free the psychologist to then acknowledge, mention, or describe publicly elsewhere the work in speeches, interviews, or related publications or in replies to responsible inquiries. Nevertheless, such utterance and responses should be limited only to the content and facts in the original authorized publication.

A CLIENT-ATHLETE HAS THE RIGHT TO REVEAL

As in any psychologist-client relationship, an

individual client-athlete has the right to reveal anything he or she wishes about the fact, the nature, and the content of the contacts, but the psychologist does not share this privilege. If the athlete, however, reveals publicly that a psychologist has helped him or her, complicated circumstances may arise. What constitutes a public revelation by the athlete?

If the athlete merely tells a friend that a psychologist is working with him or her, that does not make it a matter of public record, nor would it become necessarily widely known. However, should an athlete reveal to the news media that "Dr.—worked with me," then the psychologist may become subject to inquiries and questions from numerous formal and informal sources.

However, before the psychologist acknowledges the contact and/or describes the method as it was directly applied to the particular athlete in an article, interview, or speech or in an informal reply to interested persons, permission to do so should be obtained from the athlete.

10

TESTS & MEASUREMENTS IN PHYSICAL EDUCATION

History reveals that as humans became more civilized they also become more scientific, and subsequently sought more exact ways to measure. In the United States the history of measurement in physical education and sport has paralleled the growth and development of research and the rise of the field to a more respected position in the educational spectrum. For many decades knowledge and skills in the area of measurement have been considered important for graduate study in the field of physical education and sport. But today measurement skills and knowledge are also deemed a necessary part of the professional preparation of sport management professionals.

Testing and measuring is by no means a recent innovation in the program of physical education. Hitchcock, at Amherst, starting in 1861, and Sargent, at Harvard, beginning in 1880, were pioneers in the use of anthropometric measurements as applied to a physical development program. Sargent was also instrumental, in common with a number of other physical educators of his time, in developing the widespread popularity of strength tests during the period from approximately 1880 until around 1900. The intercollegiate strength test which was developed by Sargent and his group has been somewhat revised, first by F. R. Rogers, and second by McCloy, and in its new from is used extensively in the present-day program of physical education. Advances in knowledge concerning the physiology of the heart and circulation brought a change in emphasis from pure muscle building to improvement in physiological functioning and in all round physical condition; and with this change in viewpoint came an emphasis on cardiovascular tests.

These tests, however, failed to strike the fancy of the physical educators of that period, and although several types of such tests were developed, few have been widely used. At about the turn of the century, various types of physical ability tests began to receive widespread attention. The most popular of these consisted various combinations of the track and field type of events, and such tests have continued to grow in popularity.

Other types of ability tests, largely because they did not seem to be too directly connected with program needs to because they lacked objectivity, failed to arouse enough enthusiasm to cause them to be extensively used. These earlier testing programs, because of the strenuous nature of the physical activity programs which they encouraged, were largely restricted to the colleges and universities. Not until about 1908, when the Cleveland and New York public school systems organized their athletic leagues, was there any well-organized attempt at testing public school children. In 1913, the Playground and Recreation Association of America published the Athletic Badge Test for Boys.

This marked the first concerted effort at testing physical ability of public school children on a nationwide scale. Tests of this type, however, had been in use for some years in a number of playgrounds and school systems. During the next few years most of the larger school systems introduced some testing and measuring programs into their physical education curricula. The Detroit and the California Decathlon Tests were notable examples of early testing programs which have, with some slight modifications, retained their popularity, and they may safely be used today as models to be followed in setting up similar programs. The brief history of early testing in this country, which has just been reviewed, should convey to the reader the attitude of the pioneer leaders in physical education toward testing and measuring in this field.

A vast majority of the physical educators today do not share this enthusiasm for testing and are prone to resist attempts to set up such programs. Their chief criticisms are that many of the available tests are neither reliable nor valid and that a testing program to meet their needs would involve too much time and, in many cases, too much expense. These criticisms are rapidly being overcome through the progress that has been made in the improvement of tests for physical education.

Reliable and valid tests of various skills, abilities, and capacities are now available. One or two weeks at the most should suffice for testing every boy and girl in school, and this, in connection with the increased time allotment for physical education which is becoming more prevalent, would enable the physical educator to improve vastly his physical education program.

A Knowledge Test of Sports

This test is presented as a means of stimulating interest, and testing knowledge, in the realm of sports.

It is not assumed that it is worthwhile for a coach or a physical educator to become a walking sports-page summary, but, rather, that one is benefited by being conversant with certain aspects of sports in general. As a matter of fact, too high a score on this test may bespeak a waste of some of the precious hours of youth. By the same token, a very low score may disclose an appalling lack of interest in one of the most prominent topics of conversation in America today. This test requires 200 answers dealing with names of sports places, trophies, performers, terms, and "titles."

It purports to present a sampling of each, rather than a complete list of all phases concerned. This is not a standardized test. However, indications, based on scores made by majors in physical education classes, are that a score of 180 is excellent and a score of 100 or less is very poor.

Testing for a Purpose

Tests and measurements are useful only if they help the teacher to do a better piece of work. Consequently, except for the use of tests for research purposes, testing should be limited to those tests which are to be used to achieve a definite educational purpose. The custom in the past has too often been to test every pupil in a haphazard manner, then to file the scores away without more than a cursory examination of them. This wasteful procedure has been one cause for condemning the use of tests generally. It stamps the entire program as lacking in educational values and unworthy of professional respect.

The instructor, in fear of being accused of laziness, incompetence, or of not "being progressive," puts on a show of testing for the benefit of his administrative superior—and then neglects to utilize the results. It is no wonder that many physical educators regard such testing as unnecessary and that many educational administrators question the validity of physical education programs. One of the more common errors in interpreting test results in that of expecting a test to give information for which it was not designed. This error is a natural outcome or lack of purpose as well as of ignorance of the broad field which testing covers at the present time.

Misinterpretation of tests may be worse than not testing at all; consequently, it behooves the tester to make a careful selection of his tests, to keep in mind the purpose, or purposes, for which each test is to be utilized, and to keep in mind the inherent nature of each test. Very briefly, the entire testing program should be planned with one or more of the following purposes in mind: classification of students, guidance, grading, motivation, measuring progress toward objectives, and research. We shall discuss each of these purposes in turn.

Motivation

Most educators hold the opinion that testing and measuring are worthwhile if they have no other purpose than that of creating a greater interest in the activity program. Many self-testing devices of a stunt nature as well as the tests mentioned being made and his or her status relative to the group. If the group is a fairly homogeneous one, this will serve to motivate the vast majority of the pupils. Such increased incentives tend to raise the general level of class performance, and if, further, the grading is upon the basis of grades relative to general motor capacity, even the lower 5 or 10 per cent of the group may be encouraged and strongly motivated in spite of the fact that they will still be at the bottom of the group.

Incidentally, it is found that with good teaching, those who are, at the beginning, at the low end of a probability distribution improve very much more than those near the mean and still more than those near the top. In other words, the spread of the distribution will be greatly narrowed toward the high end. The curve becomes narrower but higher. This is a desirable outcome of both testing and teaching.

Grading

The complexity of grading methods are treated more fully elsewhere in this text, and further mention of the educational value of scientific grading may seem repetitions; however, the problem is closely related to the testing program, and its final solution must be based in part upon a sound selection of tests. In this connection in physical education, it is possible to give grades based partly upon ability relative to capacity. The correlation between tests of general motor capacity and achievement test scores is high. This would be somewhat comparable to giving grades in classroom subjects in relation to the intelligence quotient or mental age.

In school work, this is frequently not feasible. For example, one would not wish to graduate a physician from a college of medicine and license him to practice simply because he had done wonderfully we for a moron. One would not wish to have his legal practice turned over to an individual who had been graduated from law school because he had done excellent work for an individual with an I.Q. of 80. In these fields, absolute grades seem to be the most desirable. In the field of physical abilities, it may be preferable to grade the individual relative to his capacity. Thus, he is encouraged by being given full recognition for how hard he tries.

This, of course, is not in accord with the not unusual practice of requiring the scores to be distributed according to the normal curve. If, however, justice to the pupil would indicate the desirability of the departure from the academic worship of the binominal curve, it would seem the part of wisdom to so depart. In physical education testing, it is frequently feasible "to announce the examination question in advance." To give out the examination questions in arithmetic a semester before the individual was to take the examination would probably result in everyone's getting—though not necessarily deserving—an A.

To announce that the all-around score in four track and field events—naming the events—will be used as one of the term examinations does not insure that every one of the pupils will break the world's records in these events. To announce the twenty apparatus or tumbling stunts which will be used as an examination at the end of the learning period does not insure that everyone will have passed all of those tests. It does, however, give direction to the practice and give each individual an opportunity to know what his goals are to be. This type of objective testing offers possibilities in the area of physical education which are not readily achievable in the area of the classroom studies.

Guidance

The average physical educator is often at a loss to explain or to prescribe corrective measures for the shortcomings of his poorer pupils. To prescribe a program of activity which will most effectively bring about rapid improvement requires a definite knowledge of handicaps, limitations, and weaknesses. This knowledge can be obtained only through a well-planned testing program intended to give a profile of individual strengths and weaknesses. To illustrate how such a profile can be obtained from the scores recorded, let us illustrate from the tests mentioned above under the heading of the General Motor Capacity Score.

We will set up an hypothetical situation in which test scores might aid in guiding the teacher to aid his pupils. In addition to computing the General Motor Capacity Score, each of the first three test items may be assessed in terms of what is usually called a T-score. The T-score is much like a standard score but is usually computed from percentiles, assuming a normal distribution of ability, but not of the test scores. In this case, 50 will represent the average score, 60 will represent one standard deviation above the average score, 70 two standard deviations above the average score, and so forth. Forty represents one standard deviation below the average score, 30 two standard deviations below the average score, and so on.

Classification of students into homogeneous groups

Many differences exist between activity programs in physical education and in other educational fields. The chief difference, and perhaps the most fundamental, is the difference in social relationships. Learning in many of the academic subjects is more or less a subjective, individual affair. In physical education, however, the learning process is an overt one, and the results are reading apparent to all fellow students.

The boy or girl who constantly falls behind his group

in performance is apt to be regarded as inferior by them, and the individuals who are far superior to their groups tend to feel that there is little challenge to their abilities. The student's attitude toward the whole program is frequently influenced by the degree to which he is placed in a group of those of approximately his own performance level. The solution to this problem lies in a homogeneous grouping of the entire student body on the basis of sex, size, maturity, strength, speed, and skill. The simplest approach to this problem of homogeneous grouping is grouping based on sex, age, height, and weight, McCloy and Cozens and his co-workers have worked independently for the past twenty years on this problem and have obtained almost identical results.

This type of grouping, to which McCloy has given the name of The Classification Index, is more applicable to boys than to girls. McCloy gives no norms for girls in this type of index, but Cozens and his associates have given such norms, though the correlations between the index and the performance for girls are low. This type of index does not take into account strength, speed, or skill. It is, however, a very easy and convenient way to classify students. A much more accurate method of classification is that given by McCloy's test of general motor capacity.

This test is made up of the Sargent jump, the ten-second squat thrust, the Iowa brace Test, and the Classification Index. This test battery tends to give a composite measure of speed of muscular contraction, of agility, and of an all-round type of motor educability, in addition to the measurement of size and maturity offered by the Classification Index. This test results in a General Motor Capacity Score which is comparable to mental age in intelligence testing, or to a total intelligence test score.

The test score can be turned into the Motor Quotient, which is comparable to the intelligence quotient in the intellectual field, by dividing 100 times the General Motor Capacity Score by the norm for the Classification Index in boys or the norm for age in girls. In addition to this total test score, the individual items can be further analyzed. This, however, will be discussed below under the heading of guidance. A somewhat simpler test for classification is the Physical Efficiency Index, which is composed of the standing broad jump, a shot-put from a stand, and weight. These three scores, when properly combined, correlate very highly indeed with the individual's ability to perform.

The test does not tell as much or give as many facets of the individual's physical capacity as does the General Motor Capacity Score or the Motor Quotient, but it can be administered very rapidly and correlates very highly with performance in other skills.

Measuring progress toward accomplishment of objectives

Educational progress is best made by first clearly defining the objectives toward which the educational process should point. Then the educator should set up the educational processes designed to achieve those objectives. Third, he should attempt to measure pupil achievement to see whether or not his educational procedures have been successful. In the field of physical education, the tests lend themselves especially well to this end. Hence, one of the most important uses of tests is to measure progress toward the objectives. The objectives are as follows:

1. Physical objectives. The measurement of the accomplishment of physical objectives might well be classified somewhat as follows:

(a) Tests of achievement in posture and body mechanics generally. Part of these tests will be objective or semiobjective tests of posture, or position of feet; part will be the more subjective estimates of body mechanics such as are employed in the ordinary orthopedic diagnosis.

(b) Measurement of improvement in circulo-respiratory endurance. Such tests activities as the Carlson Test or tests of running endurance, particularly when equated against the speed of the individual, are excellent for this purpose.

(c) Measurement of improvement in muscular endurance. Tests such as chinning, push-ups, sit-ups, full squats or squat jumps, and activities of that type lend themselves to measurement in this area.

(d) Appraisal of nutritional status. In the larger sense of the team, this is a very difficult thing to accomplish. In the narrower sense, however, of the appraisal of weight relative to normal weight, of the amount of subcutaneous fat, and of general muscular development, this is relatively easy. Such measurements can be made by use of modern anthropometric techniques.

2. Test of knowledge. This category of tests is represented by the objective paper and pencil tests and may be used to measure progress in knowledge of rules, of techniques, and of health principles generally.

3. Improvement in general ability to develop power, as represented by the type of activities usually known as "racial activities." These are activities like running,

jumping, throwing, climbing, and vaulting, and represent improvement in the use of the physical machine up to the limits of the individual's general motor capacity. In this area, the track and field type of tests assumes an importance out of proportion to the general importance of track and field activities generally. In all power events, an increase in strength will improve the time, distance or height of the performance.

4. Measurement of improvement in characteristics usually associated with improvement in character and personality. This type of measurement is represented by ratings of character or personality qualities and is based upon comprehensive studies of how best to assess these qualities accurately.

5. Measurement of improvement in skills. One of the important objectives of physical education is to master skills of sports activities, of games and athletics, and, especially, to develop the various components of skill, such as accuracy, balance and muscular control generally. Here, the achievement tests and the tests of accuracy and balance bulk large.

Use of test for research

The foundation for progress in any science or any educational field is research. The tests mentioned in this chapter are the results of research labours by men and women who have devoted much time to these problems. Research represents the advanced stage of study in any profession; and, consequently, many years of training and experience are required before one can safely attempt to use the techniques of research for the solution of problems involving the improvement of testing and measuring methods.

The more advanced students who intend to enter the field of research, however, should become acquainted with the various techniques of research which apply to testing and to the development of tests. To the student not interested in doing research, knowledge of the techniques of research used will enable him to evaluate new tests as they appear in the literature. Physical educators untrained in such research methods should not attempt to devise standard tests; instead to competent research workers in the field of testing and physical education should fall the task of producing valid and reliable tests.

To do this well requires years of training in testing techniques plus a background of advanced statistical methods. The average physical educator should, therefore, be content to study and employ the testing techniques described and recommended by experts in this branch of physical education. For a description of the tests to be used, the student should refer to the standard textbook on tests and measurements.

Testing as an Education Procedure

Progressive physical educators agree that the education of every boy and girl is not complete without a systematic and well-organized program of physical and health education. It has been relatively easy to convince the well-trained, broad-minded educator that such a program is a necessity; but to convince him that present-day practices in physical education are educationally sound has not been as easy. The chief criticisms offered by the general educator are: (1) that physical activity programs are not well organized, and (2) that the testing and grading methods employed are not up to the standards of such testing devices for other subjects.

The latter criticism is largely occasioned by the failure of the physical educator to plan his testing program purposefully and to use the results to improve, motivate, and evaluate the results of his program in terms of his objectives. Until testing programs are more intelligently conceived, carried out, and interpreted, they will not be considered as important adjuncts to the general educational program.

Fundamental Concepts of testing. Before any teacher can serve his pupils to the best advantage, it is quite obvious that he must study each individual in terms of his or her innate capacities and present abilities. All tests are designed to measure one or other of these two factors; the vast majority are tests of general ability or of specific skills or knowledge. Tests of intelligence and aptitude are especially valuable to the classroom teacher in that they furnish an index of what to expect from each individual in the classroom. Tests of general motor capacity are equally valuable to the teacher of physical education. Intelligent procedures in testing in physical education aim at measuring not only the pupil's present ability but his ability relative to his capacity.

This measurement of ability relative to capacity gives an index to the extent of his development; in other words, it tells how good or how poor the pupil is in proportion to what he should be able to do, and, as such, this type of test score is most valuable to the teacher in his efforts to serve the individual. The importance of test interpretation is illustrated by the queries of the serious-minded pupils who, before attempting a chinning test, will ask specifically, "How many times should I be able to chin myself?" or, having been told that he had jumped a certain number of centimeters in the Sargent jump, asks, "How good is that?" or "What is a good jump?" Questions such as these are indicative of pupil interest in testing, and if this attitude upon the part of the pupil is to be maintained, it is important that the tester be able to give him intelligent answers on the sport.

This requires the use of tests for which norms or standards are available, and these norms should be kept where they can readily be refereed to when they are needed to answer questions by pupils. Another method is to post the standards where the students can read the answers. It is unfair to expect all students to achieve equal performances in any type of physical capacity or ability tests, because some may be labouring under server handicaps, and others may have distinct advantages.

The Language of Measurement

There are several key terms that often cause confusion among students beginning their study of measurement. Already in the two paragraph that you have just read, you came across the words, "tests", "inventories", "measurement", and "evaluation". We suspect that you have some idea of what is meant by each of these terms, but you may need some clarification to understand exactly how these terms are used in this area of study.

Laboratory and Field Tests

There are many highly sophisticated and precise tests, e.g., treadmill tests and reaction time tests, that can only be given in exercise physiology or motor learning laboratories. Laboratory tests typically require specialized equipment and specialized training on the part of test administrator. Another distinguishing feature of laboratory tests is that they are usually administered to only one person at a time. These features make laboratory tests impractical for use by most physical education and sport practitioners. The alternative to laboratory tests is field tests.

Additionally, they are time-effective, in that they can often be administered to a group of individuals simultaneously. Field tests must, of course, be accurate measures of the characteristic under investigation, but often these measures are less precise than laboratory tests of the same characteristic. Depending upon the intended use of the measurement, however, this lack of precision is often deemed acceptable or even preferable due to the gained advantages in practically. This text is devoted to the presentations and discussion of field tests appropriate for use by the physical education and sport practitioner in setting such as schools, camps, YMCAs, YWCAs, private clubs, and gymnasiums.

Norm-Referenced and Criterion-Referenced Tests

There are two broad classifications of measurement instruments that are referred to as norm-referenced and criterion-referenced. These are also important terms for the beginner in measurement. Norm-referenced tests are designed by the test developer to measure individual differences so one person's score on such a test can be compared to the scores of other similar persons who have taken the same test. These scores are known as norms. From tables of norms, one's score is interpreted in terms of how it compares to the scores of other similar person's scores. The standardized tests that you have taken through your years of schooling were norm-referenced tests. Perhaps you remember being told that you scored, for example, at the 85th percentile; this meant that you scored equal to or better than 85% of the similar students. The majority of physical education and sport tests that have been developed to date are norm-referenced. In recent years, however, more and more criterion-referenced tests have been developed. In this type of testing test scores are compared, not to each other; but to a standard that is referenced to a criterion behaviour.

The criterion behaviour is a satisfactory level of performance, so performers whose scores meet or exceed the standard are claimed to be masters and those whose scores fall below the standard are nonmasters. There are no limits to the number of persons who may achieve mastery on the test. In fact, a teacher may be proud indeed if all of his/her students meet or exceed the standard on a criterion-referenced test in which the standard is keyed to a meaningful criterion behaviour. American Red Cross certification tests and refereeing certification tests are examples of criterion-referenced tests.

Test, Measurement, Evaluation

For every student the word "test" surely conjures up a vivid picture of writing answers to questions presented on a page of paper. However, in the study of measurement in physical education and sport, "test" is applied in a broader sense. Test refers to any specific instrument, procedure, or technique used by a test administrator to elicit a response from the test taker. Tests, always specify a particular protocol, but vary greatly in their form. In physical education and sport contexts, some tests are paper-and-pencil instruments that require a written response directly from the student, athlete, or client.

Many of our tests, however, employ physical devices such as stop-watches, tape measures, skinfold callipers, or even treadmills. Some tests restructure the normal sport environment with cones, ropes and targets with associated point values. Many of our tests yield objective estimates of the characteristic of interest; others, known as rating scales yield subjective estimates. Most physical education and sport tests and rating scales attempt to assess a characteristic of an individual student, athlete, coach, or administrator, but some tests and rating scales are designed to assess characteristics of groups, teams, and programs. "Test" generally is used to describe instruments, procedures, and techniques that result in responses that can be evaluated in terms of their correctness.

Instruments, procedures, and techniques that assess affective qualities of one's interests, attitudes, beliefs or personal values can be included within the general definition of "test". They are however, more commonly referred to as inventories to emphasize that they do not have clearly defined right and wrong answers. In this text, measure is used to connote tests, rating scales, and inventories. When speaking collectively about different tests, scales, and inventories, "measurement instruments" and "assessment tools" are used synonymously. The term battery is used to refer to a group of several tests, scales or inventories intended to be administered in succession to the same subject or subjects. The group of measures is usually designed to accomplish a closely related set of measurement objectives. Measurement refer to the process of administering a test or inventory. The usual result of measurement is quantitative data that are characteristically expressed in numerical form. These data are referred to as scores.

Qualitative assessments usually result in assignment of words or phrases such as "excellent" or "is characteristic of the student". Evaluation refers to the process of interpreting the results of measurement. Test scores and qualitative assessments are evaluated by making comparisons with preconceived criteria in order to make judgments about people or appropriate courses of action. In other words, evaluation is the process of making qualitative judgments based upon measurement evidence. But then, these judgments are usually subjected to careful examination that often require another round of measurement and re-evaluation.

Brief History of Measurement in Physical Education and Sport

Testing and measurement in physical education and sport in America is only a little over a century old. Its history can be divided roughly into periods extending from about 1860 to the present. These periods can be loosely categorized by the prevailing interests of the times. It should be realized, however, that there are no clear-cut lines of demarcation separating them. These periods merely indicate the times when the specific measurement types came into prominence. The first three periods clearly reflected an emphasis on the physical capacity of humans, while the latter periods indicate emphases on efficiency and performance abilities, and on the "wholeness" of the physical performers.

Strength Measurement

Around 1880, interest in anthropometry began to wane as interest in strength testing waxed. Although Hitchcock had included some strength testing in his program at Amherst, the real pioneer in this area was Sargent. Sargent, along with an anthropologist named William T. Brigham, experimented with the newly invented dynamometer, and devised a strength test battery comprised of measures of the legs, back, hand grip, and arms. His strength test battery also included a measure of lung vital capacity, made possible by the invention of the spirometer. Strength testing has never truly gone out of vogue in the measurement area, although it never again received the attention that it did in the period of 1880 to 1910.

11

PHYSICAL EDUCATION AND RECREATION

The word recreation means different things to different people. To an average person, it is anything that amuses, entertains or relaxes, and it may vary fro such quite occupations as reading and handicrafts to such strenuous activities as athletic sports, hiking and mountaineering; from such group activities as team-games and folk-dancing to such solitary occupations as meditation, contemplation and admiration of beauties of nature; from such intellectual pursuits as writing or making brilliant conversation, to such humdrum occupations as cooking or visiting.

The editor of a popular weekly magazine, on inviting his readers to give their pleasurable recreations, received answers varying from enjoying the fragrance of jasmines to tabulating the stock phrases of fumbling professors and reading Charles Dickens and Agatha Christle. The activity side of the physical education programme for normal group is made up largely of five major types of work; the practice of formal exercises commonly known as calisthenics; the practice of dancing; the practice of acrobatic feats on the mats, horizontal bars, parallel bars etc., commonly known as gymnastic stunts.

Mass physical recreational activities find more universal usage perhaps than any other type of activity. It is revealed that this sort of work is in use on the playground, and the gymnasium everywhere. Different individuals find recreation in different activities, depending upon their mental make-ups. As Brightbill and Meyer say, "Recreation is as widely in variety and as deep in contact as the whole human endeavour".

The wide range of recreation activities suggests the recreation is not merely a seasoning of life but a part of its substance, not a certified list of activities but a way of living. The essence of recreation is best expressed in the attitude of the doer, and as such almost any activity can be recreational. What is work for one may mean recreation at one time and not at another to the same individual. Hence, there is no activity to which a permanent label as recreational can be attached.

There are, however, certain types of activities which have come to be commonly considered as recreational because many people attain basic satisfactions by engaging themselves in them, e.g., sports, drama, social functions, music and the entire gamut of hobbies. These activities are found to be almost universally satisfying and recreative because they provide an opportunity to exercise our body and mind in a pleasant way, giving a chance for developing skills and providing scope for the expression of creative abilities.

But the value and worth of these activities also may vary with different individuals and with the same individual in varying circumstances. All that can be asserted is that recreation is a pleasant use of leisure time which may become creative in some cases for some individuals. Due to its changing connotation, recreation as an end in its own right, as a definable, distinguishable, identifiable something, suffers from inaccurate and fragmentary interpretation. In quality it always implies the idea of choice and freedom of action. In character is may be active as in participating in sports and games and other group activities, or semi-active as in listening to music, attending games as a spectator or strolling through a beautiful park, or passive as in complete rest or relaxation or in quiet contemplation of the beauties of nature.

This wide scope of recreation makes the demarcation between recreation and other activities possible and hence the difficulty in defining the term recreation. This perhaps explain the loose use of the term in popular parlance. The layman seldom thinks of differentiating between recreation and other synonymous terms like entertainment, amusement, relaxation or diversion-all of which imply in common a pleasant feeling that accompanies such experience, and all of which denote a passive attitude on the part of individual. Recreation is popularly defined as something that amuses.

The origin of the term amuse reveals the difference between the two concepts. The verb amuse comes from the old French amuser which one meant to put into a stupid state. By the time the word entered the English language, it came to mean delude. Soldiers spoke of amusing the enemy so as to delude and divert them.

Today, amusement means another type of diversion that which pleases, beguiles and entertains. Literally, an amusement is something at which one gazes or stares, and public amusement have come to be characteristically spectacles. To a certain extent, amusement is limited to those activities that divert without requiring any effort. But the recreative and the amusing are always intermingling, and even the most mechanised amusement retains something of the recreative value, because of the pleasure-giving quality common to both.

Being amused seems different from most emotional states in that it does not indicate the need for any further effort, and in fact, inhibits, it. A defensive attitude towards this much criticised mode of human activity is taken by the Encyclopaedia of Social Sciences, when it states that most forms of amusement must have originally involved active participation of every member of the group, and that amusements are primary and spontaneous play-patterns. Even when in particular forms they may become cheap, repetitive and distorted, they never lose the impress of activities which men have passionately enjoyed. Aristotle rightly pointed out of the role amusement in human life about two thousand years ago.

In answer to the question, what ought we do when at leisure, he says clearly that we ought not to do amusing ourselves, for then amusement would be the end of life. Amusement is needed more among serious occupations, when he who is hard at work, has need of relaxation, and amusement gives relaxation. Occupation is always accompanied with exertion and effort, and some amusements at suitable times are like medicines, for the emotions they create are relaxation, and from the pleasures they afford man obtains rest. Amusements are thus essentially recuperative in character, affording rest and relaxation. But, says Aristotle, happiness does not lie in amusement, as is the popular but mistaken belief which makes man direct his quest of happiness in wrong channels and is the cause of many of his problems.

To exert and work for the sake of amusement seems to him silly and childish, but to amuse oneself in order that one may work better seem right. Amusement, therefore, is not the end but only a means. Happiness alone, according to Aristotle is the end and happiness depends upon leisure that is well occupied, in pursuit of wisdom through contemplation and in achieving self-realisation and self-expression through creative activity that is recreation. Diversion is another concept which is used synonymously with recreation but represents only aspect of it.

Just as amusement implies the recreative aspect, diversion implies change as an essential element in recreation. Pascal believed that diversion meant a complete surrender of man to self-destroying, restlessness. He says that for man without amusement, there is no joy; with amusement, there is no sadness. While condemning diversion and amusement as being no real source of happiness, Pascal does ultimately realise the need for change and relaxation when he says that man, overwhelmed with work and cares, needs some time for relaxation and amusement in play. Says he, And if he does not lower himself to this and wants always to be on the strain, he will be more foolish still, because he would raise himself above humanity.

The human need for change and relaxation after work is acknowledge but it is sought to suggest that diversion and amusement do not show the right way for its satisfaction. At best, they are incomplete remedies accepted for lack of better ones. Recreation is the answer not only affording change and relaxation but a balanced way of life through creative self-expression. One more synonymous term for pleasure-giving human experiences is entertainment.

Entertainment implies performance which is witnessed by a spectator. Amusement and diversion do not necessarily suggest or involve this spectator-performance relationship. The psychological mechanism involved in entertainment is widely accepted to be that of vicarious satisfaction through a process of identification of the spectator with the performer. In both kinds of entertainments-whether it is a display entertainment, i.e., watching the performed feasts, or representative entertainment, i.e., experiencing the imaginary situations presented in plays or novels with varying intensity, there occurs an unconscious identification of the spectator with the performed so that the impulses the former supposes the performed to be satisfying are also satisfied in him.

It must be remembered, however, that there is a wide disparity of tastes in individual preferences, and an entertainment performance may evoke enormous variations of response. What is exciting entertainment for one may be unmitigated boredom for another. Seductive music to one pair of ears may be hideous cacophony to another. Reaction to the same radio programme may vary from genuine appreciation and applause to indifference and even disgust. Objection to entertainment rest mainly on the ground that it is passive in character and does not afford the individual a chance to exercise his potential abilities and capabilities; and when it is commercialised, entertainment very frequently reaches a low standard with pecuniary goals in view.

As an antidote to fatigue, entertainment is desirable

to a certain extent, but excessive doses of it lead to a sort of addiction and bars any possibility of the individual exploring his own inner resources. Amusement, diversion and entertainment afford pleasure, and therefore, relaxation, but they do not promote human happiness. All of them come from without, and therefore, in the words of Pascal, are dependent on and subject to be distributed by a thousand accidents which bring inevitable grieves. Another activity which has a close kinship but is not identical with recreation is physical education. They are like two intersecting circles with a common area in between-the rest of the spheres remaining separate and having their own ranges.

While the sphere of recreation encompasses all such activities as physical, social and cultural, physical education is concerned with sports, games, rhythmics and other allied activities. The range of activities and the degree of emphasis is somewhat different in each field of specialisation. In its early phases the stewardship of physical educators and athletic coaches. The very word recreation suggests play, and play, to many people, is suggestive of outdoor games and physical activity, ranging from wrestling and football to athletics and hiking.

Physical education yields recreational values whenever the participant enjoys the process. Similarly, recreation in sports area pays very rich dividends in physical conditioning and physical education. Broadly speaking, physical education may be called the sum-total of man's big muscle activities, conducted for certain valuable outcomes viz., physical fitness, mental alertness and socialising influences. The idea of physical education is not merely to build a powerful and healthy body but also to evoke and foster those personal and civic virtues which make the participants better citizens.

No physical training can have any abiding value unless it also contributes towards mental and social education. Physical education is thus an integral part of the total education process and has, as its aim, the development of physically, mentally and socially fit citizen through the medium of physical activities, selected with a view to realising these outcomes. There is a philosophy behind physical education which is lacking in what is called physical culture which aims only at the development of the body.

Physical education, along with physical fitness, aims at improved coordination between systems of the body, wider activity horizons, development of skills, mental alertness and socialisation, all of which are conducive to successful group living. The educational value of physical education is summed up by Brace who feels that it has become that phase of education that is particularly assigned the function of guiding that is particularly assigned the function of guiding youth in development skills in form of physical recreation and attitudes favourable to continuing in after-school years leisure-time recreation activities which will be mentally sound and emotionally satisfying and which will at the same time contribute to the maintenance of health and physical fitness.

Objectives of physical education are the following: physical fitness, mastery over a variety of bodily skills and development of personally rewarding, and socially acceptable standards of behaviour. These ideas and objectives of physical education are almost the same as ideals and objectives of recreation with aims at providing relaxation through change and development of individual's physical and mental abilities, thus making for a balanced living.

Athletics, a part of physical education, present the greatest opportunity in modern life for exercise of ancient activities of human race and for exercise of ancient activities of human race and for fostering desirable human tendencies. They are a means of conditioning the physical, social and ethical character traits of a worthy citizen, and have a significant role to play especially in modern life, when work involving physical exertion has been so largely displaced. In cities where industrialisation has absorbed men in specialised jobs involving little physical activity, physical education has an important role to play in helping recreation to realise the values it aims to achieve. A large variety of physical education activities is ordinarily called recreation because they afford satisfaction and opportunity for growth and development to the majority.

No recreation programme is complete without the inclusion of physical education activities. The most popular item in any recreation programme is physical activities as indicate by numerous survey in western world. Our primeval ancestors had to pursue big-muscle activities daily in securing food, in preserving and protecting themselves and in the general struggle for survival amidst the stronger and more powerful forces of nature. A dominant instinct operating was that of self-preservation connected with fundamental emotions of fear and anger and courage. Associated with these emotions were big-muscles activities like running, jumping, climbing, throwing and fighting-the last being the most comprehensive and combining all the rest.

The function of physical education then was not very significant. It is when becomes civilised, when necessities and amenities of life come easily that the need for exercise of big muscles becomes evident, and hence the need for physical education activities. The fighting-team games of today would be explained by the stimulation of those fundamental emotions. These are the activities of which employ the big muscles of the body and contribute to physical vigour and vitality. In this, physical education shares two important characteristics of recreation-the element of change and the pleasure giving quality. In our country, the indigenous type of physical education has grown out of practice and experience extending over centuries, and is well adapted to our climatic, economic and social conditions.

Dands, Baithaks Wrestling, Lathi, Hututu, Kho-Kho and the various types of rhythmic activities have been practised and developed since centuries. The yogic system of exercises have been found useful not only for toning-up and developing the vital organs but even for counteracting disorders and diseases. Under the British influence, many games and physical activities of the West are adopted, and little effort and energy was devoted to popularise the Indian games.

With the awakening of the national spirit and as a phase of the entire cultural revival, the indigenous physical activities are coming to the forefront again, and the National Planning Commission has emphasised the need for research in this field. At the same time it must be said that for our adolescent and young people, the team-games adopted from the West will ever be the great rewarding type of exercise-a source of health as well as of social contacts-in schools, industries and neighbourhood groups. Some of the major problems of investigation are the relative values of different sports, games and exercises from physiological, psychological, social and educational point of view, the value of yogic system of exercises and the appropriate syllabus of physical education for different ages and vocational groups. The need for and importance of recreation in our country has been brought to light by the Physical Education Movement.

As the National Plan for Physical Education and Recreation, prepared by the Central Advisory Board of Physical Education and Recreation in 1956 suggests, it is desirable to blend Physical Education and Recreation together so that a happy combination of the two may lead to a fuller enrichment of personality. For instance, games, sports, mass drills and exercises and even folk-dances can all be so organised as to provide good physical education as well as good recreation. In Bombay State, the various Physical Education Committec, set up from time to time, have emphasised in their recommendations and reports the need for recreation and suggest ways and means of providing recreational services on community basis. These have consequently led to the creation of a Recreation Board and a Recreation Committee by the Government of Bombay. The creative aspect of recreation has been recognised and emphasised by almost all writers.

It has been called the satisfaction of creative urge through socially accepted channels, or creative, recreative, constructive and cooperative expression of personality through a wide range of enjoyable activities, and effective utilisation of leisure time in the interests of higher level of individual development and community culture, because creative recreation promotes and is promoted by cultural, artistic and intellectual activities. The forms of creative recreation are derived from the higher activities of man-art and culture. Creative recreation will make man-as the Germans say—"self-active" in his leisure and not merely a passive receptacle for pleasant experience that have to be poured from outside.

Self-activity in skill and creation is the singular function of human nature, and the role of creative recreation in this context was recognised by the great social thinker Aristotle, more than two thousand years ago. The social function of recreation may not be included in the essential elements providing a basis for defining recreation, as recreation may or may not involve social contact depending on the individual temperament and circumstances.

However, individualistic the concept of recreation may be, its social implications cannot be denied, at least in so far as it is a socially accepted leisure experience and should be no means involve any anti-social consequences. More significant is the fact that recreation not only partakes of the cultural content of a social group but also is an important means of enriching it. The determination of essential elements of recreation or the criteria of recreational activity involves a question of values.

There are degrees of recreational values yielded by different kinds of experiences. Recreation, as we have seen, contribute to the satisfaction of some basic human needs like the need for change of activity, for relaxation and recuperation after work, for recognition and for creative achievement, which promote individual, and therefore, social well-being. For fullness in living, man must grow through doing, achieving and creating. Keeping in view the points that recreation is essentially a leisure-time experience and has a creative and recreative function which may yield rich benefits to the individual and the society, it may be defined as that form of leisure activity which is chosen by the individual for the immediate and inherent satisfaction it brings him by providing an opportunity for self-expression and self-realisation through creative use of leisure on the one hand, and restorations or recuperation of lost energy through a change of activity on the other.

In both its creative and recreative aspects, recreation is beneficial to society-in the first, by enriching the culture of a group, and in the second, by paving way for a mentally and physical healthier society. Leisure and recreation are so closely connected as to be identified at times, though they are not identical. There are many leisure pursuits which cannot be called recreation by any sketch of imagination. Many anti-social activities are pursued during leisure time when time and energy are utilised in wrong channels. Such leisure activities deteriorate rather than develop personality.

Recreation is not just killing time, nor is it a philosophy of derived from those basis may be fun, but that fun which is derived from those satisfactions which are returned to the individual through the creative use of leisure and which do not involve consequences that are socially unacceptable or undesirable. Both leisure and recreation, however, involve freedom of choice and voluntary participation in any activity. But leisure can be harmful if the right kind of activity is not chosen. To make a judicious use of leisure, recreation becomes necessary.

While the emphasis in leisure is on the time element, recreation refers to the way in which that time is spent. Leisure implies tie and freedom of choice, and the ways of spending leisure are conditioned by age, sex, economic status, educational and cultural backgrounds. A balance between the use of man's leisure and the worthwhileness of the activities he engages in during this free time will of necessity become not only the nature but the function of the recreation. Recreation thus become the ideal way of spending leisure, and if one attributes to recreation the characteristics discerned above, it provides an answer to the problem of leisure in modern society. Along with leisure, two other modes of human activities in their relationship to recreation may be considered: work and play.

Work differs from play not in the nature of motions but rather in the motivational and in the form of the compensation. One works for money, power or prestige. In play and recreation, one is paid throughout the participation in terms of immediate satisfaction and gratification of fun and enjoyment. Any activity becomes recreational when the participant chosen to do it in his time off the job the fun of it. The elements of continuity and effort are common to both work and recreation, and they make it possible to derive from recreation, a sense of achievement and a feeling of restful satisfaction, lacking in more passive enjoyment.

The important differentiating factor between work and recreation is, that while in work the goal is not the activity itself but remuneration, received, in play and recreation the goal is inherent and part of the act itself. Dewey means the same thing when he says that interest in play centres in the activity with little regard to the outcome, while interest in work centres in the result and thereby controls the means. Man seeks to express himself both in his work and play, hence work and recreation are two sides of the same whole, and at their highest levels one becomes indistinguishable from the other. Like recreation, it is difficult to define play.

Play represents no concrete, describable and definable unitary or structural fact, unless it connotes a concrete method of playing. It is a word in abstraction, a synthetic concept, a word image, symbolising all or more than one of the concrete ways of playing. It has unlimited number of aspects, variety of forms, and involves many elements and far reaching and subtle results. Hence, the in adequacy of the attempts to define play. It is too comprehensive a concept to be defined in a few words. Like other terms in the loosely connected groups of ideas such as laughter, wit, jest, comic, etc. play resists any attempt to reduce it to the terms. Their rationale and their mutual relationship are to deep to be fathomable. Whether activity is play or not, depends upon the attitude of the individual towards the activity.

Some of the factors which generally contribute towards play attitude are: (i) absence of routine, (ii) presence of an element of suspense and of make-believe; (iii) an opportunity for spontaneity and imagination and new experiences, and above all, (iv) a probability of success. Unless a person can do a thing well, or at least gain skill through the process of trial and error, the satisfaction or enjoyment will not be derived from the activity. A sense of mastery is often what man looks for in his play. Various attempts have been made to explain the phenomenon of play from biological, psychological and sociological view-points.

In traditional education, play has always been considered as a kind of mental waste matter or at least a pseudo-activity without functional significance, and even harmful to children. Common sense saw in play only a relaxation or a drain for superfluous energy. The oldest theory of play was put forward by Schiller as a blowing off of steam, and was defined by him as aimless expenditure of exuberant energy.

Spencer went a little further and connected the idea of imitation with surplus energy. This theory has been criticised on many grounds-that it is wrong to consider all play without aim because the player is not aware of it, that children want to contribute to play at times even after complete exhaustion, that it does not distinguish between adult and child play, that it fails to account for various forms of play and especially those which are relaxing and restore the depleted energy.

True, that surplus energy is a favourable condition to play, and the animal or child possessing it may play harder and longer, but no one can accept the theory today as a complete explanation. The second attempt to explain play was made by Karl Groos, known as the Instinct Practice theory. It is said that the young of a given species obtain practice in those forms of activity which in life are necessary to sustenance, and instinct is the motivating factor in play. Play may be considered as preparation for adult life at the animal or primeval level but it is definitely not applicable to civilised life.

The play of today's children cannot be regarded as training for future vocation; it rather resembles the pursuits of prehistoric man and sometimes the sports of adults of present day. Analysing the larger number of observations of play activities of children. Piaget writes that far from being preparatory exercise, most of children's games either reproduce what has struck the child, evoke what has pleased him or enabled him to be more fully part of his environment.

This theory, therefore, is incomplete in so far as it leaves the play of adults unexplained. Quite the contrary is the explanation offered by Stanley Hall in his theory of what he called the Recapitulation theory: that in play, the individual rehearses the activities of his ancestors, repeating their life-work in summative and adumbrative ways. According to Hall in the content of play interests is inherited while later investigations, especially those of Lehmann and Witty, show that the content of the game variest with the child's natural and social environment.

So far as the content of play is concerned, play is rather a matter of participation in the environment than of hereditary reourrcction. Certain games may have had their origin in distant past, but through social transmission and not heredity. It may be admitted that man cannot cut himself off entirely from his past, but theoretically and scientifically, there is no proof of the definite, well-marked stages in evolution of human mind through which mankind traversed, nor of the different cultural epochs during which these characteristics of play are said to have been acquired. The Recreation theory which was first put forward by Guts Muths emphasised the recreative aspect of play and defined play as an occupation engaged in for recreation rather than for business and necessary for man to refresh himself after labour.

After the necessary amount of rest and sleep, change of stimulating and interesting activity is more relaxing than complete inactivity. It gives a valuable concept of one of the functions of play. G.T.W. Patrick modified and elaborated it and related it to the conditions in modern industrialised society where highly skilled activities involve small muscles had replaced the big-muscle activities which were less fatiguing because they were racially older. He sounded a timely warning against the nerve-racking hurry and rush, and rightly pointed out that mental activities like concentration and monotonous repetition were more fatiguing than big muscle responses to which man is naturally suited, and that change of occupation always brings rest and relaxation. The fact that it is in effort to explain motivation of play in terms of race habits detracts its value, and it is generally felt that Patrick's postulate of inherited racial characteristics is not justifiable.

The physiological structure and the mental make-up of man are naturally inclined to change of activity after a certain period, and play could have been explained better as the need for growth in children and self-development in adults and as the need for change of activity rather than idle inactivity in both. Such an explanation would have the benefit of being applicable to all play responses and not only those which tend to relax and re-create and human organism. There are some of the important orthodox and traditional explanations of play which have been criticised, as already seen, in many ways.

There are other efforts too, at explaining plays-as having a cathartic value, as a safety-valve for pent-up emotions, and as an instinct, as William James and McDougall saw it. The common criticisms of all of them is that they are all partially valid, containing a kernel of truth, but inadequate as a complete explanation of play. They all start from the assumption that play must serve something which is not play, which is mistaken, and they do not give any real understanding of the problem, or say what plan in itself is, nor do they give any idea of its intensity and absorption of the individual. In these lies that very essence, the primordial quality of play, with its intensity of mirth and fun. It is fun which characterises the essence of play, and which eludes explanation and definition.

Having dealt in short with the traditional theories of play, and their critical evaluation, we may consider three more recent explanation of play from the biological, psychological and social-cultural view points, which might give us a comprehensive idea of the motive and function of play. The biological aspect of play is represented by Thorpe, and it includes or rather starts with the play of animals.

According to Thorpe, there is now a substantial and precise evidence for a general manipulation or exploration drive in higher mammals. Play is not treated by Thorpe as a drive by itself but as originating in this drive for manipulation, which is strong and persistent and a sufficient incentive for learning. This drive is innate and involves complex and highly rigid patterns of behaviour evoked by particular environmental situations. The co-ordination mechanism of each of these fixed patterns tends to build up a kind of specific tension in the central nervous system, and if the animal does not find itself in appropriate situation for the action pattern to be released, this specific action potential is, as it were, damped up.

If continued long enough, the tension may accumulate to the point at which the action pattern goes off without any external stimulus, giving rise to overflow activity, e.g., constant activity of the hunting dog and the pouncing cat, often quite unrelated to the state of hunger-these instances suggest what we call play. Thus the appetitive behaviour, i.e., the flexible or variable introduction of an instinctive behaviour pattern or sequence, when released from the restriction of the drive and necessity of attaining the goals of consummatory act, that is, the final act which completes a reaction chains, becomes play.

The most important implication inherent in the meaning of the word Play, i.e., a sense of freedom is given a biological basis here. In the pure play, like the gambollings of lambs and puppies and young children, there is no striving towards a goal. Applying this idea to ethology, play may be expected in those situations where appetitive behaviour is emancipated temporarily or permanently from the restriction imposed by the necessity of attaining a specific goal, as in the young animals with prolonged post-embryonic development, and where primary needs are satisfied by the care of parents, as in meticulous birds and some mammals, and above all, under the conditions of dometication. Under such abnormally easy conditions of life are found the beginnings of a general exploration of environment which often takes the form of play.